The Institute of British Geographers
Studies in Geography

Critical Issues in Tourism

IBG STUDIES IN GEOGRAPHY

General Editors
Felix Driver and Neil Roberts

IBG Studies in Geography are a range of stimulating texts which critically summarize the latest developments across the entire field of geography. Intended for students around the world, the series is published by Blackwell Publishers on behalf of the Institute of British Geographers.

Published

Debt and Development
Stuart Corbridge

The Changing Geography of China
Frank Leeming

Critical Issues in Tourism
Gareth Shaw and Allan M. Williams

The European Community
Allan M. Williams

In preparation

Geography and Gender
Liz Bondi

Population Geography
A. G. Champion, A. Findlay and E. Graham

Rural Geography
Paul Cloke

The Geography of Crime and Policing
Nick Fyfe

Fluvial Geomorphology
Keith Richards

Russia in the Modern World
Denis Shaw

A Geography of Housing
Susan Smith

The Sources and Uses of Energy
John Soussan

Retail Restructuring
Neil Wrigley

CRITICAL ISSUES IN TOURISM

A Geographical Perspective

Gareth Shaw and Allan M. Williams

BLACKWELL
Oxford UK & Cambridge USA

First published 1994

Blackwell Publishers
108 Cowley Road
Oxford OX4 1JF
UK

238 Main Street
Cambridge, Massachusetts 02142
USA

British Library Cataloguing in Publication Data

A CIP catalogue record for this book is available from the British Library.

Library of Congress Cataloging-in-Publication Data

Shaw, Gareth.
Critical issues in tourism : a geographical perspective / Gareth
Shaw and Allan M. Williams.
p. cm.— (IBG studies in geography)
Includes bibliographical references and index.
ISBN 0-631-17676-4 (acid-free).— ISBN 0-631-18131-8 (pbk. : acid-free)
1. Tourist trade. I. Williams, Allan M. II. Title.
III. Series.
G155.A1S48 1994
338.4'791—dc20

93-10288

Typeset in 10 on 12pt Plantin
by Acorn Bookwork, Salisbury, Wiltshire
Printed in Great Britain by T.J. Press Ltd, Padstow, Cornwall
This book is printed on acid-free paper

Contents

List of Tables

List of Boxes

List of Figures

Acknowledgements

The authors wish to give their thanks to the following people at the University of Exeter: Terry Bacon for drawing all the diagrams, and Jane, Judy and Jo for all the long hours they spent on the word processor.

G.S. and A.M.W.

PART I

An Approach to Tourism

One

Introduction

Tourism and Leisure: Definitions and Relationships

The aim of this book is to outline critical issues in the study of the geography of tourism. While an interdisciplinary approach is adopted, the principal focus is on acknowledged areas of concern of geography, namely landscape space, place and locality. These are approached via tourism, and of resultant and contextual tourism environments. In addition, tourism is placed within the context of leisure.

Leisure and tourism are closely related and one of the themes of this book is the links between them. There is, therefore, a need to set out their definitions. This is more difficult than first appears as there are a number of definitions of both concepts. Turning first to leisure, there are three main competing definitions to note (see de Grazia 1964; Kelly 1982; Patmore 1983, 5–6; Stockdale 1985, 13–14). These are based on time, activity and experience:

- Leisure is juxtaposed with time which is functionally obligated to work, to biological needs such as eating or sleeping, or to other commitments such as travel to work. The residual time is considered to be free time, and this is equated with leisure. Surveys suggest that in the European Community 15.7 per cent of an individual's time, on average, is free time (figure 1.1). However, the notion of free time is itself ambiguous. Free time is usually used in the sense of 'freedom from' obligations such as work. This is quite different from the concept of 'freedom to' enjoy leisure; hence Rojek (1985, 13) states that '. . . the concept of free time has no intrinsic meaning' with respect to leisure. It ignores the quality of the time available and the resources to allow participation in lei-

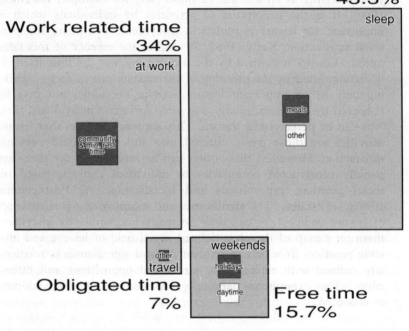

Figure 1.1   Individuals' use of time in EC countries
Source: World Tourism Organization (1983, 16)

sure. Human agency is important, so that these vary between individuals, while also having structural determinates such as class, life-cycle, race and gender. For example, the role of married women in the dual labour process (home and external workplace) means that the quality of time available to them is more fragmented, as well as more spatially and socially constrained, than is the time available to married men (Hudson and Williams 1989, 112–15).

• Leisure is the time during which leisure activities are undertaken. This overlaps with the definition of recreation as the activities undertaken during leisure time. In this definition leisure takes on a strictly objective form – it is a list of activities proscribed by an external object such as a researcher or government department. Apart from a certain circularity in the argument, this definition is unsatisfactory because it assumes a false objectivity. Activities such as gardening or do-it-yourself home repairs may be regarded by different individuals as leisure or obligations.

- In response to the previous criticism, most recent research has viewed leisure as an attitude of mind (see, for example, Isa-Ahola 1980). It is the perception of activities by individuals which is important, for leisure is rooted in enjoyment, well-being and personal satisfaction. Kelly (1982, 7) catches the essence of this definition: 'Leisure is defined by the use of time, not the time itself. It is distinguished by the meaning of the activity not its form'. Walking may be an important leisure activity for some, but may be abhorred by others. Similarly, for some fortunate individuals, their jobs can be perceived as leisure. This approach implies that leisure activities are those freely entered into and which yield personal satisfaction. However, this notion can be misleading, for there are socially constructed boundaries to individual choices, based on social position, expectations and socialization. As Featherstone (1987, 115) states, 'The significance and meaning of a particular set of leisure choices . . . can only be made intelligible by inscribing them on a map of the class-defined social field of leisure and lifestyle practices in which their meaning and significance is relationally defined with reference to structured oppositions and differences'. This experiential definition is the one that we have adopted in this book.

The definition of tourism is also problematic. Gunn (1988), for example, considers that tourism includes all travelling except commuting. This is too all-embracing, for it would involve not only all out-of-home recreation but also travelling for such purposes as visiting doctors. Another definition stresses that tourism involves travelling away from home for leisure purposes. It is therefore seen as a subset of leisure and of recreation. For example, Kelly (1985) writes that tourism is '. . . recreation on the move, engaging in activity away from home in which the travel is at least part of the satisfaction sought'. There is ambiguity here in that it is not clear whether 'away from home' begins at the front door, involves a substantial journey of a minimum length or implies an overnight stay away from home. The definition that we follow here is that preferred by international organizations such as the World Tourism Office, which is that tourism includes all travel that involves a stay of at least one night, but less than one year, away from home. This therefore includes travel for such purposes as visiting friends or relatives, or to undertake business.

The definition of tourism adopted is an objective one which stands in contrast to the experiential definition that we have favoured for leisure. However, it is the definition most commonly in use within

the literature on tourism. More importantly, we do not believe that
pleasure tourism can be studied in isolation from other forms of
tourism such as business travel. The economics of the air travel and
the accommodation industries, for example, are based on the carriage
of both business and holiday tourists. Furthermore, it is common for
business tourists to enjoy leisure activities during their trips. We have
therefore made the leisure tourist the principal focus of this book.
But we also argue that this sector cannot be adequately understood
without considering leisure as a whole, as well as the tangential and
sometimes overlapping business tourism sector (see figure 1.2).

Much of the previous literature on tourism, leisure and recreation
has developed as separate strands of research and teaching, often with
very few points of contacts (see Fedler 1987). One of the aims of this
book is to help to rectify this imbalance. We would not go so far as
to agree with Jansen-Verbeke and Dietvorst (1987, 263) that '. . . in
the perception of the individual at least, the distinction between
recreation and tourism is becoming irrelevant', but the perceptions
are increasingly linked. There are a number of points at which tourism and (non-tourism) leisure are interrelated, and neither can be

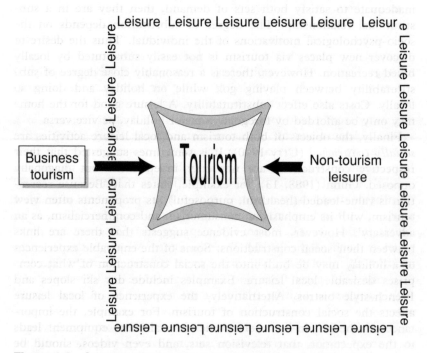

Figure 1.2   Conceptualization of tourism, leisure and recreation study

adequately understood without reference to the other. First, they are tied together in the same *time–space framework*. Individuals' lives, measured as trajectories through time, have a certain structure. Work and other functional obligations mean that there is a rhythm to the time available for leisure – leastwise for most people. The total amount and the quality (degree of fragmentation, possibility of interruptions by functional obligations such as family care etc.) varies through the day, the week, the year and the life-cycle. Work and family/household obligations are the most important influences, but these are not deterministic. Most individuals have the potential to vary the amount of time that they devote to leisure, by reorganizing the time that they spend on other activities. As tourism involves a minimum of one night spent away from home, this activity is only possible during certain blocks of time available for leisure. While this is an absolute irreducible, the propensity to participate in tourism during certain blocks of time changes with levels of economic development. For example, technological advances in travel may make it attractive to take short tourism breaks.

In addition, tourism and non-tourism leisure make demands upon the same *household budget*. If the disposable income available is inadequate to satisfy both sets of demand, then they are in a substitutional relationship. The degree of substitution depends on the socio-psychological motivations of the individual. Thus the desire to discover new places via tourism is not easily substituted by locally based recreation. However, there is a reasonably close degree of substitutability between playing golf while on holiday and doing so locally. Costs also effect substitutability. A leisure good for the home may only be afforded by foregoing a major holiday, or vice versa.

Finally, the objects of both tourism and local leisure activities are *socially constructed* (Urry 1990). It is sometimes suggested that their respective constructions are not only independent but diagonally opposed. Gunn (1988, 13), for example, states that 'Because recreation is value-loaded (healthful, purposeful), its proponents often view tourism, with its emphasis on consumerism and commercialism, as an adversary'. However, most evidence suggests that there are links between their social constructions. Some of the enjoyable experiences of a holiday may be built into the social construction of what comprises desirable local leisure. Examples include dry ski slopes and French-style bistros. Alternatively, the experience of local leisure affects the social construction of tourism. For example, the importance attached to in-home electronic entertainment equipment leads to the expectation that television sets, and even videos, should be provided in tourist accommodation. More fundamentally, Urry

(1990) argues that innovations in local leisure – such as theme parks and leisure centres – have contributed to British seaside holiday resorts losing their exotic allure, appearing to offer only commonplace experiences. The relationship between tourism and locally based leisure is not fixed: it is culturally and economically contingent. The expectations of participation in leisure and tourism, as well as the economics of their supply, change over time and between societies: this is only to be expected as they are socially constructed. Furthermore, leisure is culturally specific, being influenced by culture as well as being an important element in culture. One of the most obvious examples was the prioritization given by Protestantism to work over most forms of leisure.

The relationship between tourism and leisure is also historically specific (Rojek 1985, 23–9). Until the twentieth century, for example, the costs of travel, the limited availability of holidays, and the absolute levels of incomes meant that tourism was essentially a preserve of the upper classes and some of the middle classes, even in the most developed countries. There was, therefore, a clear class basis as to who could participate in both tourism and leisure. The relationship between tourism and leisure has also been affected by what has been termed 'time-deepening'. There are three aspects of time-deepening; '. . . undertaking an activity more quickly or satisfying some need through an activity more quickly, undertaking more than one activity simultaneously, and using time more precisely' (Gobey 1985, 19). The post-1950 era of mass consumption in the developed countries saw an increase not only in the number of goods that people owned but also in the number of leisure activities that they participated in. This was greatly facilitated by improvements in personal mobility, especially the extension of car ownership. At least of equal importance was a change in people's aspirations.

There was a parallel, and linked, series of changes in tourism in the developed world in the post-1950 period. Mass tourism only came into existence in the 1950s, but it was part of the major shift which occurred in consumption and in expectations regarding consumption. This was to change further in the 1960s with the growth of mass international tourism, particularly from Europe and the USA. At first, the destination countries were mainly in the Caribbean or involved other European countries. However, by the 1980s mass tourism from these countries, and from new sources such as Japan, was being extended to a wide range of countries in the Third World. This affected both the attraction of traditional tourist destinations and participation in local leisure activities.

One of the central contentions of this volume is the need to place the study of tourism in context of leisure. The following sections underline this point by briefly reviewing their interrelated roles in economic development, the quality of life and lifestyles, and culture. This also serves to emphasize that tourism is not a peripheral aspect of local, national or global economy and society. Instead, it is critical to all of these and to the spheres of both production and consumption.

Economic Structures: Commodification and Privatization

The importance of the services sector has grown in both absolute and relative terms in most countries in recent decades. In the USA, for example, there was a 12 per cent increase between 1947 and 1980 in the proportion of all employment which was in this sector (Knox and Agnew 1989, 183). While this is often linked to the process of deindustrialization, this is an ethnocentric view founded in the experiences of the developed countries. For example, because of the impact of technological change, many of the more recently industrialized countries have not developed large manufacturing sectors in employment terms (Urry 1987, 5–6). In addition, some less developed countries have based their development strategies on the service industries – whether offshore financial services as in the Bahamas, or tourism as in the Seychelles.

The previous neglect of the services sector has been remedied to some extent in recent years. In particular, the producer services have been extensively analysed for their role in capital accumulation and uneven development (see, for example, Marshall 1989). However, the consumer services have tended to be ignored, despite the fact that they consistently feature amongst the most rapid growth sectors in most developed countries (see Urry 1987, 11). One of the sectors of most rapid growth is undoubtedly tourism and leisure services (see Champion and Townsend 1990, on the UK). Their economic importance is considerable. Thus, in 1985 international and domestic tourism alone accounted for global expenditure equivalent to $1800 billion (Gunn 1988, 3), and the leisure industries for an even higher level.

Tourism and leisure are also important elements in labour markets, with tourism accounting for more than one million jobs in the UK alone. Although there is a considerable debate about the nature of tourism employment (Williams and Shaw 1988), this has not diminished its attraction to politicians and economic planners seeking rapid responses to the growth of unemployment which has accompanied the recurrent crises in capitalist economies. There is also a need to look at the wider labour-market impacts of leisure and tourism, particularly the implications for other sectors such as agriculture (Smith 1977b, 4–5).

In common with all other economic sectors, tourism and leisure have *linkages* with other forms of production. These may be complementary (backward, forward or horizontal linkages), or competitive (as in negative externalities, labour-market shortages and land-price inflation).

Given the definition adopted in this book, tourism is necessarily a non-basic economic sector, in that it has the capacity to generate *export* income for an area. This has long been recognized in the analysis of international tourism (see Williams and Shaw 1988, chapter 2, on Western Europe). More recently, its role in local economic development has also been recognized (Townsend 1992). This has been enhanced by the ubiquity of socially constructed tourism attractions (Urry 1990, chapters 5 and 6) and by the speed of development (Williams and Shaw 1988).

Furthermore, tourism and leisure developments can have major local *environmental impacts*. In areas of mass tourism these are usually considered to be negative, but they can also be positive. In particular, they can play a critical role in the social reconstruction of places. Outstanding examples are provided by waterfront redevelopments such as in Baltimore, Liverpool and Sydney. Within this context, tourism and leisure are also intimately connected with *public-sector economics*. They generate tax and other revenues for local and central governments, but also require expenditures on health care, infrastructures, pollution control etc. As such, there is inevitably a struggle between factions of capital (say, industrialists versus tourist interests) over control of public policy.

The neglect of tourism and leisure is particularly marked in the geography of production. Manufacturing, and even some consumer services such as retailing, have been extensively analysed by economic geographers. The geography of the production of leisure and tourism services has many features in common with these other sectors; for example, product cycles, changes in the labour process, and the concentration and internationalization of capital. While there has been considerable empirical work on the economics of these industries (see chapter 8) there has been relatively little critical, theoretical analysis of those features listed above. Urry (1987, 22–3) considers that, in terms of the restructuring literature, there is a particular need to address the issues of partial self-provisioning, investment and technical change, rationalization, changes in labour input, enhancement of quality and centralization.

While it is not possible to develop all of the themes identified by Urry, there are five critical features of the production of tourism and leisure services which can be noted at this point:

- The first is that tourism and leisure are subject to *commodification*. Newman (1983, 100) argues that 'On the one hand, leisure time appears as a form of free time, holding out the promise of spontaneity and periodic liberalization. On the other, leisure is seen as assimilated into the values prevailing elsewhere, and hence is equally marked by the materialist imperative motivating consumption and work'. Informally organized leisure pursuits are increasingly being converted into products and services to be traded. For example, walkers are confronted with more and more equipment which can be purchased, while the growth in the 1980s of electronic equipment for in-home entertainment has been truly remarkable. The opportunities for the realization of profits have been seized upon by private capital. Harvey (1987, 273–6) argues that in order to take advantage of new flexible production methods, and the considerable consumer expenditure of the expanding middle class, there has been the growth of cultural or symbolic capital. This is the investment of capital in the consumption and collection of commodities and cultural values which are intended manifestly to demonstrate taste or status. In other words, private capital exploits the fact that the ownership of certain goods (or participating in certain activities) comes not only directly from these but also from their conspicuous consumption.
- A second feature is that private capital cannot guarantee the sustained production of those tourism and leisure services that a society values, whether for economic, social or cultural purposes. There is, therefore, marked *state intervention* in their production and, in capitalist societies, these are mixed public–private sectors.
- Third, despite the commodification of tourism and leisure, the total production of these services usually incorporates *a mix of the formal economy, informal production and households*. These are linked together by flows of money, goods, services and labour. For example, the informal economy may produce services such as pirate videos and non-declared rented holiday accommodation. And households, of course, continue to produce their own leisure and tourism services such as family games or outings.
- A fourth important feature is that there has been *privatization* of leisure services (Rojek 1985, 19) which have tended to become more home based. Gershuny and Miles (1983) argue that this is

related to the substitution of goods (such as videos) for services (such as cinema attendance).

- This leads on to the final feature, which is that the production of most *local leisure and tourism services is interdependent*. Their facilities are rarely exclusive in terms of market segments, with a few exceptions such as accommodation. In addition, many large companies, such as Ladbroke in the UK (owners of betting shops as well as a major hotel chain), are strongly diversified into both local leisure and tourism markets.

Social Well-being and Lifestyles

Social well-being and quality of life are terms open to a variety of interpretations, but they centre on the satisfaction that people obtain from their lives. This can be measured both subjectively and in terms of objective indicators. Subjective research on the quality of life tends to identify leisure as an important element, but secondary to such items as health, family life and marriage (see, for example, Andrews and Withey 1976). Detailed empirical research in the UK, however, confirms the '. . . existence of identifiable groups who suffer leisure disadvantage or even privation, often in the context of economic constraints and limited job satisfaction' (Stockdale 1985, 117). There is also the need to look at the wider ramifications of leisure. Smith (1987, 83) for example, argues that leisure serves two fundamental needs: '. . . the need for the leisure space in which to construct ongoing close relationships, and also the need for the leisure space to renew individual energy and potential'. This is reflected in the role of state provision in leisure and, in some countries, in social tourism programmes (see chapter 3).

Geographers have also contributed to the debate on the quality of life and social well-being. There have been a number of attempts to derive objective measures of these concepts and to use these social indicators to measure spatial variations in their distribution. These include both indirect measures pertaining to leisure and tourism – such as overcrowding and car ownership – and direct measures. With regard to the latter, Knox (1974) includes the availability of public libraries and cinemas in his synthetic index of 'the level of living'. This is then used to map out the spatial distribution of the level of living in the UK, which highlights both rural–urban and north–south differences. Such an approach is essentially descriptive, and although later attempts have been made to ground this work in theories of social and economic differentiation (Smith 1977a; Coates et al. 1977) these have not been entirely successful. At the very least, the approach is subject to two fundamental criticisms: first, that the quality of life is essentially a subjective matter and that it is therefore not amenable to objective statistical analysis; and second, that the spatial focus has diverted attention away from important social differences in the quality of life. There is a thesis that developed countries have been moving towards being 'leisure democracies' (see, for example, Golbey 1985, 38). This takes the view that people's leisure activities are determined less by status and income and more by personality and individual lifestyle. We reject this perspective in favour of the idea that gender, race, life-cycle and other social dimensions – acting in combination – are critical filters which condition social access to tourism and leisure (see chapter 3).

These different dimensions of access to leisure and tourism do not operate independently of each other. The class experience of leisure is conditioned by gender, stage of life-cycle, race and location. However, there are fundamental tendencies which tend to cut across social divides. A high level of disposable income, for example, provides a means to compensate for some of the systematic leisure disadvantages of being a woman, being elderly, being black or living in a poorly serviced area. This is why leisure and tourism are important elements of the quality of life.

However, leisure and tourism are more than just elements in social well-being, since they are also indicators of lifestyle and of an individual's position in society. Weber (1968) argued that a specific style of life is expected from those who wish to belong to a particular social circle. Rojek (1985, 73) adds that while the composition of life-style varies with empirically given circumstances, 'One important dimension of it in all cases and at all times is the conspicuous consumption of commodities and leisure time'. In this sense the lifestyle attached to a given leisure form is a symbolic expression of power. Belonging to the 'right' club, wearing the 'right' designer leisure clothes, and being seen in a fashionable resort help define your position in the status hierarchy, and also indicate your power base (see Featherstone 1987). The epitome of this was Veblen's (1925) 'leisure class' who used their leisure time to display their wealth and status in society. Similarly, youth subcultures are partly defined by their leisure, whether it be biking, drugs, alcohol, music or voluntary work. In this way leisure becomes one of the weapons in intergenerational conflicts.

Culture and Internationalization

Leisure helps to shape culture and is culturally contingent. This is evident in the books that are read as well as in the sports that are played (whether individualistic or collective) both within and between countries. Over time there has been a tendency to greater homogeneity in culture. This is linked to the growth of mass culture which is '. . . part of the process of the development of common unifying cultural values and attitudes in the new and vast population of modern national units' (Theodorson and Theodorson 1969, 245). The mass media play a critical role in the creation of mass culture. Consequently, the internationalization of the mass media – whether in terms of broadcasting, films or print – has contributed to the internationalization of culture. The process is, of course, not monolithic and many groups retain distinctive leisure interests even in the most developed countries. For example, in the North West of England there is a tendency for Asian workers to be employed on night shift work. Aubrey et al. (1986 133) comment that '. . . the pattern of Asian recruitment and the hours which they worked appeared to set them apart in many ways from the normal leisure patterns of the native white community, and to maintain or reinforce their cultural isolation'.

Tourism is a particularly potent agent of cultural change, especially of internationalization. Lanfant (1980, 34) argues that 'we are dealing, in tourism, with an all-embracing social phenomenon characterized by the introduction of new systems of relationships in all sectors of activity, bringing about structural changes at all levels of social life and increasingly affecting all regions of the world'. In a later paper (Lanfant 1989, 182–3) she argues that Euro-Disney represents an extreme example of this process:

> This firm unites into one industrial whole the development of leisure parks, a cable communications network for press and television, the manufacture of pictures, models and all the apparatus essential to the creation of illusion. The new industry incorporates the most up-to-date scientific discoveries in communications, and is marshalling all the knowledge required to create a *planetary culture* of universal influence.

Conceptualization of the cultural impact of tourism can be further extended to take into account reverse cultural flows (figure 1.3). There is a cycle of cultural impacts even if the flows are asymmetrical. Gobey (1985, 131) argues that tourism produces 'a wanderlust, not for other places but for other lives'; in other words, for new, more pleasing self-images. MacCannell (1976) goes further and argues that one reaction to the harshness of modern, mass-produced life has been the belief that 'authentic' life is occurring elsewhere in the world. Holidays offer a transient opportunity to capture some of

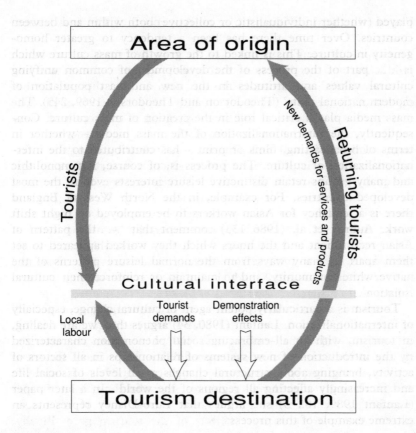

Figure 1.3   The tourism and culture cycle

this 'authenticity', at least for some groups of tourists (see chapter 4). It is hardly surprising, therefore, that there should be some attempt to transfer back to the home communities some aspects of this authenticity. This is most obviously evident in the demand for Spanish *tapas* bars in Britain, or in the purchase of London Bridge for use as a tourist attraction in the USA. However, it is also present in the demand for more ecologically sound lifestyles or the attempts to recreate French country cooking in British homes. It is little wonder, consequently, that the European Community in the 1980s and 1990s has been promoting tourism as a means of facilitating the process of European integration.

Production and Consumption: an Approach to Critical Issues

The approach adopted in this book is to study critical issues in the production and consumption of tourism. We have already touched upon some of these aspects in the introduction, and they are further elaborated in the next two parts of the volume. In terms of production there is a complex of industries involved in the supply of these services and goods. They tend to have a dualistic structure, with large numbers of small, independent firms operating alongside a few large transnationals. The nature of production is distinctive in that the quality of labour at the point of service delivery is an essential part of the labour process. Tourism and leisure services (but not necessarily goods) also have to be delivered directly to consumers where they reside permanently, or temporarily, while on holiday. This poses particular requirements in terms of assembling the necessary labour force to fulfil this objective. Production is also distinctive in that tourism involves a high degree of self-provisioning; this also applies more generally to leisure.

There are also distinctive features of the consumption of tourism services. There is a degree of complimentarity/substitutability in the consumption of some tourism and leisure services; for example, cycling in the home area or while on holiday. In addition, the social construction of tourism is particularly well-developed and is linked to an exceptionally high level of market segmentation. There is also increasingly rapid change in the social construction of what constitutes the (more attractive) objects of the tourism gaze. Finally, tourism and, more generally, leisure are critical elements in the construction of lifestyles and in social differentiation.

While there is nothing new in the study of the production and consumption features as such (see, for example, Jansen-Verbeke and Dietvorst 1987), we believe that the book does contribute to redefining the geography of tourism in some important respects. First, it emphasizes the need to analyse tourism within the context of leisure as a whole; this is important given the traditional segmentation of the literature in these two fields. Second, we have attempted to link some of the issues in tourism to wider issues in the social science literature. In effect, this is what de Kadt (1979) was calling for when he warned researchers against concentrating on the 'unique' problems associated with tourism. The holistic nature of much of the recent development of critical social science has been particularly helpful in widening the analytical frame of reference. Third, we have sought to link the analyses of production and consumption by examining how these come together to produce particular types of tourism environments (part

IV). In this volume it is not possible to be comprehensive in this respect and, instead, we concentrate on rural, urban and mass tourism environments. The actual form that any one of these tourism environment types assumes in a particular locality is, of course, contingent. Our aim therefore has been to identify relevant issues in each case rather than to proscribe their characteristics in any deterministic sense.

Finally, in terms of geographical coverage we have principally focused the book on the tourism of the developed capitalist societies. We therefore make scant reference to tourism in the old 'socialist' block of countries, and are mainly concerned with the less developed countries in so far as they are affected by tourism from the more developed economies. Therefore, the book does not claim to provide a comprehensive perspective on tourism geography. Instead, our aim is to review some of the critical issues in the geography of tourism which have been, are or should be the main objects of analysis.

PART II

Access to Tourism Consumption

TWO

The International Dimension

International Comparisons of Tourism and Leisure

There has been changing availability of 'free' time in most countries, whether they are classified as 'developed' or 'less developed'. There is a lack of precise comparative data, but a World Tourism Organization (1983) survey indicates aggregate changes in the length of the working week (table 2.1). Whereas in the developed countries the average length of the working week has been falling, it has been increasing in many less developed countries. The data have to be interpreted carefully, as different sets of countries are included in the 1960 and the 1980 samples. There are also major differences in the distribution of leisure time between men and women, and amongst age cohorts and social classes (see chapter 3).

There is a general tendency towards internationalization in the content of leisure time. Purchases of mass consumer goods, such as electronic audio and visual equipment, together with media presentations of 'desirable' lifestyles, are leading to greater universalization in both active and passive leisure time. Tourism services are also becoming increasingly internationalized. Todaro's (1977, 271) comments on the implications of the internationalization of trade, in general, are relevant here. They apply at least as much to tourism, and to most of the developed as well as the developing countries:

... international trade and finance must be understood in a much broader perspective than simply the inter-country flow of commodities and financial resources. By 'opening' their economies and societies to world trade and commerce and by 'looking outward' to the rest of the world, Third World countries invite not only the transfer of goods, services and financial resources, but also the 'developmental' or 'anti-

Table 2.1 Trends in the length of the working week, 1960-80: the percentage of countries in which the average working week is less than 40 hours

	1960	1980
Africa	55	47
Americas	0	32
East Asia and the Pacific	80	55
Europe	0	44
Middle East	25	0
South Asia	NA	33

Source: World Tourism Organization

developmental' influences of the transfer of production technologies, consumption patterns, institutional and organizational arrangements, educational, health and social systems, and the more general values, ideals, and lifestyles of the developed nations of the world, both capitalist and socialist.

The internationalization of tourism is a process with long roots. It can be traced back to the earliest trading, to the pilgrimages of medieval times, and the Grand Tours of the aristocracy and the upper middle classes in the eighteenth and nineteenth centuries. Mass international tourism is a product of the twentieth century, especially of the period since the Second World War (see chapter 9). In most countries the vast majority of tourists are still domestic tourists but, as table 2.2 shows, there are several countries in which international tourists outnumber the domestic ones. These are mostly located in Western Europe, where international travel is facilitated by relatively high disposable incomes, political and social stability, and the relatively small geographical size of most states. In the USA, by contrast the sheer size of that country, and the vast range of climatic regions and landforms which it encompasses, means that international tourism is dwarfed by domestic tourism.

In 1948 there were 14 million international tourists, in 1955 there were 46 million, in 1965 144 million, and in 1989 there were 403 million (World Tourism Organization 1990). Such trends led Cosgrove and Jackson (1972, 42) to comment that 'The pioneer fringe of international tourism ostentatiously flutters almost throughout the world'. They were right then – and even more so in the 1990s – that there are very few regions, let alone countries, which have not been touched, in some way, by international tourism. However, this should

Table 2.2   Domestic tourism: share of all hotel and similar accommodation nights accounted for by domestic tourists

	Per cent
Kenya	20.6
Zaire	35.3
Morocco	17.7
Denmark	50.3
Greece	22.3
Italy	61.7
Spain	33.4
Austria	20.5
France	69.0
Syria	52.6

Source: World Tourism Organization (1989a, 61–3)

not be taken to imply that global mass tourism has now arrived and that the populations of most countries are caught up in the whirl of international travel.

There are a number of important features in the geographical pattern of international tourism movements. Mansfield (1990) provides an overview of spatial interaction within the 'tourist space', and distinguishes between aggregated and disaggregated perspectives. The latter are subdivided into those that emphasize sociodemographic variables and behavioural segmentation. Here, we limit ourselves to some brief comments on the aggregate patterns (but see chapters 3 and 4 for disaggregation perspectives). First, the international movements of tourists are highly *polarized*. All of the major (larger than one million) international movements of visitors are shown in figure 2.1. These figures include day visitors, international labour migrants, business and holiday tourists. They therefore exaggerate the importance of some of the tourism flows, but despite this they provide a picture of the geographical pattern of international movement. As would be expected, the moves are primarily amongst the more developed countries (that is, intra- or inter-core) or from these to less developed ones which offer relatively accessible holiday destinations (that is, core–periphery). Two of the three largest international flows are between the USA and Canada. There are also important trans-North Atlantic flows and large movements from Japan.

Second, most of these international movements are *regionalized* and are especially concentrated within Europe. There were two separate systems within Europe in 1987, involving Western and Eastern

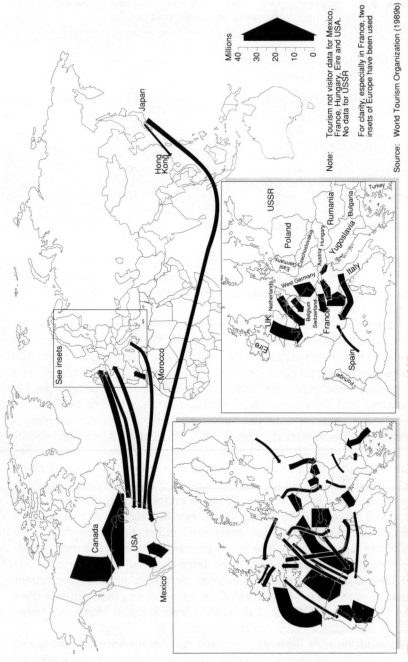

Figure 2.1 Major international visitor movements, 1987
Source: World tourism Organization (1989b)

Europe; this will have been modified to some extent by the collapse of the Communist regimes in Eastern Europe. The cut-off point of one million means that only the largest flows are shown on this map, and there are several other subsystems of international movements which are not so apparent. These include Japan and East Asia, the USA and the Caribbean, South Africa and southern Africa, and Europe and North Africa. For example, the relatively modest tourism flows into the Caribbean are highly dominated by the USA; it accounts for more than half of the tourists in most of the Caribbean islands, while in Bermuda and the British Virgin Islands the figure exceeds 90 per cent.

Third, the *overall dominance of Europe continues but is in relative decline* (table 2.3a). International tourism expanded rapidly in Europe in the 1960s, but its world share peaked at 75 per cent in the early 1970s. Subsequently, this share has fallen back, to 62 per cent in 1989. The share of the Americas (especially the USA) has also fallen back, although it has been relatively stable at about one fifth of the

Table 2.3 International tourism: global macro-regions
(a) Tourism arrivals by region – percentage distribution

	1950	1971	1989
Europe	66	75	62
Americas	30	19	20
Africa	2	1	4
Asia/Pacific	1	3 }	15
Middle East	1	2 }	
	100	100	

(b) Tourism growth rates, 1980–89

	Percentage change, 1980–89
Africa	+ 81.36
Americas	+ 48.43
Asia	+ 102.37
Europe	+ 28.75
Oceania	+ 123.61
World	+ 41.69

Sources: World Tourism Organization, various reports; (b) World Tourism Organization (1990, 11–12)

total since the early 1970s. In contrast, there has been steady growth in tourism arrivals in Africa, and quite spectacular growth in Asia/Pacific. This is underlined by the percentage change data for the 1980s (table 2.3b). Oceania and Asia have had far higher growth rates than the other world regions. In part, this reflects the 'discovery' of these regions by the tour companies and the tourists of the developed countries in the Northern Hemisphere. However, it also reflects rising real incomes in some of the newly industrializing countries of Asia and, more especially, Japan. In 1987, for example, there were 577 700 Japanese tourists to China and 341 900 to Thailand. Japanese tourism has been fuelled by rising living standards, appreciation of the yen, and government promotion of foreign tourism as a gesture towards reduction of the balance of payments surplus. The latter is the so-called 'Ten Million' programme launched in 1987.

The Uneven International Trade in Tourism

Tourism is an important element of international trade and, not surprisingly, has attracted the interest of national governments. There is a high and positive income elasticity of demand for tourism. This has been translated into strong growth in the volume of international tourism and in the foreign exchange transfers generated by the industry. Between 1965 and 1987 the growth of tourism's foreign exchange earnings matched the overall growth of world exports. The significance of this is underlined by the realization that the growth of world trade itself has outstripped that of GDP since the 1950s (Knox and Agnew 1989). While this in itself is impressive, a disaggregation of temporal trends reveals a major shift in the composition of trade in recent years. Between 1980 and 1989 international tourism expenditure increased by 104 per cent, which was double the 52 per cent growth in global exports (World Tourism Organization 1990). The economic importance of international tourism can also be provided with a theoretical perspective – albeit a simplistic one – in the form of the export base theory. This argues that economic growth stems from income generated from outside an area; that is, from exports.

Another reason for the growing importance of international tourism is deindustrialization in the developed countries. This means that the service sector – including tourism – has become more important in these economies. This is particularly the case with employment; for example, in the USA 80 per cent of job growth between 1975 and 1985 was concentrated in just four service sectors (Knox and Agnew 1989, 183). Ricardo's concept of comparative advantage provides an interesting theoretical perspective on specialization in tourism. The argument is that an area should specialize in producing and exporting those products in which it has competitive or relative cost advantages compared to other countries. This would seem to rule out international tourism in the more developed countries of northern Europe. However, the application of this economic principle to tourism is limited because of the nature of tourism attractions, which are – to a large extent – socially constructed. Faced with deindustrialization in the late twentieth century, many developed countries set about reconstructing their tourism images as a means of generating alternative sources of employment.

In addition, the conditions surrounding the production of tourism services are distinctive. Tourism requires relatively low initial capital investment, especially if it is integrated with existing settlements and infrastructure. Obviously, the development of large-scale tourism will require greater capital investments (perhaps in a new airport, in attractions or in new hotels) but even these are usually easier to facilitate than a major investment in manufacturing capacity. Generally, tourism requires lower per capita investment, lower technological and labour skills, and faces less protectionism in world markets than does manufacturing. Not surprisingly, for these reasons tourism tends to be attractive to less developed regions and countries in search of strategies for economic development.

Establishing the importance of international tourism receipts and expenditures is easier than quantifying them in any detail. Data for different countries for the same time period can be inconsistent because of differences in definitions and in data collection methods. There are two main methods for estimating tourism expenditures, and these are often used in conjunction:

> The direct method relies on information provided by tourists themselves and by financial institutions. The indirect method multiplies the number of tourist nights by an average of daily expenditures. These procedures involve errors in generating the net balance on 'tourist' expenditures abroad (the balance on tourism) and fail to include the related transactions which owe their existence to tourism (Baretje 1982, 59).

There are considerable problems in providing such estimates: poor reporting by financial institutions, incomplete records of tourist numbers and tourist nights, and inaccurate estimates of tourism spend levels. There is also a need to take into account net financial transfers related to tourism such as foreign investments, transport costs, imports of goods, remittance by migrant workers, and so on. International tour companies add an additional layer of complexity to international tourism trade flows. For example, Bull (1990, 325) provides an estimate that, on average, only 31 per cent of the money spent on a British package holiday in Spain is received by that country, whereas 50 per cent is received by the UK tour company, and the remaining 19 per cent is received by other UK businesses. Within the receiving country, the tourism receipts are distributed across a number of sectors. In the UK in 1980, for example, the distribution was as follows: 27 per cent on shopping, 21 per cent on each of accommodation and travel to the UK, 11 per cent on eating out, and 9 per cent on travel in the UK (Gratton and Taylor 1987, 70).

Table 2.4 The ideal calculation of the national tourism balance

	Sum		Sum
Tourism expenditures (outlays of national citizens abroad)	—	Tourism receipts (expenditures of foreign tourists)	—
Importation of commodities (chiefly foodstuffs and instrumental goods)	—	Exportation (goods, durables or semi-durables, handicraft products)	—
Transportation (share of international travel by national citizens)	—	Transportation (share of international travel by non-nationals)	—
Tourism investments abroad	—	Foreign tourism investments within the nation	—
Interest payments on foreign Investments and refund of capital	—	Income from tourism investments made abroad	—
Repatriation of income paid to foreign tourism workers	—	Repatriation of income paid to national tourism workers residing abroad	—
Publicity, advertising, etc.	—	Publicity, advertising, etc.	—
DEBIT BALANCE = deficit		CREDIT BALANCE = surplus	
Total		Total	

Source: Sessa (1983, 136)

These, and other such financial transactions, must be taken into account to calculate the net tourism balance, what Baretje (1982) terms 'Tourism's External Account' or what Sessa (1983) calls the 'Ideal Tourism Balance': the latter is summarized in table 2.4. Arguably, even this broader calculation is incomplete in that, for example, it fails to take into account the social and environmental costs of international tourism, whether in terms of traffic congestion or the damage to the ecosystem of the Mediterranean and the Caribbean. Despite such shortcomings, these arguments are important in providing a broader conceptual framework for analysing the economic importance of international tourism trade flows, although in practice it is very difficult to obtain comparable international statistics for the Ideal Tourism Balance. Instead, we have to rely on the less complete estimates of receipts and expenditure which are collated by the World Tourism Organization and by the OECD.

Earnings from international tourism have long been important to a number of economies. As early as 1966, it was estimated that $13.1 billion of $60 billion tourism spend was international (Cosgrove and Jackson 1972, 45). Subsequently, the importance of the international component has almost certainly increased substantially. In the following discussion some of the salient features of the international trade in tourism services are analysed. There has been a tendency within tourism research to view tourism trade in isolation from general trends in trade. This perspective is limited and we, therefore, provide some references to the literature on this topic.

The present distribution of tourism receipts between world regions is summarized in table 2.5. There is a broad but imperfect association between the numbers of international tourists and the share of total tourism receipts accounted for by the major world regions. Africa

Table 2.5 Global regions: percentage shares of international tourism arrivals and receipts, 1989

	Arrivals	Receipts
Africa	3.8	3.2
Americas	19.8	26.9
Asia	13.6	17.1
Europe	61.8	50.4
Oceania	1.1	2.5
World total	100.0	100.0

Source: World Tourism Organization (1990)

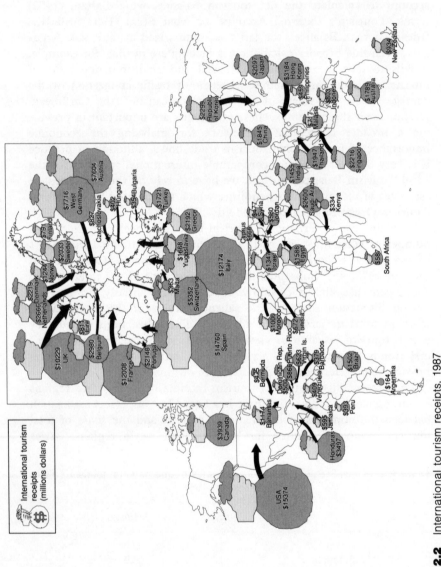

Figure 2.2 International tourism receipts, 1987
Source: World Tourism Organization (1989b)

and Oceania have relatively small shares of both, while 94 per cent of receipts are accounted for by Europe, the Americas and Asia. Both the Americas and Asia account for a larger share of receipts than of tourists, reflecting a relatively efficient income-extracting industry. In comparison, Europe has 11 per cent more arrivals than receipts; this is accounted for by shorter distances and shorter trips, and by the organization of a mass tourism industry based on all-inclusive holiday packages (see chapter 9). In addition, over time the shares of receipts accounted for by both Europe and the Americas have declined; their respective shares in 1965 had been 62 per cent and 29 per cent (Cosgrove and Jackson 1972, 43). This reflects the globalization of the tourism industry in the 1970s and 1980s, as well as the rise of Japan as a major source of tourism expenditures.

A more detailed disaggregation of international tourism financial flows also reveals a number of features. In terms of total receipts (figure 2.2), the USA is the world leader. However, with this exception, the main feature of the distribution is strong regionalization. For the reasons noted earlier, European countries are dominant, particularly the UK, Italy, Spain and France. In addition, the other two main geographical nodes are in the Americas, largely driven by tourism from the USA, and in East Asia, through Japanese tourism. This strong tourism relationship between a core economic area and an adjacent peripheral economic area has parallels with the world pattern of industrial trade (Knox and Agnew 1989). The rise in importance of Japanese tourism also mirrors the growing significance of Japan in world industrial production. Between 1950 and 1981 Japan's share of world exports increased from 1.4 per cent to 8.2 per cent, and its share of world tourism trade has followed this trend, although at lower levels.

Overall receipts need, however, to be set against tourism expenditures, as some countries, notably the USA, Japan, the UK and, above all, Germany have large net outflows of tourism expenditures. As a result, the geographical distribution of the net balances on the tourism account (figure 2.3) reveal a quite different pattern. Reflecting the north–south pattern of tourism, the less developed countries make a far stronger showing in terms of net receipts than of gross receipts. Europe also appears more polarized. Northern Europe mostly has large deficits, while southern Europe records large surpluses. Another feature of note is the large deficit on the tourism account of the USA, Japan and especially Germany. The latter had a net deficit of $15 835 in 1987. In the case of both Germany and Japan these deficits partly counterbalance large surpluses on the balances of trade. In the case of the USA, tourism adds significantly to the current account deficit of a country with a large recurrent trade imbalance.

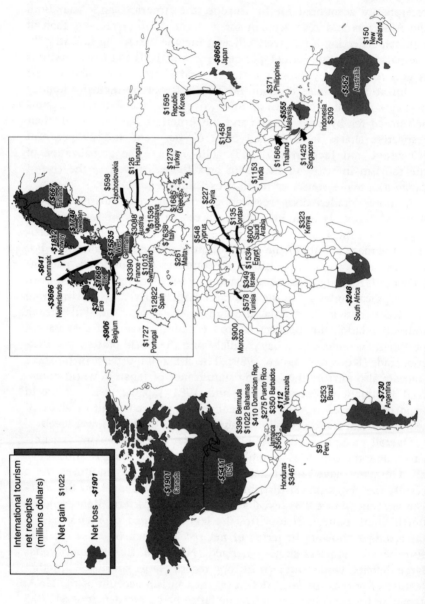

Figure 2.3 Net international tourism receipts, 1987

Source: World Tourism Organization (1989b)

The overall importance of tourism to these different economies is, of course, a function of several contingent conditions, and is not simply related to the absolute size of the net balance. A deficit of $8 billion is relatively insignificant to Japan given its trade surpluses, while a small positive balance can be of major importance to a less developed economy. This is dependent on the absolute size of the economies as well as the degree of diversification which exists. For example, in Mexico the share of tourism earnings in total exports declined from 52 per cent to 6 per cent between 1954 and 1982, largely as a function of industrialization and increased revenue from oil exports (Truett and Truett 1987). The degree of diversity is reflected in the experiences of the Caribbean as shown in figure 2.4. In 1985 gross receipts of $97 million represented 97 per cent of the exports of the Bahamas, while receipts of $407 million in Jamaica represented just 37 per cent of exports. In summary, the overall position is one in which tourism accounts for a relatively large share of exports in the developing countries compared to both Asia and Eastern Europe (table 2.6). The developed market economies, *en masse*, occupy an intermediate position but, especially within Europe, this conceals considerable variations amongst individual states.

The pattern of commodity trade is mainly inter-core or intra-core trade, in that it centres on North America, Europe and Japan. For example, the industrial core economies have dominated international commodity trade, accounting for 60–70 per cent of world exports and imports in every decade since 1950 (McConnell 1986). In general, there has been an intensification of this long-standing dominance at the expense of core–periphery trade, with the exception of the oil-producing states. Tourism trade is different, however, in that some of the peripheral or semi-peripheral economies located in the Caribbean or on the fringes of the Mediterranean have secured important shares of the international tourism trade. Moreover, this share has increased over time. Finally, there is broad similarity between trade in tourism and in commodities, in that both bring vulnerability (Keohane and Nye 1977) to the less developed countries. Vulnerability can be interpreted as structural dependence (Gill and Law 1988, chapter 6), implying reduced scope for national policy.

International Tourism and the Pursuit of Business

While most tourism is a form of leisure, it does have other important functions such as visits to friends and relatives, as well as educational or religious trips. Tourism is also generated by business require-

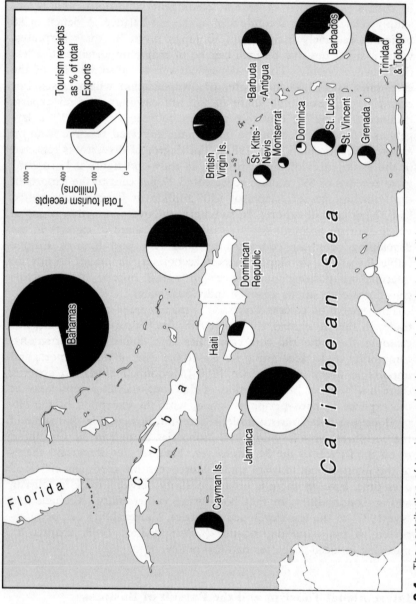

Figure 2.4 The contribution of tourism receipts to exports in selected Caribbean countries, 1985

Table 2.6   International tourism receipts as a percentage of all exports, 1987: global regions

	Per cent
Developed market economies	6.4
(Europe)	(8.0)
(Americas)	(5.7)
Developing countries	8.0
European socialist countries	1.0
Asian socialist countries	5.0

Source: World Tourism Organization (1989a, 17–18)

ments. If tourism is defined in terms of overnight stays, then international business tourism has existed since the early emergence of international trading. As the internationalization of the world economy developed, so international business tourism increased in importance. According to Palloix (1975), the internationalization of the world economy passed through a historical sequence from commodity capital (trade), to money capital (investment), through to productive capital (foreign direct investment as part of a global strategy by multinationals). Each of these stages has generated new forms and levels of international tourism. Trade required travel abroad to buy, sell and distribute products; portfolio investment also required travel for management purposes; and foreign direct investment demanded foreign travel to coordinate intra-company organization. Similarly, international subcontracting also generates foreign travel to maintain an integrated economic system.

In the late twentieth century, international business tourism has become a sophisticated industry. There are three constituent elements: incentive travel, conference tourism and business travel. Their economic importance is underlined by two facts. First, the per capita spending power of the business tourist is considerably higher than that of the leisure tourist, and the ratio between these has been estimated to be as much as three to one (Lawson 1982). Second, the sheer volume of international business tourism has reached an impressive level, with the World Tourism Organization (1991) estimating that this now accounts for 30 per cent of all international tourism.

Unfortunately, comprehensive statistics on business tourism are not available, although the World Tourism Organization collation of travel data provides information for some countries on the basis of tourist motivations (figure 2.5). There is considerable variation in the

A   Holiday tourism is *overwhelmingly* dominant

B   Business tourism is important and holiday tourism is little developed

C   Business and holiday tourism are *relatively* important

Figure 2.5   Tourist motivations: selected international examples, 1987

importance of business tourism. Some countries in both the semi-periphery (Portugal) and the periphery (Seychelles) have well-developed holiday tourism industries which account for more than 90 per cent of international tourism. In the case of Portugal this makes a large absolute level of international business arrivals seem relatively unimportant. There are also some Third World countries (such as Bangladesh) with very limited holiday tourism; as a result, even modest levels of business tourism become important in relative terms. Finally, there are countries in the developed world (the USA) and amongst the newly industrializing countries (Singapore) where both business and holiday tourism are relatively important.

Amongst the three main types of international business tourism, *incentive travel* is probably the least important. It is also the least researched. Incentive travel is an employment perk used to reward or motivate employees. It is used by such diverse organizations as major sporting clubs, and by large business corporations. Above all, it relies on the socially constructed nature of tourism and on the powers of the image-creating industry. The destinations may be relatively prosaic – a weekend on the golf courses of the Algarve or the beaches of Mallorca for exhausted footballers or executives. Alternatively, it may involve '. . . an individually tailored fantasy which cannot be bought in an ordinary package' (*Financial Times* 2 September 1986). There is often an important gender dimension to these fantasy packages. They may be designed for the mostly female spouses of a largely male group of executives, and may represent a symbolic exchange for long hours spent at work and away from families. Whether the package is prosaic or fantastic, it is of considerable importance in economic terms. It has been estimated that one third of the UK's top companies use tourism as a perk, and that the UK incentive travel industry was valued at £400 million, while that of the USA is worth over $2 billion (Smith 1990). Moreover, 80 per cent of these incentive packages involve trips within Europe, so that their geographical distribution, as with tourism in general, is largely intra-core.

Conference tourism represents big business at both the national (see chapter 10) and the international scale; the North American market alone is valued at around $45 billion (Smith 1990):

> The Austrians like to claim that modern, organized conferences began with the Congress of Vienna in 1815, an influential affair which, like modern conventions, had a substantial social programme in addition to its working sessions. Perhaps it is more accurate though to look to the USA for the development of the modern convention industry. In North America, attending meetings has become something of a way of life (Smith 1989, 61).

By the early 1980s there were an estimated 14 000 international conferences each year (Law 1985a). These also have an overwhelmingly inter- and intra-core spatial distribution. Within Europe, the primary international conference centres are Paris, London, Madrid, Geneva and Brussels (figure 2.6). Outside of Europe the main venues are Sydney, Singapore, Washington and New York. International conferences vary in size from brief meetings of a handful of individuals in an informal setting, to major assemblages of delegates and associated commercial exhibitors in large purpose-built conference centres. One of the largest international conferences held to date was the International Rotary meeting at the National Exhibition Centre in Birmingham, which was attended by 23 000 delegates. This was a notable success for Birmingham in its attempt to establish itself as a

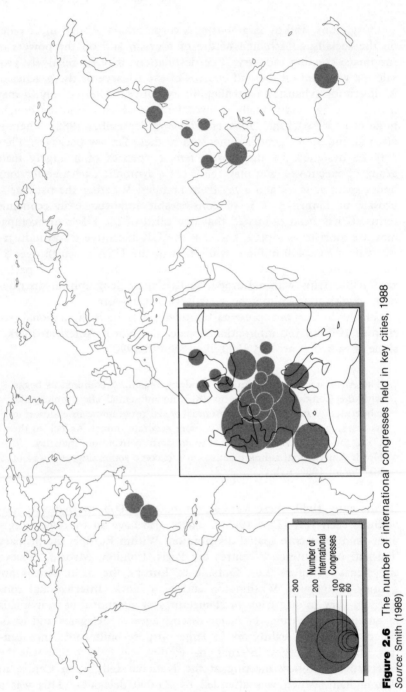

Figure 2.6 The number of international congresses held in key cities, 1988

Source: Smith (1989)

major international conference venue. However, this is a highly competitive market and within Western Europe alone there is competition from centres from as far apart as Vienna, Helsinki and Belem (Lisbon). Furthermore, the competition is becoming more intense. Smith (1990, 211) writes:

> The last 20 years have seen considerable changes in the meetings industry, in itself a new phrase. . . . Now every sizeable town in the world sees itself as a meeting place, promotes its facilities for conferences and seminars, pays at least a little attention to the search for friends among meeting planners, welcomes their delegates, provides overt and covert inducements which can range from a free deckchair to a no-charge convention centre for 1000 people for a week.

While there is a strong element of regionalization in the international conference market, this coexists with a growing tendency to globalization. For example, the American Law Association has held its conference in London, and there are increasing numbers of truly world conferences, such as the Rio 'Earth Summit'. In some market segments, therefore, Birmingham is in competition not only with Brussels and Barcelona, but also with Baltimore, Bangkok and Bali. The requirements for success as an international conference centre are demanding: a high degree of accessibility, especially in terms of air travel; modern, well-equipped conference facilities; a large stock of adjacent high-quality accommodation; and an attractive tourism image which will attract not only the delegates but also their 'accompanying persons'.

International business travel has expanded considerably in recent years as a result of the globalization of the world economy. In 1989 the world business travel market had an estimated value in excess of $320 billion (Petersen and Belchambers 1990). Its geographical distribution closely resembles that for trade in goods and services, and therefore accords strongly with the core–periphery model of economic development. The most important elements are regionalization within the cores of the Americas and Europe, global linkages between the cores, and core–adjacent periphery movements. In addition, international business tourism is predicated by the internal organization of transnational companies themselves.

Transnational companies are involved in a global search to maintain capital accumulation. They seek out new international locations which offer access to markets, advantageous production costs, or the opportunity to secure strategic advantages over other transnationals. Given changes in technology and factor costs, transnationals have tended increasingly to spread their operations across international boundaries. This often involves the spatial separation of different stages of production: in extreme form, headquarters are located in one continent, while production and regional management are located in others.

Hymer (1975) is most closely associated with the conceptualization of this model (figure 2.7). The model has been criticized for ignoring the possible existence of production in all zones, and for the location of lower level management in the major metropolitan centre. However, if this fuller model is taken into account, then it can provide a simple framework for understanding the geographical distribution of international business travel. Not least, this new international division of labour is predicated on 'enabling technologies' (Dicken 1986), which provide a 'permissive environment' (Knox and Agnew 1989, 92) for decentralization while maintaining central coordination. The main 'enabling technologies' are technological developments in transport and communications, and developments in company organizational methods.

The role of business travel in this model of spatial organization is

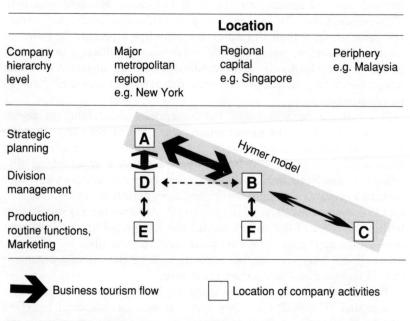

Figure 2.7   The business tourism potential of the spatial organization of transnational companies
Source: adapted from Hymer (1975)

somewhat ambivalent. Improved international travel was a precondition for the development of more sophisticated international divisions
of labour. However, improvements in information technology
(videoconferencing, faxes, satellite link-ups etc.) are challenging the
need for travel between company branches. This tendency does exist
but, at the same time, there continues to be a need for face-to-face
contact. This can be understood in terms of the hierarchy of contacts
in the structure of businesses (Goddard 1973). At the highest levels
of company management, there is a need for a high intensity of face-
to-face contact in the process of strategic decision-making. As you
descend through management hierarchies, and as decision-making
becomes more routine, the requirement for face-to-face contact
diminishes. This is one of the principal reasons for the spatial concentration of company headquarters within national economic spaces,
in metropoli such as New York, Tokyo, Milan and Paris.

An important element of international business tourism involves
the linking together of global headquarters cities (Cohen 1981).
Indeed, Dicken (1986, 193) writes that the corporate headquarters of
the global company '. . . requires, above all, a strategic location on
the global transport and communications network in order to keep in
touch with its far flung empire'. Regional headquarters have '. . . to
be accessible both to their corporate headquarters and also to the
affiliates under their immediate control.' Therefore, while some of the
more routine international business travel may be replaced in the
near future by new forms of information technology, business tourism is likely to become even more important as transnationals continue to extend their global reach.

Tourism and the Less Developed Countries

The less developed countries are in the process of being incorporated
into the world economy. This is an uneven and contingent process,
and it does not necessarily follow a set sequence. Nevertheless, it is
useful to conceptualize these economies as lying along a continuum,
for which Hall (1986) provides a working typology (table 2.7). There
are four stages of incorporation – none, weak, moderate and strong.
These are defined in terms of market articulation, the impact of the
core on the periphery, and the impact of the periphery on the core.
The form and level of tourism development in a Third World country is partly dependent on the stage of incorporation (because of the
need for infrastructure and certain social relationship) but it also
contributes to the process of incorporation.

Table 2.7   The continuum of geographical incorporation

	The continuum of incorporation			
	None	Weak	Moderate	Strong
Type of periphery	External arena	Contact periphery	Marginal periphery	Dependent periphery
Market articulation	None	Weak	Moderate	Strong
Impact of core on periphery	None	Strong	Stronger	Strongest
Impact of periphery on core	None	Low	Moderate	Significant

Source: Hall (1986, 392)

In most respects, Hall's typology could be used to model the role of tourism incorporation. The greater the incorporation, then the greater is the market articulation, and the greater the impact of the core on the periphery. This broadly accords with models of tourism development in the Third World (see chapter 4). The main difference is that, with tourism, the impact of the core on the periphery remains limited even when there is strong incorporation of its tourism economy. This is because the tourism flows – unlike those of industrial trade – remain highly asymmetrical; that is, from the developed countries to the less developed countries. However, at the same time, the fact that tourism moves people rather than goods between the First and the Third Worlds means that 'There is no other international trading activity which involves such critical interplay among economic, political, environmental, and social elements as tourism' (Lea 1988, 2). In this section we provide a brief overview of some of the critical issues in Third World tourism, although most of these themes will be developed in greater detail elsewhere in the text. There are five major issues to which we draw general attention here:

1 International tourism is characterized by asymmetrical power relationships, with most of the power and influence residing in the more developed countries. This is symbolized by the nature of the exchange which takes place: tourists from the developed countries demand high levels of luxury at prices below those which they are willing to pay in their home countries. These are provided by indigenous labour (and some enterprises) which

require hard foreign currency and which usually lack alternative sources of income.

2 The relationships between Third World countries and the tourist markets in the developed world are mediated by a group of organizations such as travel agencies, tour companies and airlines. Even more so than in the case of the semi-peripheral economies, such as Greece or Mexico, the less developed countries lack the means of excluding the intermediaries from these relationships. This is partly related to their colonial backgrounds and the historical underdevelopment of indigenous capital. The result is not only structural dependence but also a high level of income leakage. For example, in Gambia only 10 per cent of gross earnings from tourism are retained by the local population (Cater 1987). This is reinforced by the enclave nature of many tourism developments, which limits the spatial and social dispersion of expenditure.

3 Tourism brings both positive and negative economic benefits (table 2.8). These centre on its effects on other sectors of the economy, the demand for and development of facilities and infrastructures which will affect the local populace, foreign exchange earnings, GDP, employment, and net government revenue.

4 There are also both social and cultural effects of international tourism. The social effects centre on the modernization of society and polarization, the family, and the broadening of social horizons/ social pathology. The cultural effects centre on indigenous culture, the natural environment, landscapes, the built environment and demonstration effects.

5 The assessment of the economic, social and cultural effects listed above has been left open-ended at this stage because of the difficulty of making generalizations about the impact of tourism. This, in turn, is related to the multilinear nature of tourism (Cohen 1979b). Tourism can have organic growth rooted in the indigenous economy and society, or it can be externally driven. This, together with variations in the nature of the tourism inflows and the economic, social and cultural character of the recipient areas, means that the impacts of tourism in the less developed countries are highly contingent.

Finally, it can be observed that there has been a tendency within the tourism literature to treat tourism as a unique force for economic, social and cultural change. While there are some unique features of tourism as an agent of change, de Kadt's (1979, 12) dictum that 'tourism is not a unique devil' is certainly worthy of note. There is a need to assess the opportunity costs of tourism, both in the sense of

Table 2.8   The economic, social and cultural impacts of tourism

Positive	Negative
Economic	
Agricultural stimulus	Distention of agricultural production
Create new markets for their products in the developed countries	Decline of certain products not in international demand
Stimulus to fishing	Disturbance of traditional fishing ports and beaches
Stimulus to manufacturing	Manufactured goods/imported
Creation of new tourism attractions such as beaches or swimming pools, which can be used by locals	Over-use of existing attractions
Funds new infrastructure: water, roads, power and telephones	Saturates existing infrastructure
Earns foreign exchange	Leakage of foreign exchange income to intermediaries, and to purchase imported goods
Increases GDP, directly and indirectly via multiplier	Brings greater external control over the economy
Increases government revenues from taxation	Increased government expenditure
Creates employment	In-migrants hold many key management jobs; seasonal nature of employment
Offers jobs requiring little training or previous skills	Condemns labour force to low-skilled jobs
External source of growth	Dependence
Social	
Modernization of society	Polarization of social structure and increased income inequalities
Modernization of the family, via new gender and intergenerational conflicts	Disintegration of the family
Broadening social horizons and reduced prejudices among the tourists	Social pathology, including prostitution, drugs, etc.

Table 2.8   (Continued)

Positive	Negative
Cultural	
Development of indigenous culture	Disappearance of indigenous culture under the impact of commercialization
Greater protection of the natural environment	Destruction of the natural environment
Improve landscapes and architectural standards	Destroys landscapes, and leads to non-integrated tourism complexes
Contributes to conservation of monuments and buildings	Degradation of monuments and buildings
Positive demonstration effects	Negative demonstration effects

Source: elaboration on a classification developed in World Tourism Organization (1981, 9–13)

the diversion of resources from other sectors, and in the sense of evaluating what other economic strategies are open to a particular country or region. In the latter context, the 'green revolution' and rapid industrialization – even if achievable – have their own well-catalogued mixtures of positive and negative economic, social and cultural impacts, which also require careful consideration (see, for example, Knox and Agnew 1989).

THREE

Social Access to Tourism and Leisure

Socio-economic Change and Leisure Development

The links between levels of socio-economic development and the growth in demand for tourism and leisure are relatively easy to describe in a general historical context, but more difficult to analyse in any detail. Most perspectives have focused on stage-type models, such as that by Maslow (1954) based on changing societal needs, to discuss increases in leisure demand. More recently, attention has been focused on using 'lifestyle economics' (Mitchell 1983; Earl 1986), through the construction of 'values and lifestyles' (VALS) typologies, to study changes in consumption. The original VALS typology, developed in North America (Mitchell 1983), consists of nine types arranged hierarchically, as shown in figure 3.1. However, for our purposes we need only be concerned with the broad categories; need driven, outer- and inner-directed, and integrated.

This model can be used in two basic ways; to explore the nature of demand in any particular society, or as a framework to examine broad changes over time. Within a developed, high-level economy, it is considered that there will be a hierarchy of VALS types and that these will range from need-driven individuals, concerned mainly with satisfying food and shelter needs, through to outer- and inner-directed individuals, while at the top of the system are the integrated types. In general terms, outer-directed individuals are mainly motivated by the search for esteem and status, as they are materialistic in nature. Those categorized as inner-directed are motivated by the desire for stimulating experiences, having little interest in displays of status. The majority of people in Western societies tend to fall into the outer- and inner-directed groups. In the USA, for example, it has been estimated that around 87 per cent of the population fall within

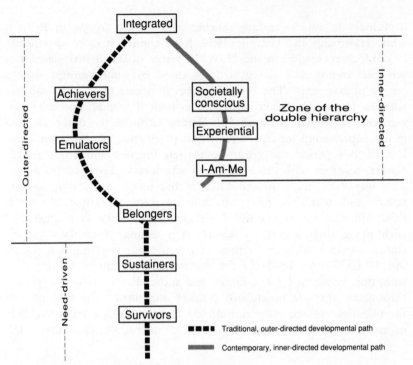

Figure 3.1   The value and lifestyle hierarchy

these two categories (Hartmann and Hennig 1989). Similarly, studies in the UK by MacNulty (1985) have examined such VALS types in terms of socio-economic groups. It was found that the needs-driven category is comprised mainly of groups of unskilled and skilled manual workers, together with the unemployed, while outer- and inner-directed covered those employed within professional, managerial and clerical activities, with a small number of skilled manual workers. In general terms, it is the inner-directed types that are growing most rapidly in British society, accounting for an estimated 38 per cent of the population in 1989, compared with 34 per cent outer-directed and 28 per cent needs-driven (MacNulty 1985).

In many developed Western societies the inner-directed types, whom MacNulty terms 'skilled consumers', have emerged relatively recently – in Britain, for example, from the 1960s onwards. The VALS model has been used in an evolutionary context in tracing the development of these different groups and their relationships with leisure patterns.

Gratton (1990) has provided a wide-ranging review of the model's usefulness in understanding tourism and leisure trends in Britain, while Hartmann and Hennig (1989) have applied it more specifically to outdoor recreation in the USA. In terms of the British case, it is possible to postulate the growth of these consumer groups over a period of 200 years. The broad changes in access to tourism and leisure in Britain, together with the estimated trends amongst consumers, are shown in figure 3.2. Before 1870–80 the outer-directed group represented an extremely small proportion of the population. During this period the group comprised the new industrial middle classes, together with the established aristocracy. Their access to leisure was very much routed towards the newly developing seaside resorts and, when the European political scene permitted, the wealthier still went on the 'Grand Tour'. Generally, they were concerned with using their access to leisure as a means of displaying their status, together with an element of conspicuous consumption (Gratton 1990). These trends in the materialistic nature of leisure consumption intensified for a larger and more diverse range of people throughout the late nineteenth century and during the first part of the twentieth century (figure 3.2). By the early 1950s small numbers of inner-directed consumers could be identified, whose access to lei-

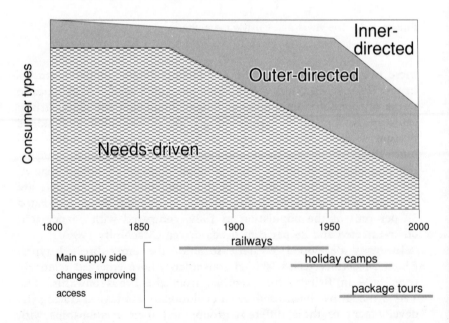

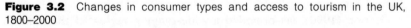

Figure 3.2   Changes in consumer types and access to tourism in the UK, 1800–2000

sure was similar to the larger outer-directed group, but whose consumption patterns was very different. These individuals started to look for new holiday experiences, and by the 1970s activity and cultural holidays had become very important to them. As MacNulty (1985) and Gratton (1990) argue, these leisure activities require greater consumer skills than those characteristic of the outer-directed group. Krippendorf (1986) has termed these people 'critical consumer tourists' who have a new consciousness of holiday travel and are more critical in their demand for tourist experiences.

In Britain, during the period after 1870, increased access to leisure and tourism was provided by improvements in overall real income, the growth of paid holidays for workers, and the provision of cheaper travel to seaside resorts by rail (Walvin 1978). Under such changes, a good many people moved from the needs-driven group into the outer-directed one, as the process of leisure access was achieved through the filtering down of activities from the controlling middle classes. Such access was also brought about by key institutional changes in the supply of holidays. Probably the two most important of these were the development during the 1930s of holiday camps (Burkart and Medlik 1981), and the later introduction of overseas package holidays (see chapter 9). The influence of the latter may be seen in the changing proportion of UK residents holidaying abroad, which increased from just 3.3 per cent in 1947 to 30 per cent 40 years later (Seaton 1992). Gratton (1990) argues that particular foreign destinations became a new source of conspicuous consumption for the more wealthy outer-directed consumers, that is, until some destinations became overcrowded, and the leading members of this consumer group then moved to newer, more distant locations.

Inequalities in Tourism and Leisure Access

Structural features and individual circumstances obviously condition people's ability to participate in tourism and leisure: these include the stage in the family life-cycle, gender, cultural conditions, the amount of leisure time available, access to tourist areas and disposable income.

Such structural features not only condition access but also represent considerable differences in the quality of experience. There is a world of difference between taking your holiday in Puerto Banus rather than in Torremolinos. From a sociological perspective, Newman (1983, 102) comments that, 'To rank the working classes as equal members of "leisure society" is clearly absurd. Even their sole brief interlude from routinization – the annual holiday – is subject to the grossest commercialization. . . . In common with other facets of social existence, their leisure experience is stratified and no less alienated than that of family, life chances, or avenues for social participation'. Such a perspective is particularly true of the underclass in many capitalist societies, especially the increasing numbers of long-term unemployed who may be regarded as 'leisure or tourism poor'. As we shall see later in this chapter, some governments have recognized the leisure problems faced by this group and attempt to offer potential help.

Socio-economic influencs on access to tourism and leisure have been given prominence. For example, surveys by the Commission of the European Communities (1987) have shown strong correlations between GDP per capita and the proportion of people taking holidays. Furthermore, tourism is characterized by a positive income elasticity of demand. In other words, the demand for holidays rises proportionately more than increases in personal income. Such relationships have been highlighted within the economies of the EC, where in 1985 an estimated 56 per cent of the population (140 million tourists) took at least one holiday, of four or more days, away from home (European Commission 1987). Within Scandinavia, even higher proportions have been recorded, reaching 83 per cent in Sweden in 1981, and 77 per cent in Norway in 1978 (Sundelin 1983).

A closer inspection of the EC reveals that the Community average hides considerable variations ranging from only 31 per cent of Portugal's population who take a holiday, to 65 per cent of Dutch people. These differences highlight the whole issue of access to tourism and leisure, particularly since some 40 per cent of the Community's population did not take a holiday in 1985. As table 3.1 shows, a variety of reasons appear to condition this access, although, with the exception of Denmark, economic constraints were cited most frequently. More specifically, we can recognize a group of countries within which economic constraints seem to play a major role in controlling holiday-taking; these are Greece, Portugal and Ireland (table 3.1).

Within the EC survey, some 49 per cent of manual workers stayed at home, compared with only 18 per cent of those in professional occupations. The survey also showed that older people, those with large families and those living in rural areas were less likely to take holidays away from home. For example, 66 per cent of Europeans living in large towns went on holiday, compared with 45 per cent living in villages. Furthermore, such differences appear to be far greater in the less-developed economies, such as Italy, Spain, Greece

Table 3.1 Reasons for West Europeans not taking a holiday during 1985
(per cent)

	(a)	(b)	(c)	(d)	(e)	(f)
Belgium	32	7	40	14	*	4
Denmark	38	8	23	16	*	16
West Germany	27	12	41	29	1	3
Greece	12	24	55	35	*	—
Spain	14	22	50	15	*	9
France	22	23	44	25	1	2
Ireland	14	10	61	10	1	6
Italy	30	22	31	21	2	2
Luxembourg	23	16	20	31	*	10
The Netherlands	22	9	32	27	1	14
Portugal	12	19	67	14	1	2
United Kingdom	14	6	50	21	1	16
EC12	22	16	44	22	1	6

(a) Preferred to stay at home
(b) Not able to get away from work
(c) Couldn't afford it
(d) Special reasons (health, moving house, family reasons, etc.)
(e) Worry about safety, terrorism, etc.
(f) Other reasons

Notes: in each country the sample comprised 100 people who did not take a holiday away from home in 1985. Because some respondents gave more than one answer, the total for each country generally exceeds 100. * Less than 0.5 per cent

Source: Commission of the European Communities (1987)

and Portugal, than in the more developed ones. Travis (1982) has shown that in Italy there is generally a low level of holiday-taking, but that there is also considerable divergence between different socio-economic groups. In the UK, by comparison, the proportion of people taking holidays shows less variation when related to age and socio-economic class (Mihovilovic 1980).

With a developed economy such as the UK, there are variations in access to tourism and, more particularly, to certain forms of holiday tourism. The social class and geographical dimensions of such variations are partly shown in table 3.2. From these data, based on large-scale surveys at a national level, it can be seen that socio-economic factors do relate to the consumption of holidays. While those from social class groups D and E (including unskilled workers) account for 31 per cent of the population, they make up 43 per cent of adults not taking any holidays. Conversely, those in professional and managerial occupations (groups A and B) comprise 17 per cent of the population,

Table 3.2   Social class, age and regional influences on holidaymaking in the UK, 1987

	Adult population of UK (%)[a]	Adults taking no holiday (%)	Holidays in Britain (%)[b]	Holidays abroad (%)[c]
Social class				
AB – professional/managerial	17	9	21	33
C1 – clerical/supervisory	22	19	24	25
C2 – skilled manual	29	29	30	26
DE – unskilled/pensioners etc.	31	43	25	15
Region of residence				
North	6	6	6	6
North Yorkshire and Humberside	9	9	10	9
North West	12	13	11	12
East Midlands	7	7	8	5
West Midlands	9	10	10	9
East Anglia	3	3	3	2
South East				
London	13	14	11	14
Rest of South East	18	15	21	24
South West	8	7	8	8
Wales	5	5	5	4
Scotland	9	11	8	7
Age				
16–24	18	20	11	18
25–34	18	15	19	18
35–44	15	12	17	19
45–54	15	13	13	19
55–64	15	14	18	14
65+	20	25	22	12

Note: regions of residence are the Registrar General's regions.
[a]Based on the characteristics of the British resident adults who formed the basis of the sample survey
[b]Holidays of four+ nights
[c]Holidays of one+ nights

but only 9 per cent of those not taking holidays. In addition, there are some regional variations, although these are slight, with the South East of England standing out as a region with a higher than average consumption of holidays. Such patterns obviously relate back to levels of household income rather than to any distinct cultural differences. More general discussions seem to suggest that these class influences are also responsible for quite 'different attitudes and values towards tourism' (Seaton 1992, 108) that result in much higher priority being given to holiday-taking by the middle classes.

Table 3.2 suggests that inequalities in holiday-taking amongst socio-economic groups are as much to do with the type of holiday taken as with participation rates. For example, socio-economic groups A and B (professional and managerial employment) are much more likely to holiday abroad than are groups D and E (unskilled workers and pensioners); the latter only accounted for 15 per cent of overseas holidays, compared with 33 per cent for the former group. This is despite the impact of cheaper overseas packages which, according to Thurot and Thurot (1983), have allowed holidaymakers from lower social classes to emulate those with higher incomes, thereby 'democratizing' foreign travel. The use of such packages is, in fact, linked to socio-economic factors, with higher-status consumers being associated with greater levels of independent travel, compared with the stronger use of organized packages by lower socio-economic groups (Seaton 1992). Such differences are becoming most readily identifiable with the growth of short-break holidays (trips of between one and three nights) which, as shown in table 3.2, are very much the domain of socio-economic groups A and B, who account for 33 per cent of the market compared with just 11 per cent from groups D and E. Short break holidays tend to be taken more evenly throughout the year than long holidays, especially in the Easter–May and September–October periods. Furthermore, they tend to be related to special events, exhibitions or interest holidays. It would seem, therefore, that financial constraints, timing and the types of activities that are offered limit access for certain socio-economic groups. Gratton (1990) goes further and suggests that the growth of short-break holidays is indicative of the demands from an increasing inner-directed group of consumers, since they involve more skilled consumption than conventional holidays.

Variations in holiday-taking are also strongly related to age and stage in the family life-cycle, which is clearly recognized by the way in which many holiday companies strongly segment their product by age of tourist. Holidays tailored to meet the demands of young people, family groups and retired people figure prominently in the marketing of tour companies. As well as being offered and seeking different holiday products, inequalities also exist between different age groups, as shown in table 3.2. For example, in terms of the ages of people taking no holidays, the highest proportions are to be found in the 16–24 group and those over 65 years old. Similarly, the retired age group generates a large proportion of domestic holidays rather than foreign trips – 22 per cent compared with 12 per cent (table

3.2). The importance of stage in the family life-cycle is suggested in the middle age groups, which have relatively high family incomes and high demand expectations. The 35–44 and 45–54 age groups each represent 15 per cent of the population, but account in total for 38 per cent of the overseas holidays taken by UK residents.

While retired people are less likely to take a holiday than other adults, when they do have access to the holiday market they are equally likely to take two or more holidays. This select group of retired people take holidays more frequently than the rest of the adult population. Socio-economic differences do, of course, play a part in accounting for such variations. This is indicated by the fact that almost two out of three retired people, formerly in professional or managerial jobs, take at least one long holiday per year, while only one in three of formerly unskilled workers do so. Of course, many retired people have moved to live in seaside areas and, in a sense, are trying to recreate a holiday-type experience all year round (Karn 1977). In a way, these individuals have gained total access to a particular leisure environment, although the reality of the experience often fails to match expectations.

Leisure Patterns and Constraints on Leisure Participation

Many commentators have argued that because of the institutional changes in tourism (including cheaper air travel, package tours and holiday camps) access has been improved for large sectors of society (Pimlott 1976; Thurot and Thurot 1983; Hughes 1987). In contrast, much of the literature suggests that there are far greater inequalities in access to certain types of leisure activities.

The interest and concern over such issues has become sufficiently focused to spawn a new subfield of investigations on leisure constraints research (Jackson 1988 and 1991 provide wide-ranging reviews). This work includes diverse studies, with attention being given to specific forms of leisure, levels of constraint, and variations in access by different subgroups in society. Thus, McGuire (1984) has focused on the elderly, Willits and Willits (1986) on adolescents, and Henderson (1990) on constraints to womens' leisure. The picture that emerges is one of variable access, with constraints being related to socio-economic, gender, life-cycle, racial and cultural features.

Initial work in both North America and the UK (Rapoport and Rapoport 1975; Kelly 1978) indicated that leisure behaviour is strongly influenced by class, together with individual orientation and family–home–local relationships (Smith 1987). More specifically,

---

Box 3.1   Main findings in gender differences of leisure activity in the UK

- Women were more likely than men to have no leisure activities
- Women appear to engage in fewer leisure activities than men
- Women have a lower level of active participation in physical pursuits, apart from walking, dancing and swimming
- Women appear to attach greater importance to cultural and social pursuits in their leisure

Source: modified from Smith (1987) and based on General Household Survey data

---

early emphasis was given to the importance of family life-cycle, especially through the research of Young and Willmott (1973), who focused on the concept of the symmetrical family. From their studies of leisure in the London region, they argued that social class was far less of an influence on leisure behaviour than were age, marriage and gender. Their views were strongly coloured by two underlying assumptions: one was the belief in a process of stratified diffusion, whereby middle-class lifestyles were being adopted by the working classes; while the other was associated with the rise of the symmetrical family. As Smith (1987) demonstrates, however, such perspectives give a false reading of the nature of leisure patterns, especially concerning differences relating to gender and household structure. For example, the idea of gains from more shared family roles between men and women (the symmetrical family) have been offset by more females taking employment outside the home. While this may have re-orientated some women away from purely home-based leisure activities, its more general impact has been to reduce the total amount of time that working women with children have for leisure. Such reductions have an obvious impact on leisure access and, together with broader structural factors, act as a powerful constraint.

At the heart of these structural factors is the relationship between the family and leisure which in turn conditions gender differences. Smith (1987), using reworked data from the General Household Survey, identified a number of key differences between male and female leisure, including the major inequalities of time (box 3.1). Similarly, earlier studies by Sillitoe (1969) and Talbot (1979) identified three main characteristics of womens' leisure: (i) its strong home-based nature, with more women likely to engage in crafts, (ii) the emphasis that women themselves place on family duties curtailing their leisure pursuits, and (iii) the very different leisure activities engaged in by men and women (box 3.1). Taken together, these factors condition and produce strong gender differences in many areas of leisure. In this respect, Aubrey et al. (1986, 133) write about women's leisure being vulnerable since 'it is subordinate to the demands of men's and children's domestic and leisure needs. Women are unable to organize their time to reconcile 'normal' leisure with unorthodox schedules'.

Of course, access to leisure both for women and men is potentially improved considerably by increased disposable income. Such a factor has been mainly examined by socio-economic class variables, although when using such measures we should be aware of work–leisure relationships. Evidence seems to suggest that occupational variables are important in conditioning leisure behaviour, but that these appear to operate through a series of attitudinal relationships linking work patterns to leisure (Kelly 1982; Parker 1983). Spreitzer and Snyder (1987) have identified four basic perspectives on these relationships, including, spillover, compensation, segmentation and joint determination (box 3.2). As yet, empirical work has not provided any clear fit between these work–leisure relationships and particular occupations, or socio-economic groups. However, the limited evidence does suggest that compensation or segmentation, covering the case in which work and leisure are seen as autonomous spheres of experience, are more likely to be found in mass-production, manual occupations, where many jobs are extremely repetitive. Conversely, in many professional occupations, there may be a strong tendency for attitudes and interests to flow from work to leisure, as described in the spillover relationship.

Specific attempts to relate social-class variables to constraints on leisure have also highlighted the complexity of assuming simple

---

Box 3.2   Main perspectives on work–leisure relationships

• *Spillover*: a basic continuity of attitudes, interests and activities flowing from the work context to a person's leisure

• *Compensation*: involvement in leisure activities that are the complete opposite of a person's work, thereby providing satisfaction not gained from work environment

• *Segmentation*: work and leisure as autonomous spheres of experience; experiences in work and leisure are completely unrelated

• *Joint determination*: work and leisure are reciprocally related: there is a two-way influence between these two spheres of experience

Source: modified from Spreitzer and Snyder (1987)

causal relationships. Work in the UK by Kay and Jackson (1991) has attempted to relate leisure constraints to different social areas: (i) inner-city environments that cover low-status, stable older communities; (ii) inner-city areas of a more transitional nature (dominated by bedsitters, higher proportions of young people and non-indigenous groups); (iii) local-authority housing estates containing low-status occupants and having all the indications of relative deprivation; (iv) middle-class suburban areas dominated by younger families; (v) high-status, prestigious areas characterized by a mature age structure. Survey work in each of these areas revealed a number of constraints affecting leisure participation, with money, time, family responsibilities and work being the main ones cited (Kay and Jackson 1991). However, very few of the major constraints appeared to vary significantly between the different social areas. However, the largest proportions reporting that they experienced such constraints on leisure did come from the inner-city transitional area (80 per cent of respondents), followed by the local-authority estate (77 per cent) and the middle-class suburban area (76 per cent). Clearly, complex influences are at work, including not only income, family life-cycle, gender and location but also culture.

The impacts of working- and middle-class cultures on leisure patterns do have important constraining effects that operate through a range of variables. Wynne's (1990) study of leisure lifestyles on housing estates in northern England illustrates part of these effects, while more broadly based studies (Bourdieu 1984) suggest that these cultural differences relate to status and occupation. Bourdieu (1984) argues that substantial, available capital, often related to industrial and commercial management jobs, is used mainly to pursue more commercial types of leisure interests, such as tastes for second homes, the use of sports clubs and the commercial theatre. In contrast, many of those people in occupations related to higher education tend to have higher volumes of cultural capital, which is used to pursue interests in art, classical music and opera. More specifically, Dimaggio and Useem (1978) put forward a model for understanding variations in the consumption of arts-based leisure, which is strongly related to social class differences and the notions of social control. This projects the idea that variations in cultural consumption reflect the appreciation of arts-based leisure activities by certain social groups as a method not only of identifying such classes, but also of excluding others. Access is controlled by flows of information, expected norms of behaviour, high costs of attending concerts, and the physical environment of opera and concert halls (Hughes 1987). In turn, such ideas take the discussion back to a consideration of the cultural relationship between work and leisure, which appears to be critical in understanding the use of leisure.

Leisure patterns and participation rates also seem to vary with ethnicity, although here the situation is again complicated by a range of socio-economic and life-cycle influences. However, in many capitalist societies access to leisure by many racial minorities is limited by their position in the underclass. In extreme cases, such as South Africa under apartheid, such differences are clear to see; while on average 63 per cent of Whites go on holiday in any one year, only 10.5 per cent of urban Blacks and just 3.5 per cent of other Blacks do so (Ferrario

Table 3.3   Comparative studies of racial differences in leisure behaviour in North America

Authors	Methodology	Main findings
Meeker et al. (1973)	Historical analysis	Blacks, who are more group oriented, are more likely than whites to utilize urban recreational activities; while whites, who are more individualistic, are more likely to participate in wildlife recreation
Cheek et al. (1976)	Sample of urban blacks and whites	Small differences exist and whites between central-city blacks and whites in outdoor recreation, with the exception that whites more than blacks are involved in various sports
Washburne (1978)	Sample of low-income urban families	From a theoretical perspective, blacks should have limited accessibility to leisure because of poverty and discrimination; and that variations in leisure, based on race are due to ethnicity
Kelly (1980)	Regionally stratified national sample of 4029 individuals	White participation in winter sports, camping, waterskiing, and golf higher than black participation
Edwards (1981)	Random sample of 819 households	Ethnicity a factor in leisure; however, ethnicity ceases to be a factor when blacks live in white areas – blacks living in black areas are more likely than blacks or whites living in white areas to participate in outdoor recreation and belong to recreational association

1988, 24). Much of the specific work examining race and leisure has been undertaken in North America, where a number of comparative studies exist (table 3.3). As Stamps and Stamps (1985) argue, while the literature highlights differences between the leisure activities of non-white and white Americans, it is far less clear in delineating the leisure patterns of middle and lower social class blacks. In their study of race and leisure activities, they found race not to be a conclusive variable, although there were differences in leisure participation between middle-class blacks and whites. Such variations may very well be the result of past experiences, in this case the rural origins of many urban blacks in North America who brought with them limited leisure experiences (Craig 1972). Thus, in Stamps and Stamps' (1985) sample, some 40 per cent of black respondents had been born and brought up in the rural South before moving into urban areas. For many, the past limitations had affected current leisure activities and acted as a constraining background influence.

Obviously, a certain amount of leisure activity takes place away from the home environment. In the UK, for example, this is of the order of 30 per cent in terms of total time spent on leisure (Gershuny and Jones 1987). Such out-of-home activities are affected by the

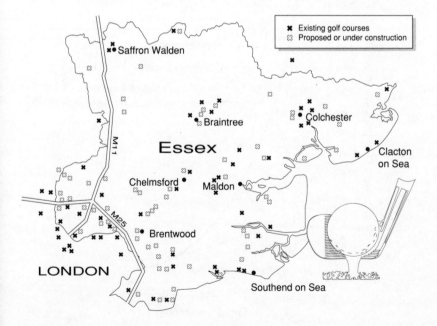

Figure 3.3   The distribution of golf courses in part of South East England, 1990

availability and spatial distribution of leisure facilities, bringing distance into play as a constraining factor. Activities dependent on specific facilities can be termed 'confined activities', where participation is only possible at some given purpose-built leisure resource (Veal 1987a). In these cases constraints are caused not only by distance, but very often also by defined capacities within the leisure facilities. In these circumstances increased access involves both changes in the leisure attitudes of potential participants, and the increased provision of facilities. Policies for sport centre provision by local government, as well as efforts to develop more golf courses within the commercial sector, reflect the range of such needs. For example, in the latter case insufficient facilities in the UK mean that in most regions there are considerable waiting lists to join golf clubs, with the highest levels of constraint being in London and the South East of England, despite relatively large numbers of existing and planned golf developments (figure 3.3). Evidence from work on spatial patterns of leisure beha-

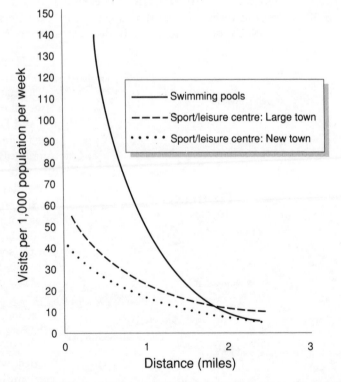

Figure 3.4 The effect of distance on the use of sports centres in the UK
Source: after Veal (1987b)

viour is that distance, travel time and travel costs all constrain access. Relationships vary depending on the size and nature of the leisure facility, as well as with the type of consumers (Veal 1987b). As can be seen from figure 3.4, there is a marked decline in the rates of visiting, which is also strongly related to the type of leisure facility on offer, as well as the characteristics of the urban environment. Of course, not all leisure away from home takes place in confined activities. Many people also use a range of so-called 'unconfined facilities', such as trips to the countryside, walking and jogging. In relative terms, these may have fewer constraints, depending on where people live.

Improving Access to Leisure and Tourism: the Role of the State

Many researchers have identified the important role of leisure activities and free time for both the individual and society. Leisure, in all its forms, is part of the individual and collective needs of a society, complementing work, reinforcing group or family relationships, and providing for many a therapy or even a preventative medicine to the pressures of everyday living (Roberts 1981; see also chapter 4 for a discussion of tourist motivations). Such values have been increasingly recognized by many governments and labour organizations; while more recently they have also formed the basis of a series of international statements on the individual's right to rest, leisure and holidays (World Tourism Organization 1983). The first of these formed part of the United Nations' 'Universal Declaration of Human Rights', which emphasized that 'everyone has the right to rest and leisure' (table 3.4). More specific statements on the rights to holidays have followed this 1948 declaration, as is shown in table 3.4: the so-called 'Manila Declaration' supports the view that 'Tourism is considered an activity essential to the life of nations because of its direct effects on social, cultural, educational and economic sectors of societies' (World Tourism Organization 1983).

Goals such as the provision of the right to holidays are usually encompassed by the term 'social tourism' (Murphy 1985). This refers to the situation in which deprived, disadvantaged or economically weak sections of society are provided with the means of taking a holiday. In one sense it highlights the increasing importance placed on tourism as a leisure activity and its duality in many societies, where it is perceived both as a luxury and as a basic right of each individual. The international organizations certainly support the latter view, with

Table 3.4 International statements on the right to rest, leisure and holidays

Date	Organization	Statement	Basic principle(s)
1948	United Nations	Universal Declaration of Human Rights	Everyone has the right to rest and leisure, including reasonable limitations of working hours and periodic holidays with pay
1966	United Nations	International Covenant on Economic, Social and Cultural Rights	The right to periodic holidays with pay, as well as public holidays
1980	World Tourism Organization	Manila Declaration	Tourism is considered an activity essential to the life of nations because of its direct effects on the social, cultural, educational and economic sectors of societies. Its development can only be possible if people have access to creative rest and holidays
1982	World Tourism Organization	Acapulco Document	This stresses the essential nature of the right to holidays for all

Source: modified from World Tourism Organization (1983)

the World Tourism Organization suggesting specific measures to encourage the development of holidays. These range from the encouragement of low-cost accommodation and cheap travel, through to incentives for producing package holidays adapted to the needs of all wage-earners (World Tourist Organization 1983, 41).

The effectiveness of these international declarations is of course restricted by the actions of individual governments, very few of which operate any comprehensive form of social tourism. As Murphy (1985) points out, while the aim of social tourism is unitarian in philosophy, it is expressed in a variety of ways, either through government involvement or, more probably by some form of voluntary means.

At the most informal level, access to holidays has been improved through the activities of church organizations and youth movements, such as the YMCA, scouts and guides, which often provide subsidized holiday centres and summer camps. Similarly, labour and trade union organizations have sought to provide cheap holiday centres for their members, while in some countries (Germany and Japan) a number of companies make contributions towards the cost of their employees' holidays. Within this context, one of the earliest and most progressive social tourism schemes was in Switzerland, where the Swiss Travel Saving Fund (REKA) was established in 1939. Teuscher (1983) has shown how this scheme, and developments of a less formal nature in other European countries, came about largely in response to the increases in workers' holiday leave during the 1930s. In Switzerland, for example, access to holidays was greatly increased for many workers between 1910, when only 8 per cent of factory employees were entitled to a holiday, and 1937, when the figure had risen to 66 per cent. REKA itself was established as a co-operative by the tourism and transport industries, trades unions, employers and consumer co-operative associations, with the aim of improving real access to holidays for many of the country's lowest paid workers. Its initial areas of activity focused on providing a method of saving for holidays, and giving information on low-cost holidays (Teuscher 1983). By the 1950s, however, REKA had widened its operations and had constructed its own holiday centres which, together with its leased apartments, provide more than 4000 guest beds. Other countries provide similar, although less comprehensive, schemes. For example, Brazil has holiday camps run by workers' associations, while Israel has holiday chalets operated by both trades unions and employers (World Tourism Organization 1983, Annex III).

Government involvement in increasing access to holidays often assumes an indirect approach, usually through increasing statutory rights to paid holiday leave. This does widen access to tourism, as was witnessed in the UK after the passing of the 1938 Holidays with Pay Act, which proposed a minimum of three consecutive days of paid holiday. When the Act was fully implemented after 1945, it provided an important growth stimulus to British tourism. However, despite discussions in 1974 between the English Tourist Board and the Trades Union Congress, which established the 'Social Tourism Study Group', no formal action has been taken in the UK to establish a social tourism scheme. This contrasts with the situation in France, where central government and regional authorities created the Villages-Vacances-Familiales in 1959; this scheme now provides subsidized serviced and self-catering accommodation for low-income families, either in villages or on camp sites.

If most governments have steered away from direct involvement in social tourism programmes, they have, in contrast, been more likely to involve themselves in some type of general leisure policy. This has taken many forms, ranging from the subsidy of arts and cultural activities, through to establishing access to the countryside, putting into place policies for greater involvement in sport and, more recently, the development of leisure programmes for deprived sectors of society. In all of these cases, there are strong grounds for arguing that such 'leisure policies' are far from being either politically or socially neutral. As Bramham et al. (1989, 17) point out, such issues are 'inherently connected to a wide range of political tensions and contrasts' and especially 'to the ways in which these [policies] mediate existing socio-economic differences'.

At the level of national governments, Bramham and Henry (1985) have shown how successive British governments have adopted the view that state intervention in leisure should be kept at arms length, and should not intrude into the private lives of individuals. In contrast, Hantrais (1989) argues that the coming to power of a socialist government in France during the 1980s put leisure policies firmly on the political agenda. After appointing a Minister of 'Free Time', the French government went on to proclaim a programme in which leisure was seen as both a public good as well as a citizen's right. During the early 1980s a number of urban leisure programmes were developed to provide better access for young people and also to prevent the private sector from gaining a monopoly over leisure services. Attempts were also made to solve problems of regional disparity in leisure provision, with central government promoting and partly funding 300 new leisure centres in under-resourced smaller towns between 1982 and 1984 (Hantrais 1989). In addition, the socialist government also sought to decentralize culture by allocating 70 per cent of the Ministry of Culture's budget to projects outside the Paris region. This latter fact also highlights the class and political conflict generated by what was seen as the paternalistic tradition of 'cultural heritage' pursued by previous conservative governments in France (Hantrais 1989).

The whole notion of class divisions in leisure access has led many authors to conclude that most subsidies of leisure activities have been largely to the benefit of the middle classes, at the expense of the 'leisure-poor' (Hughes 1987; Bramham et al. 1989). Thus, many central governments have traditionally aided the arts, heritage and cultural sectors, while leaving improvements in access to other leisure activities to local government. At this local level, it is possible to detect the development of distinct urban leisure policies directed at improving conditions for both young people and the unemployed. Within the British context, Glyptis (see Glyptis and Riddington 1983, Glyptis 1989) has examined the provision of sports facilities for the unemployed by local authorities, 64 per cent of whom were operating such schemes by the mid-1980s. In many urban areas this service was based on the possibility that unemployment was not a temporary feature of economic adjustment and that, consequently, longer-term policies were needed. This, as Bramham et al. (1989) argue, raises the central question of whether, if work is no longer the main role of community organization, leisure could, and should, take its place. If this should be the case in many urban communities, then not only does the issue of social access need to be more seriously addressed, but such policies will also need to cover a much wider sector of the 'leisure-poor'.

Increased sports facilities will cater for some needs, but such activities will not fit everyone's needs. Indeed, the provision of increased leisure access through local policies still appears to suffer from the same kinds of limitation that operate in the commercially driven market. This has been clearly highlighted by Dietvorst's (1989) research in Nijmegen, Holland which strongly suggests that class biases exist in the organization of local projects for the unemployed; these tend to reproduce the interests of the better-educated amongst those out of work. With this in mind, it has been argued that local leisure policies must be structured as a response to existing local ways of life, and aimed as widely as possible at the full range of 'leisure poor' (Bramham et al. 1989, 296). Before this can happen, however, it may well be that we require much more understanding of, and agreement on, the whole notion of what constitutes leisure.

FOUR

Individual Consumption of Tourism

In Search of the Tourist

In the previous chapter a broad discussion was introduced concerning the patterns and constraints of tourism in leisure. By contrast, this chapter will focus in much greater depth on some of the more specific factors and relationships involved in tourism consumption. This approach is taken to guide the reader through the much more detailed literature on tourists and their behaviour.

It is significant that some of the earliest sustained attempts to identify the tourist came not from academics but from official organizations interested in monitoring the growth of international tourism. In this context, the League of Nations in 1937 recommended that a tourist be defined as someone 'who travels for a period of 24 hours or more in a country other than that in which he usually resides'. Of course, such simple definitions tell us little about tourist behaviour and completely ignore the importance of domestic tourism. Broader, and at an international level, more meaningful definitions put forward by the World Tourism Organization (previously the International Union of Official Travel Organizations) have, through the UN Conference on International Travel and Tourism (1963), agreed the term 'visitors'. This covers two main categories: tourists – temporary visitors staying for at least 24 hours, whose purpose could be defined as either leisure or business; and excursionists – temporary visitors staying less than 24 hours, including cruise ship travellers, but excluding travellers in transit. Such ideas have been greatly extended into the construction of more comprehensive and elaborate classifications that relate types of travellers with scale and purpose of journey (figure 4.1). Within this perspective many trips are multipurpose, involving a range of primary and secondary activities.

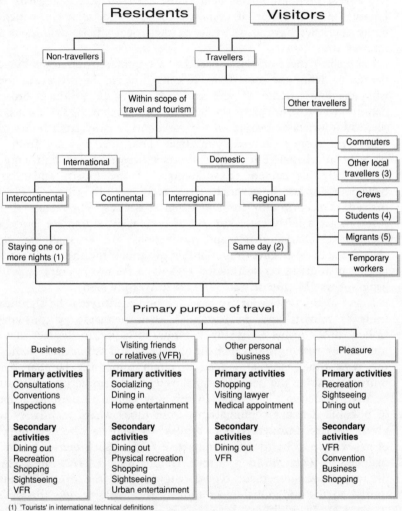

(1) 'Tourists' in international technical definitions
(2) 'Excursionists' in international technical definitions
(3) Travellers whose trips are shorter than those which qualify for travel and tourism, e.g. under 50 miles (80km) from home
(4) Students travelling between home and school only - other travel of students is within scope of travel and tourism
(5) All persons moving to a new place of residence including all one-way travellers such as emigrants, immigrants, refugees, domestic migrants and nomads

Figure 4.1 A classification of travellers
Source: Chadwick (1987)

Such definitions are important when attempting comparative studies of international tourism. Their purpose is to provide an international standard, but not to explain or examine tourist behaviour. Moreover, even as official definitions, such adopted standards still ignore the wide range of domestic tourists and, as a consequence, many countries have also developed their own official definitions for internal use.

Set against these official approaches are numerous attempts by academics to define the tourist and to conceptualize the process of tourist behaviour. Some of the early attempts to produce broader definitions were similar to the official ones. Ogilvie (1933), for example, saw tourists as people on temporary trips away from home who also spent money derived from their home area and not from the place being visited. Put simply, tourists were travellers and, equally importantly, consumers. Examinations of the tourist and tourist behaviour did not, however, figure in early work by geographers and, instead, come primarily from sociological studies. The results of this research are a fairly close-knit set of typologies of tourists, based on their travel characteristics and motivations. As we shall see, such classifications also have important implications for the study of the impact of tourism on destination regions, a feature re-emphasized by geographers (Mathieson and Wall 1982; Murphy 1985).

Many of the typologies are based around identifying the significant traits of tourists and, in particular, their demands as consumers. Cohen (1972), in his early studies, draws attention to the fact that all tourists are seeking some element of novelty and strangeness while, at the same time, most also need to retain something familiar. How tourists combine the demands for novelty with familiarity can in turn be used to derive a typology. In this way Cohen recognized a range of possible demand combinations, from those where familiarity was given priority, through to ones typified by tourists who held novelty of experience to be the most important factor. Such demands can be matched by a classification of tourists. In Cohen's (1972) initial study he recognized four main types, ranging from the organized mass tourist to the individual mass tourist, the explorer and the drifter (table 4.1). In addition, these groups were also differentiated along the lines of contact with the tourism industry, with mass tourists being termed 'institutionalized' and the more individualistic tourists regarded as non-institutionalized.

Cohen's tourist typology, and the more detailed variant developed by Smith (1977b) which identifies seven categories of tourist (table 4.1), focus on the relationships between tourists and their destinations; as such they have been termed 'interactional typologies'

Table 4.1 The main typologies of tourists

Experience	Demands	Destination impacts
Interactional models		
Cohen (1972): a theoretically derived approach not based on any empirical survey:		
Non-institutionalized traveller		
Drifter	Search for exotic and strange environment	Little because of small numbers
Explorer	Arrange own trip and try to get off the beaten track	Local facilities sufficient and contact with residents high
Institutionalized traveller		
Individual mass tourist	Arrangements made through tourist agency to popular destinations	Growing commercialization and specialization as demand grows
Organized mass tourist	Search for familiar, travel in the security of own 'environmental bubble' and guided tour	Development of 'artificial facilities, growth of foreign investment, reduced local control
Smith (1977): a theoretical approach limited to empirical information:		
Explorer	Quest for discovery and desire to interact with hosts	Easy to accommodate in terms of numbers, acceptance of local norms
Elite	Tour of unusual places, using pre-arranged native facilities	Small in number and easily adapted into surrounding environments

Table 4.1 (Continued)

Experience	Demands	Destination impacts
Off-beat	Get away from the crowds	Minor because willing to put up with simple accommodation and service
Unusual	Occasional side trips to explore more isolated area or undertake more risky activity	Temporary destinations can be simple but support base needs to have full range of services
Incipient mass	Travel as individuals or small groups, seeking combination of amenities and and authenticity	Numbers increasing as as destination becomes popular, growing demand for services and facilities
Mass	Middle-class income and values leads to development of a 'tourist bubble'	Tourism now a major industry, little interaction with local people beyond commercial links
Charter	Search for relaxation and good times in a new but familiar environment	Massive arrivals; to avoid complaints, hotels and facilities standardized to Western tastes

Table 4.1 (Continued)

	Experience	Demands	Destination impacts
Cognitive–normative models			
Plog (1972): based on original work for 16 airline and travel companies:			
	Allocentric	Adventuresome and individual exploration	Small in number, board with local residents
	Mid-centric	Individual travel to areas with facilities and growing reputation	Increased commercialization of visitor–host relationship
	Psychocentric	Organized package holiday to 'popular' destinations	Large-scale business, with facilities similar to visitors' home area
Cohen (1979a): a theoretically based approach:			
Modern pilgrimage	Existential	Leave world of everyday life and practicality to escape to 'elective centre' for spiritual sustenance	Few participants who are absorbed into community: little impact on local life
	Experimental	Quest for alternative lifestyle and to engage in authentic life of others	Assimilated into destination areas because of small numbers and desire
	Experimental	Look for meaning in life of others, enjoyment of authenticity	Some impact as destination provides accommodation and facilities to 'show' local culture

Table 4.1 (Continued)

	Experience	Demands	Destination impacts
Search for pleasure	Diversionary	Escape from boredom and routine of everyday existence, therapy which makes alienation endurable	Mass tourism with large demand for recreation and leisure facilities, large impact because of numbers and commercialization
	Recreational	Trip as entertainment, relaxation to restore physical and mental powers	Artificial pleasure environment created; major impact on local lifestyles

American Express (1989): based on results from a classification of 6500 respondents in USA, UK, West Germany and Japan:

	Experience	Demands	Destination impacts
	Adventurers	New experiences of different cultures and activities	Independent travellers affluent and better educated; limited impact
	Worriers	Mainly domestic-based trips, limited travel	Older, less educated; limited impact
	Dreamers	Attach great importance to meaning of travel and experiences: orientated towards relaxation	Modest income group rely on guidebook and stick to main tourist areas

Table 4.1 (Continued)

Experience	Demands	Destination impacts
Economists	Travel a routine outlet for relaxation rather than experience	Average income: mainly go to established tourist areas
Indulgers	High demand for travel, making above average trips	Generally stay in large hotel and resort complexes; willing to pay for better services

Sources: modified from Murphy (1985) and Lowyck et al. (1990)

(Murphy 1985, 5–6). In contrast, other studies have stressed the motivations that lie behind tourist travel, and have been described as 'cognitive–normative models'. In some cases, these approaches to identifying and classifying tourists have their roots in the commercial needs of the tourism industry, with typologies often being established for a specific study. We find, for example, that Plog's (1972) typology, which recognizes three main groups of tourists – the allocentric, mid-centric and psychocentric – was initially constructed to enable airline and travel companies to broaden their market. As shown in table 4.1, the basis of this typology is the idea of a norm or centre around which more diverse patterns of tourist motivation can be recognized. Such work also draws heavily on the concepts of 'lifestyle' in an attempt to explain tourist motivations and relates to the ideas associated with the VALS hierarchy, as discussed in chapter 3.

Typologies, such as the one devised by Plog, are based on asking tourists about their general 'lifestyles' or value systems, often using perceptual information derived from interviews (Holman 1984; Lowyck et al. 1990). This psychographic research (Plog 1987) can be used to examine tourist motivations as well as attitudes to particular destinations and modes of travel. In terms of the latter, a tourist typology developed for American Express (1989) has categorized travellers into five distinct groups – adventurers, worriers, dreamers, economizers and indulgers – all of whom viewed their travel experiences in very different ways (table 4.1).

These tourist typologies, only a few of which have been presented here, are not without their problems, chief amongst which is that they are rather static models based on fairly limited information (Lowyck et al. 1990). It is certainly the case that such perspectives assume that tourists belong to one type or another, and that individuals remain within a particular category for all time. Set against this, sociologists such as MacCannell (1976) have called for more detailed studies of how people experience tourist settings, so as to provide a better understanding of tourists. Perhaps of even greater importance in identifying different types of tourists is the need to learn more about how individuals change as tourists over time. This can be achieved by taking a biographical approach, as introduced in the concept of a tourist's travel career (Pearce 1982). This would involve longitudinal studies of changing patterns of tourist behaviour which, at the present time, do not exist in sufficient detail or scale. Therefore, such critical issues remain to be researched, and we are left with nothing more than the generalities of the tourist typologies.

Despite their limitations, the tourist typology models remain useful for three main reasons. First, they highlight the broad diversity of tourists, their demands and consumption. Second, they provide an insight into the motivations of tourists and their behaviour. Finally, and most importantly, such perspectives provide a platform from which to explore the relationships between tourist consumption and the sociocultural fabric of destination areas. The remainder of this chapter will focus on the latter two themes.

Tourist Motivation and Decision-making

The understanding of tourist motivation and decison-making processes is important for a number of reasons, but not least because it links to the impact on destination areas (Crompton 1979). In addition, there are strong economic considerations related to the promotion of tourism and tourism planning that are highly reliant on an understanding of tourist decision-making. For example, in terms of tourism marketing and promotion, it enables the identification of market segmentation and target marketing. The tourist travel market is extremely competitive, especially within the area of mass tourism, and the market is highly segmented. Similarly, the potential to control or strongly influence tourist decisions is important in tourism planning as, for example, in diverting tourists from sensitive areas.

Set against these practical reasons for understanding tourist decision-making, we should recognize at the outset that the question of measuring motivation is extremely problematic (Dann 1977), and little in the way of a common understanding has emerged (Jafari 1987). In this context researchers have stressed different combinations of factors; Thomas (1964) for example, listed 18 reasons, Gray (1970) discussed just two distinct motivations, 'wanderlust' and 'sunlust', and Lundberg (1972) identified 20 factors, while Crompton (1979) recognised nine different motives.

From empirical studies of tourists, Crompton (1979) also conceptualized states of disequilibrium or homeostasis which could be rectified by taking a break away from the routine. As shown in figure 4.2, there are four main components of this process, starting with an initial state of disequilibrium, followed by the recognition of the need to break from routine behaviour. The third component involves three behavioural alternatives, which range from leisure activities in the local area, to taking a holiday or travel to see friends and relatives, to travelling for business purposes. Finally, there is the recognition that particular motives obviously determine the nature and destination of the leisure trip. Such motives can either be classified as socio-psychological (push factors) or cultural (pull factors), as shown in more

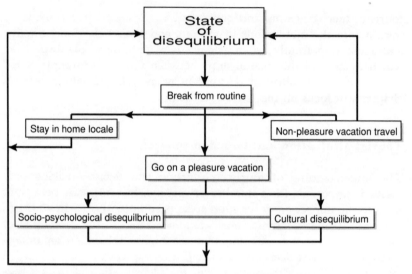

State
of
disequilibrium

Break from routine

Stay in home locale

Non-pleasure vacation travel

Go on a pleasure vacation

Socio-psychological disequilbrium

Cultural disequilibrium

Figure 4.2 Possible resposes to personal disequilibrium
Source: Crompton (1979)

detail in box 4.1. These broad ideas have, to some extent, been confirmed through larger empirical studies; for example, by Schmidhauser (1989) in Switzerland, who has shown that a single leisure trip
cannot satisfy all the touristic motives of an individual.

The recognition of push and pull factors within tourist motivation
forms a critical issue in much of the literature, although little attention has been directed at any cross-cultural comparisons. Dann
(1977) has stressed the initial importance of push factors which

---

Box 4.1 The dimensions of tourist motivation

Push factors

Motivation *per se* why people decide to take a holiday:

- desire for something different
- anomie in origin society
- ego-enhancement, usually associated with relative status deprivation
  in an individual – holiday offers temporary alleviation from this
- peer pressure to take a holiday, especially amongst middle classes

Pull factors

Refer to destination 'pull', why tourists decide to visit a particular resort
destination

determine the need for travel, while the pull factors tend to affect the choice of destination. The need for leisure travel is, according to Dann (1977), the consequence of anonymity and ego-enhancement. The first cause is somewhat similar to Crompton's disequilibrium in the sense that it identifies a sociological need to move away from the home–work environment. In contrast, ego-enhancement relates to motives of relative status deprivation or prestige, including the need for people to impress their friends, which in itself can also lead to to disequilibrium or homeostasis (Mill and Morrison 1985).

The ideas of escaping from particular environments, as well as seeking personal rewards, have been explored in greater depth by Iso-Ahola (1984) and Mannell and Iso-Ahola (1987) who defined leisure travel in terms of 'escaping' and 'seeking' dimensions (figure 4.3). At the two extremes they identify those individuals who have a high level of stimulation in their working lives and therefore seek to 'escape' stimulation on holiday. In contrast, those with low levels of stimulation at work have a tendency to seek greater novelty and sti-

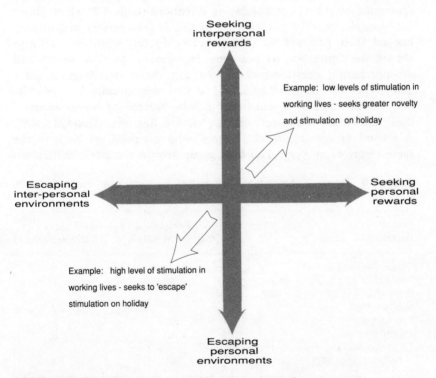

Figure 4.3 The escaping and seeking dimensions of tourist travel
Source: after Iso-Ahola (1984)

mulation on holiday. But, of course, leisure preferences also depend to a great extent on personality traits, as well as lifestyle experiences. Furthermore, many of the authors writing on tourism motivation highlight the complexity of individual's real motives, in that many people have a hidden agenda (Krippendorf 1987).

As with other forms of consumption, there are particular stages in which tourists particpate, such as the buying process. However, unlike other consumer purchases, the holiday has some very distinctive features. The tourist product is an experience rather than a good, and there is therefore no tangible return on the investment. It also involves a relatively large expenditure and a high degree of planning. Finally, many tourists are not distance minimizers; for most people the travel element is an important part of the holiday product.

Buying a holiday is, for many families, a high-risk decision, and for this reason pre-purchase planning assumes a greater role (Gitelson and Crompton 1983). The degree of planning obviously varies between different types of tourists but, in the Northern Hemisphere, it is often in full swing by January. The timing of this process can be illustrated by surveys of holidaying intentions (table 4.2) which show, for example, that 59 per cent of British holidaymakers had already booked their holidays in Britain before Easter, while for holidays abroad the figure was 64 per cent. In terms of tourists' search and pre-purchasing decision-making, we can therefore recognize three main types of buyer behaviour. The first are 'impulse buyers' who may be attracted by a 'cut-price' holiday offered by travel agents – these individuals have very short planning horizons (Goodall 1988). A second group are 'repeat buyers' who generally go back to the same resort every year. The final group are the so-called 'meticulous

Table 4.2   Holiday intentions: the reservations of commercial accommodation made by British holidaymakers, 1988

Reservations made	Percentage of holidaymakers	
	Holidays in Britain	Holidays overseas
Before September 1987	6	5
September and October 1987	3	7
November and December 1987	10	9
January 1988	24	22
February 1988	12	9
March 1988	6	8
Total reservations before Easter 1988	59	64

Source: English Tourist Board (1990)

Table 4.3   Sources of information used by holidaymakers visiting Cornwall, England, 1988

Source	Percentage of sample[a]
Previous visit	57.8
Personal recommendation	29.7
Tour operator's brochure	20.6
Tourist board guide	12.2
Local resort guide	11.8
Newspaper advertisement	6.3
Magazine advertisement	6.9
TV holiday programme	6.7

Note: percentages do not sum to 100 as many respondents used more than one source
[a]Based on a sample of 902 holidaymakers
Source: Greenwood et al. (1989)

planners', who obtain specific and up-to-date information, and make detailed comparisons; as a consequence they tend to have fairly long planning horizons.

These search processes are obviously strongly influenced by the media and the images projected of various destination areas. Most individuals have a preferential image of their ideal holiday, clearly influenced by their motives. According to Goodall (1988, 3), this 'conditions their expectations setting an aspiration level or evaluative image, against which actual holiday opportunities are compared'. The information and images of destination areas are provided by a large media industry (formal sources), and informal recommendations from friends (Nolan 1976). In some destination areas, informal sources figure highly (table 4.3). It should be recognized, however, that most people use a combination of formal and informal sources to construct an image of each destination area. Clearly, the matching of preferential, evaluative and factual images will determine what type of holidaymaker goes to which type of destination, and how they travel there in terms of the type of holiday selected (i.e. package or non-package tour).

Tourist Behaviour: at the Scene of their Dreams

Patterns of tourist behaviour have an important impact both on the structure of facilities within particular resorts and the relationships that tourists have with the host population. The tourist typologies explored at the start of this chapter obviously go part way to suggesting possible ranges of behaviour, although they say little about the detailed leisure activities and patterns of consumption indulged in by holidaymakers.

According to Krippendorf (1987, 32), having 'arrived at the scene of their dreams', many tourists behave in much the same way as they do at home. For them the break with routine is a functional and spatial one, in that they do not have to work and are away from home. The holiday resort is an 'exotic backdrop' (Krippendorf 1987, 32), against which they can play out the usual patterns of behaviour. Such traits are common, however, only to the point of enjoying home comforts as, for many tourists, aggressive – almost colonialist – behaviour becomes a norm while on holiday. Holidaymakers become totally self-oriented, having little regard for others, especially the host population. Such anti-social behaviour, in its most extreme form, has become an increasing feature of many of the mass tourism resorts on Spain's costas.

Table 4.4   The importance of activities to holidaymakers in Cornwall, England, 1988

Activity	Taken part in only – no rating (%)	Very important (%)	Fairly important (%)	Not very important (%)
Going to the beach	6.1	52.0	30.9	11.0
Walking around town	7.3	26.5	53.0	13.2
Strolling in the countryside	6.2	47.5	37.3	8.9
Climbing/hiking/rambling	3.5	29.0	24.3	43.3
Sightseeing coach	6.7	50.0	35.5	7.8
Shopping	7.7	21.6	47.9	22.8
Visiting pubs/bars	5.7	22.6	37.4	34.3
Visiting restaurants	5.7	26.2	43.3	24.8
Cinema/theatre	2.4	9.2	25.9	62.5
Festivals/outdoor show	2.2	13.5	35.4	48.9
Historic buildings/country houses	5.6	34.5	43.4	16.4
Fun fair/amusement arcades	3.6	8.5	25.2	62.7
Dancing/disco	2.3	9.9	21.3	66.6
Museum/art galleries	3.4	22.6	50.1	24.0
Theme parks	4.2	16.9	44.0	35.0
Scenic railways	4.3	13.0	34.6	48.0
Miniature golf/putting	4.0	13.0	33.1	49.9
Other	6.1	59.1	22.7	12.2

Source: Greenwood et al. (1989)

Approaches to the study of tourist behaviour have focused on two main themes, namely, general tourist activities and more detailed analysis based on tourist time-budgets (Cooper 1981). Much of the published material falls into the former category and presents generalized lists of tourist pursuits derived from basic questionnaire surveys, usually of people on holiday (table 4.4). In the example taken from research in Cornwall, the emphasis for many visitors is on 'sightseeing', with 85.5 per cent rating it as very or fairly important; also significant were 'strolling in the countryside' (84.8 per cent) and 'going to the beach' (82.9 per cent). On the surface, such activities look passive and harmless, but closer inspection reveals the potential for problems. Thus, according to MacCannell (1976, 13), the focus of sightseeing is part of a systematic scavenge of 'the earth for new experiences to be woven into a collective, touristic version of other peoples and other places'. However, this touristic integration is nothing more than a catalogue of displaced forms as both modernization and tourism separate out objects from the societies and places that produced them. At a broader level, Krippendorf (1987) draws attention to the contradiction between tourist motives (involving the desire for peace and something different) and actual tourist behaviour, which for many holidaymakers tends to be focused in congested resorts.

One of the difficulties in interpreting tourist behaviour from the data contained in table 4.4 is that activities vary markedly over time and space. Tourist time-budgets allow an insight into such variations, and the few studies undertaken using such techniques have revealed some interesting variations. Thus, Pearce (1982) showed an increase in self-initiated activities (walking, reading and admiring views) by holidaymakers after four or five days of being on holiday in Australian resorts that provided structured activities. Similarly, a diary-based study of a sample of visitors to the South Pacific island of Vanuatu found variations in activities even over a four-day period, although strong regular diurnal rhythms were also evident (Pearce 1988b). Also significant in the Vanuatu study was the strong spatial concentration of tourist activity in and around their hotels (figure 4.4).

Unfortunately, despite its importance, the consideration of the spatial patterns of tourist behaviour has received little attention. Indeed, one of the significant behavioural issues on which geographers are uniquely qualified to comment has seen them remain largely silent. One of the few significant contributions has been by Cooper (1981), who examined the space time-budgets of tourists on Jersey over a five-day period. This revealed that most tourists determined an hier-

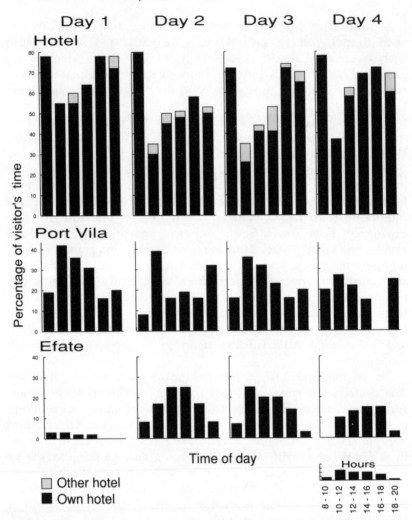

Figure 4.4 The percentage of time spent by visitors in hotels and visiting resorts on Vanuata (South Pacific)
Source: Pearce (1988b, 110)

archy of sites on the basis of the facilities provided at each one, while over time there was a progressive filtering down this hierarchy of sites. The decision to visit the largest, most important sites first and then move down the hierarchy suggests, first, that tourists reduce uncertainty at the expense of effort (Cooper 1981) and, second, that their time is discretionary.

Finally, it is worth stressing that such time-budgets will obviously vary between different types of tourists (however we may define such differences). Thus, Cooper (1981) found variations between different tourists, as defined by social class, with the lower social groups tending to limit their visits to only the major sites. Unfortunately, more detailed anlaysis of such variations are precluded in many of the time-budget studies because of small sample sizes (Pearce 1988b).

Hosts and Guests: Making and Remaking Relationships

Leaving aside economic considerations, in most societies tourists tend to be viewed in a negative way. Many studies have commented on the disdain in which tourists are held, and as MacCannell (1976, 9) explains, it 'is intellectually chic nowadays to deride tourists'. Even tourists dislike tourists, who are 'reproached for being satisfied with superficial experiences of other peoples and other places' (MacCannell 1976, 10). Similarly, Krippendorf (1987, 41) explains that whatever 'the tourist does he does it wrong' by being the 'rich tourist', the 'uncultured tourist', the 'exploiting tourist', the 'polluting tourist' and so on. This critique of tourists is related to larger issues associated with the culture of tourism, and with the fact that many tourists want to have a deeper involvement with the society and culture they are visiting, but very often on their terms. Krippendorf (1987) feels that the blame is too narrowly focused on the tourist, and that the negative effects of worldwide tourism are its massiveness, which has much to do with the international institutions that control tourism. Whatever the rights and wrongs of the argument, the fact remains that tourists are mainly perceived in a negative way.

Much of the established literature holds that tourists bring with them positive and negative impacts, but the latter dominate host–guest relations. Such views are most extreme when tourists come into contact with marginal or peripheral economies and sensitive cultures. These perspectives stress the exploitative view of tourism which, in extremes, is perceived as a form of imperialism or the 'prostitution' of developing economies. This is grounded in the idea that developing nations have few alternatives to tourism with which to earn much needed foreign exchange. As host nations they have to sell their 'beauty', which is then often desecrated by mass tourism. The analogies with prostitution come, it is claimed, at a psychological level as developing nations are forced into a servile role in order to secure foreign exchange (Nash 1977). Another equally exploitative view is provided by the so-called 'self-destruct' theory of tourism that postulates the rise and decline of resorts in a cyclical fashion (box 4.2).

Box 4.2   The self-destruct theory of tourism development (based on Caribbean studies)

These are four phases of development and decline:

Phase 1   Remote and exotic location offers rest and relaxation – provides an escape for rich tourists

Phase 2   Tourism promotion attracts tourists of middle incomes – come for rest and to imitate the rich. More hotels built, transforms original character away from an 'escape paradise'

Phase 3   Area develops mass tourism, attracting a wide variety of tourists and lead to social and environmental degradation

Phase 4   As resort sinks under the weight of social and environmental problems most tourists exit – leaving behind derelict tourism facilities. Most of population cannot return to original way of life

More recent reviews have recognized both the critical or cautionary platform on the impact of tourists, as well as the so-called advocacy platform as shown in table 4.5 (Jafari 1989).

Perhaps more constructively, we can examine the sociocultural impact of tourists at three different levels, not all of which are necessarily negative. First, we can explore the nature of host–guest encounters. Second, we can follow through a functional view of those elements of the host society experiencing change due to tourism. Third, we can examine aspects of cultural change that are due to the influence of tourists (Mathieson and Wall 1982; Lea 1988).

A generally held view is that the impact of tourism on a host community will vary according to the differences between the tourists and their hosts. Such differences may be measured in terms of race, culture and social outlook, while the number of tourists is also significant. At this juncture we can turn back to the tourist typologies examined earlier in this chapter, especially those developed by Cohen and Smith, both of whom directed their identification of tourists towards an understanding of their potential impact on host communities (table 4.5). As can be seen from these typologies, the impact of tourism on host–guest relations becomes most prominent and critical under the influx of mass tourists to underdeveloped countries. Under such conditions, as a Unesco (1976) report points out, relations between tourists and the host community tend to be characterized by four main features: the transitory nature of encounters between hosts and guests; temporal and spatial constraints on encounters; a lack of

Table 4.5 The advocacy and cautionary perspectives of the impacts of tourism

Economic	Sociocultural
Advocacy perspectives	
Is labour intensive	Broadens education
Generates foreign earnings	Promotes international peace
Can be built on existing	Breaks down racial and
infrastructure	cultural barriers
Can be development with local	Reinforces preservation of
products and resources	heritage and traditions
Spreads development	Enhances an appreciation of
	cultural traditions
Complements other economic	
activities	
Important multiplier effects	
Cautionary perspectives	
Causes local inflation	Generates stereotypes of the
	host and guest
High leakage of money from local	Leads to xenophobia
economies	
Highly seasonal and contributes	Results in social pollution
to seasonality of employment	
Very susceptible to change and	Commodifies culture, and
economic fluctuations	traditional ways of life
Results in unbalanced spatial	Threatens traditional family
development	life in host communities
Leads to extraneous dependency	Contributes to prostitution
Increases demonstration effects	Produces conflicts in the host
	community
Destroys resources and creates	
environmental pollution	

Source: modified from Jafari (1989)

spontaneity in most encounters; and, finally, unequal or unbalanced relationships (box 4.3).

At the root of these differences and their related problems is the fact that hosts and guests not only have diverse sociocultural backgrounds but also very different perceptions. The tourist is living in what Jafari (1989, 32) terms 'non-ordinary time and place', while to the host it is ordinary life and home. Furthermore, these non-ordinary worlds are structured and conditioned by their respective cultures. The degree of contrasting values and conflict will obviously depend on levels of differences, together with the inherent flexibility of 'each world' to adapt. As we have seen, the least flexible tourists

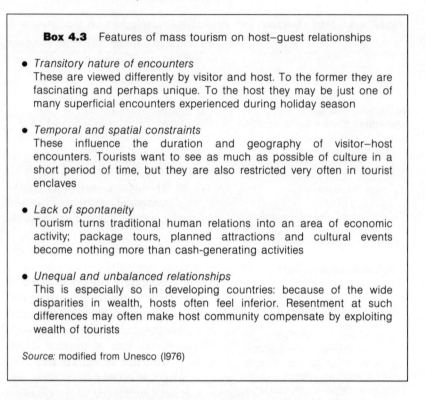

Box 4.3   Features of mass tourism on host–guest relationships

- *Transitory nature of encounters*
  These are viewed differently by visitor and host. To the former they are fascinating and perhaps unique. To the host they may be just one of many superficial encounters experienced during holiday season

- *Temporal and spatial constraints*
  These influence the duration and geography of visitor–host encounters. Tourists want to see as much as possible of culture in a short period of time, but they are also restricted very often in tourist enclaves

- *Lack of spontaneity*
  Tourism turns traditional human relations into an area of economic activity; package tours, planned attractions and cultural events become nothing more than cash-generating activities

- *Unequal and unbalanced relationships*
  This is especially so in developing countries: because of the wide disparities in wealth, hosts often feel inferior. Resentment at such differences may often make host community compensate by exploiting wealth of tourists

Source: modified from Unesco (1976)

are those involved via some form of mass tourism. While such contrasts have received considerable attention, far less interest has been directed at the receiving system, which is comprised of the host community and the host culture (Jafari 1989). Of particular importance in examining host–guest encounters is the structure of the community – its openness to other cultures and its traditions of hospitality. The main operating force within the community is the host culture, which structures community life and defines the degree of outside influence. As Jafari points out, some host communities are multicultural, which produces a far more complex response to tourists.

The non-ordinary world of the tourist is, in turn, structured by both the tourist culture and their residual culture. Despite the fact that tourists come from diverse social, ethnic and cultural backgrounds, the 'observable rituals, behaviours and pursuits . . . bind them into one collectivity' (Jafari 1989, 37; Gottlieb 1982; Krippendorf 1987). In contrast, residual culture stresses the differences between tourists, since it denotes the 'cultural baggage' that tourists bring from their home cultures. Such residual culture shapes the behaviour of tourists and can play an important role in the host community. The whole nature of host–guest relations is therefore conditioned by the complex interactions between these different elements of culture, together with the level and nature of tourism development (see also chapter 6 and figure 6.3).

The Sociocultural Impact of Tourists

The changes brought about by host–guest encounters are transmitted through both social and cultural impacts, the dimensions of which are indicated in figure 4.5. In reality, as Mathieson and Wall (1982) explain, it is extremely difficult to disentangle such sociocultural impacts, although for the sake of clarity we can examine some of the specific areas of change.

One of the simplest but most widely used frameworks for describing the effects of tourists on a host society is Doxey's (1976) so-called index of irritation. This represents the changing attitudes of the host population to tourism in terms of a linear sequence of increasing irritation as the number of tourists grows (figure 4.6). In this perspective host societies in tourist destinations pass through stages of euphoria, apathy, irritation, antagonism and loss in the face of tourism development. The progression through this sequence is determined both by the compatability of each group – which is related to culture, economic status, race and nationality – as well as by the sheer numbers of tourists (Turner and Ash 1975). Indeed, one of the most important factors in the growth of hostility to tourism relates to the physical

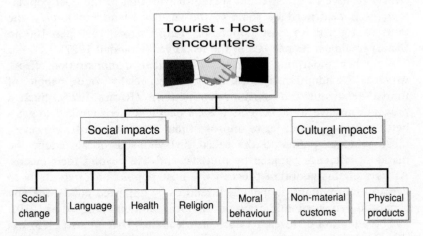

Figure 4.5 The dimensions of tourist–host encounters
Source: modified from Lea (1988)

Levels of host irritation

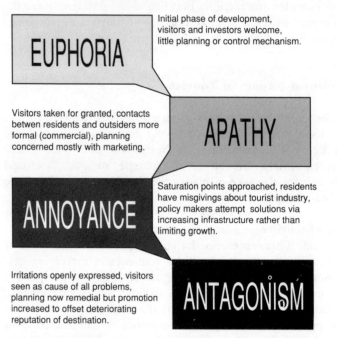

EUPHORIA — Initial phase of development, visitors and investors welcome, little planning or control mechanism.

Visitors taken for granted, contacts betwen residents and outsiders more formal (commercial), planning concerned mostly with marketing. — **APATHY**

ANNOYANCE — Saturation points approached, residents have misgivings about tourist industry, policy makers attempt solutions via increasing infrastructure rather than limiting growth.

Irritations openly expressed, visitors seen as cause of all problems, planning now remedial but promotion increased to offset deteriorating reputation of destination. — **ANTAGONISM**

Figure 4.6   Doxey's index of irritation

presence of large numbers of tourists. This numerical impact is clearly relative to the size and spatial distribution of the host population, as is evidenced by some of the smaller island ecomomies: the ratio of tourists to host population ranges from 15.4 per 100 in Samoa to almost 33 per 100 in the Maldives (Crandall 1987).

A further underlying factor is the so-called 'demonstration effect', which is the adoption by local residents, especially young people, of tourist behaviour and consumption patterns (Rivers 1973). Such a process can have some benefits if local people are encouraged to get a better education in order to improve their living standards. However, most evidence points to the social disbenefits as locals adopt the marks of affluence paraded by tourists, and live beyond their means. As part of this adoption process, the host population often starts to demand more luxury items which tend to be imported goods, thereby generating an ecomomic drain on the local ecomomy (Clevedon 1979).

The adoption of foreign values also leads to what Jafari (1973) has described as a premature departure to modernization, producing rapid and disruptive changes in the host society. Under these circumstances social tension develops as the hosts become subdivided between those adopting new values (usually young people and those deeply involved in the local tourism economy), as opposed to those retaining a traditional way of life. Such social dualism has been recorded by Smith (1977b) in her study of Eskimo communities, and by Greenwood (1976) in rural Spain; while Lundberg's (1974) studies of Hawaii and Cowan's (1977) work on the Cook Islands detected societal disruptions in the form of increases in divorce rates and split families. These changes in family life are often brought about through increases in rural–urban (resort) migration, as individuals search for employment, and an increasing number of women enter the paid workforce.

The societal changes brought about by tourists are not always easy to isolate from other 'modernizing' influences, but they appear to impact on a range of social elements (figure 4.5). It is not the intention of this chapter to review all of these, but rather to identify certain key features. Indeed, in certain areas, such as language, only limited research on the impact of tourists has been undertaken (White 1974; Mathieson and Wall 1982). In contrast, considerable and growing attention has been directed towards the moral changes attributed to tourism, particularly the rise in crime (Nicholls 1976; Pizam 1982; Chesney-Lind and Lind 1985), gambling (Pizam and Pokela 1988), prostitution (Graburn 1983; Fish, 1984) and most recently the spread of AIDS through sex tourism (Cohen 1988b).

Given the difficulties in establishing tourism's role in changing the moral standards of host societies, it is not surprising that many of the early studies were empirically based and, at the same time, cautious over their findings. However, despite some methodological problems, Jud (1975) was able to present strong evidence of a positive relationship between tourism and crime in Mexico, while studies by McPheters and Stronge (1974) in Miami focused on the seasonality of crime. Within host societies in developing countries large differences between the incomes of hosts and guests, often highlighted in the demonstration effect, lead to increased frustration in the local community, which sometimes spills over as crimes against tourists (Chesney-Lind and Lind 1985). In turn, this frustration and friction is influenced by the volume of tourists, which obviously varies over the season. Thus, Rothman's (1978) study of resorts in Delaware showed massive seasonal changes in crime, which increased fivefold over a 12-month period.

Surveys amongst British tourists by the Consumer Association have revealed that the Caribbean tops the theft league, with tourists having a 1 in 14 chance of having their property stolen. Similarly high figures are recorded in the Gambia, while in Spain the risk falls to 1 in 30. As more tourists venture to an increasing number of destinations, crime does appear to be increasing, so some travel companies, such as Hogg Robinson and Tradewinds (a specialist long-haul company), even issue warnings of world trouble-spots. As the Tradewinds brochure puts it, 'beauty seldom comes without a price', although of course the price is paid by both tourists and the local community. Not all crime is directed at the tourists; indeed, many research projects have found that local people are increasingly the victims (Rothman 1978). In some circumstances the tourists themselves behave in extremely anti-social and criminal ways: as witnessed in many Spanish coastal resorts throughout the late 1980s and early 1990s, and as recorded earlier within the provincial nature parks of Canada (White et al. 1978).

In their review of tourism and prostitution, Mathieson and Wall (1982, 149) suggested four main hypotheses that may be related. One was locational, in that tourism development often creates environments which attract prostitutes. The second was societal and related to the breaking of normal bonds of behaviour by tourists when away from home – circumstances conducive to the expansion of prostitution. A third hypothesis is related to economic aspects and the employment opportunities offered by prostitution to women, which may upgrade their economic status. Finally, they suggest that tourism may be a mere scapegoat for a general decline in moral standards. They go on to conclude their review with the idea that there is a lack of firm evidence concerning connections between tourism and prostitution. Recent reports have, however, exposed the development of a fully fledged 'sex tourist' industry (Lea 1988).

Sex tourism is largely focused on parts of South-East Asia, especially in Thailand, the Philippines and South Korea (primary areas), together with secondary areas throughout Indonesia (Seager and Olsen 1986). The clients are normally men and the prostitutes are usually women in the particular division of labour. Tourists participating in this trade – either as individuals, small groups of friends or as employees offered a company bonus (often Japanese, as Blasing (1982) points out) – are sold holidays through sex-tour brochures. These thinly disguise the actual prostitution market by images such as 'Thailand is a world full of extremes, and the possibilities are limitless. Anything goes in this exotic country – especially when it comes to girls' (Heyzer 1986, 53).

Attempts to quantify the scale of prostitution in places such as Thailand or the Philippines are difficult, considering the nature of the activity and its supposed illegality. The numbers of masseuses and prostitutes in Bangkok are estimated to be between 100 000 and 200 000 (Phongpaichit 1980), while other studies have recorded at least 977 establishments in the same city which are associated with prostitution (Heyzer 1986). The driving force behind such developments appears to be economic, since young female prostitutes can earn at least twice as much in the so-called hospitality industry as in other forms of employment. As Heyzer (1986) explains, although tourism increases the dividends of the prostitution trade it is not totally responsible for it. Certainly in Thailand the trade in female sexuality is supported by a complex network of ideological, economic and political systems. Both Graburn (1983) and Heyzer (1986) have explored these systems, identifying three main reasons why Thai society sanctions this high level of prostitution. These revolve around employment discrimination against females in most formal sectors of employment, the economic crises facing many rural areas from where most prostitutes are drawn, and the breakdown of many marriages, which leaves women cut off from traditional society. In Thailand, however, there are noticeable changes in the tourist industry, with a decrease since 1987 in single male tourists (usually associated with the sex tourism industry) and an increase in family tourism. This, as Cohen (1988b) argues, is entirely due to the fear of contracting AIDS, and to the authorities placing greater stress on the cultural and natural attractions of the country.

Most cultures hold a fascination for tourists, who tend to be attracted by a number of overlapping cultural elements (box 4.4). Of particular importance to tourists are those forms of culture which are based around physical objects, the purchasing of local crafts, visiting cultural sites, and folk culture as reflected in daily life or

---

Box 4.4 Main elements of culture that attract tourists

- Handicrafts
- Traditions
- History of a region
- Architecture
- Local food
- Art and music
- 'Ways of life'
- Religion
- Language
- Dress – traditional costumes

These tend to be ranked as most important by tourists

Source: modified from Ritchie and Zins (1978)

special festivals (Mathieson and Wall 1982, 159). There have been numerous anthropological studies on tourism and culture (see Jafari 1989), although two main areas of interest can be identified. The first follows the ideas already discussed on societal change, and concerns the processes of acculturation, which refers to the degree of cultural borrowing between two contact cultures (Nunez 1977). An alternative conceptual approach to this theme is through the concept of 'cultural drift', as discussed by Collins (1978). Under the seasonal and inter-mittent contacts that characterize host–tourist relations, cultural drift assumes that changes in the host culture are at first temporary and then exploitive. Obviously, the degree to which acculturation or cul-tural drift occurs is strongly related to the patterns of host–tourist encounters, as discussed in the previous section.

The second group of studies relates to the marketing and commo-dification of culture, as traditional ways of life become commercia-lized for tourist consumption (de Kadt 1979; Cohen 1988c). In some of the initial studies of the commoditization of culture by tourism, Greenwood (1977) observed, in the Spanish Basque town of Fuenter-rabia, that local rituals lost all meaning when repeatedly staged for money. His more general conclusions were that local culture could be commoditized by anyone, often without the consent of local people who would, in most cases, be exploited. The destruction of local cul-tural products, whether rituals or craftwork, leads to what MacCan-nell (1973) termed 'staged authencity'. In its most basic form it is associated with 'airport art', cheap imitation products sold to tourists as local craftwork (Graburn 1967) or fake rituals that stress exotic local customs (Boorstin 1964). Furthermore, Cohen (1988c) suggests that in some instances a contrived cultural product may, over time, become recognized as authentic both by tourists and, more impor-tantly, by local people. This emergent authenticity has been recorded by Cornet (1975) in the case of a supposed revival of an ancient Inca festival in Cuzco. This process is also frequently to be found at the heart of many revitalized local craft industries.

There are examples of the positive impacts of tourism on local cul-tures mainly through the revival of craft activities, and in many cir-cumstances these can be strongly related to the concept of emergent authenticity. Within this context Graburn's (1967) study of the emer-gence of Eskimo soapstone carvings provides a ready example, as does Deitch's (1977) work on the art forms of Indians in south-west America. But, of course, for each example of a more positive inter-play between tourism and culture, even though such impacts derive from the process of emergent authenticity, the literature contains many more cases of negative impacts (Mathieson and Wall 1982).

Cohen (1988c) has argued that many of these studies and, indeed, Greenwood's early categorical assertion that commoditization removed all meaning from cultural products, are over-generalizations. He believes that even though events become tourist-orientated, they may still retain meanings for local people, and he argues that such impacts need to be submitted to more detailed empirical examinations, especially of a comparative nature. Such studies would make it possible to identify the conditions under which cultural meanings are preserved or emergent, as opposed to those environments under which tourism destroys culture. This debate takes us back to an assessment of tourism consumption and behaviour, which in turn calls for a reworking of tourist typologies.

PART III

The Production of Tourism Services

FIVE

The Tourism Industry

The Tourism and Leisure Complex: Commodification, Spatial Fixity and Temporality

Sessa (1983, 59) proposes a catholic definition of the tourism industry: 'Tourism supply is the result of all those productive activities that involve the provision of the goods and services required to meet tourism demand and which are expressed in tourism consumption'. This is the tourism production system. It includes tourism resources, infrastructures (both general and those specifically devoted to tourism), receptive facilities, entertainment and sports facilities, and tourism reception services (see box 5.1). This holistic definition is important as it colours the arguments surrounding the economic, social and cultural impact of tourism. The costs of providing jobs in tourism, the income generated by tourism, and the seasonality effects of tourism have to be estimated for the complete tourism production system, not only for the most obvious tourism services such as accommodation. This also has implications for the analysis of ownership patterns in the tourism industry. While capital in the more obvious elements of tourism services is usually in private ownership within capitalist economies, this is linked to capital and services provided by the public sector and voluntary bodies.

The leisure production complex differs in important ways from the tourism production complex, as would be expected given the definitions outlined in chapter 1. Tourism resources are also leisure resources. However, some leisure resources such as lesser known beauty spots or networks of friends and neighbours may predominantly serve the leisure needs of local populations. The general infrastructure of an area is likely to serve the needs of both tourists and local residents, although international and interregional means of

---

Box 5.1 Elements of the tourism industry

Tourism resources
- Natural resources
- Human resources

General and tourism infrastructure
- Means of communication and travel
- Social installations
- Basic installations
- Telecommunications

Receptive facilities
- Hotels, guest houses, towns and villages
- Condominiums
- Complementary residences
- Residences for receptive personnel
- Food and beverage installations

Entertainment and sports facilities
- Recreational and cultural facilities
- Sports facilities

Tourism reception services
- Travel agencies
- Hotel and local promotional offices
- Information offices
- Car hire
- Guides, interpreters

Source: Sessa (1983)

---

communications are utilized by tourism rather than for local leisure. Receptive facilities and tourism reception facilities are largely devoted to tourism, although food and beverage installations, car hire firms and information services may also be elements in local leisure patterns. Entertainment and sports facilities are important to both tourism and leisure; while these may be shared – such as public swimming pools or squash courts – others are exclusive. Hotels and holiday villages may have residents only facilities, while some local facilities may be exclusive to membership groups, which by definition excludes tourists. Finally, there is a range of home based leisure pursuits, such as gardening, which – again by definition – are excluded from tourism.

One important feature is a tendency to the commodification of tourism and leisure services. Leisure and tourism enterprises tend, over time, to bring into the market products or services which traditionally were met outside the market (see Benington and White 1988, 17). Garden centres, for example, are selling more and more convenience and other products which were traditionally produced by the gardener at home. Larger numbers of guide books and leisure wear items are being produced for walkers and motorists. One notable aspect of this has been the commodification of place. Beaches or areas of countryside (such as Lands End in England or Nordkap in Norway) may be purchased by private capital and access to them may be commercialized. Where it is not possible to control access to a site – such as a historic city – it is still possible to commodify the experience of place.

The commodification process is significant in several ways. It can lead to restricted social access (predominantly by income) to a leisure or tourism resource. Alternatively, it can generate increased flows of visitors which may lead to improved accessibility to the area by both public and private transport. Commodification can generate the income to help conserve an important site, such as the town of Williamsburg (USA), or it can lead to the construction of commercial facilities, as at Niagara Falls, which detract from the intrinsic value of the place. Commodification, and in particular the introduction of private ownership into tourism and leisure services, also increases the potential for ownership of particular resources to pass into external control. In extreme cases, ownership may be acquired by large, diversified multinational corporations, the interests of which may not coincide with those of local communities.

Tourism, and to a lesser extent leisure, is also characterized by spatial fixity. Urry (1990, 40) writes that '. . . while the producers are to a significant extent spatially fixed, in that they have to provide particular services in particular places, consumers are increasingly mobile, able to consume tourist services on a global basis'. Of course, there are exceptions: large transnationals may be able to move around their capital in response to demand, while there is considerable scope to create new tourist attractions, given that these are socially constructed. However, the vast majority of entrepreneurs are small scale, and their businesses are characterized by spatial fixity in that they are associated with particular tourist attractions. As a result they are subject to the high degree of volatility in tastes in tourism and leisure, and are restricted in their ability to respond to this.

Temporal variations in demand exacerbate the difficulties associated with spatial fixity. While the demand for manufactured goods can also be temporal, producers can respond by accumulating stocks of (non-perishable) goods. However, the production capacity of a tourism service is '. . . fixed by inelastic physical and geographical

limits and by the impossibility for this kind of production to accu-
mulate stocks of products' (Sessa 1983, 68). Producers usually
respond to the temporally uneven nature of demand via differential
pricing, and temporary labour contracting. Higher prices are charged
at peak times when market demand will bear them. Lower prices will
be charged in the off-peak periods in the hope of attracting deferred,
unsatisfied peak period demand.

Tourism and leisure production systems are also composed of very
diverse elements, in terms of both ownership and scale. In tourism,
in particular, the successful development of a service complex will
depend on a partnership between the public and private sectors and
between small and large capitals (see chapter 10).

A Question of Scale: Company Structures

The tourism and leisure industries tend to be dominated by a few
large businesses operating alongside a large number of small, independent ones. For example, in the USA during the late 1980s there
were only two national bookshop chains – Daltons and Walden Books
– after a long series of mergers and acquisitions (Benington and White
1988, 14). In the American travel agency business there are some large
corporate chains, but 99 per cent of businesses – as opposed to business – are small firms (Richter 1985). In the UK fast food industry it
is estimated that small independents accounted for 55–60 per cent of
fast food sales in 1987, despite the growing presence of corporate
chains (Key Note 1988). However, fast food also illustrates the trend
to increasing scale and transnationalization in the leisure and tourism
industries. In 1987 the world's four largest chains owned or franchised
almost 28 000 outlets between them, and this number continues to
increase (see table 5.1).

Increasing scale is clearly evident in tourism within the accom-

Table 5.1   The world's five major fast food chains, 1987

Chain	Number of outlets
1. McDonalds	10 000
2. Kentucky Fried Chicken	7 600
3. Burger King	5 700
4. Pizza Hut	4 500
5. Baskin Robbins	3 500

Source: Key Note (1988)

Table 5.2   The ten corporate chains with the most hotels, 1990

Company	Number of hotels
1. Best Western International	3348
2. Choice Hotels International	2102
3. Holiday Inn Worldwide	1606
4. Accor	1421
5. Days Inns of America Inc.	1112
6. Hospitality Franchise Systems	944
7. Trusthouse Forte	838
8. Super 8 Motels Inc.	785
9. Czech Government Trade and Tourism	550
10. Marriott Hotels and Resorts	476

Source: *Hotels* (1991, 45)

modation sector. Between 1977 and 1985 all but two of the world's 16 largest hotel chains increased the average number of rooms in their hotels. The leader in terms of unit size was Westin Hotels and Restaurants of the USA, with an average of 547 rooms per hotel (Bernardi 1987). By 1990 five corporate chains owned or operated more than 1000 hotels each, with Best Western leading with 3348 hotels (table 5.2). While most of the chains are American, Holiday Inn Worldwide, Accor and Trusthouse Forte are owned by European private capital.

The scale of operations in the hotel sector continues to increase. In 1990 five corporate groups added more than 10 000 rooms to their chains, the largest being Choice Hotels International with an increase of 80 696 rooms, bringing their total up to 201 048 (*Hotels* 1991, 40). Similar trends are evident within particular countries. In the UK, for example, the first really large hotel group was formed only in 1970, following the merger of Trust Houses and Forte (Tarrant 1989). By the mid-1980s, however, corporate chains accounted for 13 per cent of all hotels and 55 per cent of all hotel rooms in the UK (Slattery and Roper 1988). This does not mean that the demise of the small independent hotel is imminent. While the large chains and hotels have access to economies of scale, the small independents can compete on the basis of costs (using low-wage family or other labour), individuality or personalized service. The critical size appears to be the medium-scale establishments with 25–60 bedrooms, which find it difficult to benefit from either individuality or economies of scale (Burkart and Medlik 1981, chapter 14).

The economies of scale available to companies in the tourism sector are not greatly different in character from those which operate in the service – and to a lesser extent the manufacturing – sector at large. There are economies of scale in production, relating to the purchase of inputs, the internal division of labour and specialization, and the use of capital. The latter is illustrated by the application of information technology. Hotels have developed relatively sophisticated information technology systems which offer cost reductions and more effective management to help counter some of the managerial disadvantages of increased scale (see figure 5.1). In air travel, computer reservation systems (CRS) which initially favoured the largest carriers, have been one of the more significant developments. The large capital costs involved in the development of these super CRS operations originally meant that only the largest airlines were able to participate. This eventual advantage was lost as the other world airlines developed their own CRS networks. However, scale remains important as the costs of the most sophisticated CRSs remains too high for most of the smaller air carriers.

There are also economies of scale to be derived in marketing. There are minimum scales of operations necessary to justify national – or even international – marketing, whether for hotels, air transport or travel agencies. Large hotels have also been able to capitalize on the advantages of 'branding'; that is, offering a standard product of known quality and price in key locations. This allows them to maximize repeat business which is important given the lower costs of attracting return visitors compared to new customers. The process of branding is assisted by the standardization of taste amongst regular travellers, so that there is a virtuous business cycle of standardized product–standardized taste–standardized product. However, successful branding requires close control and rationalization. Tarrant (1989, 188) writes:

> . . . the need to maintain brand consistency has led to substantial programmes of hotel refurbishment by many operators. Where refurbishment is not a viable option this has led some operators to dispose of properties, even when in major commercial centers.

In some sectors of the tourism industry there are minimum capital requirements for successful operation. Airline operations, for example, require large initial capital outlays to purchase aircraft and supporting installations. Furthermore, to compete in the international air carrier business, major investments are required subsequently to update the fleet. Small companies cannot hope to compete in these sectors, especially if large research and development costs are

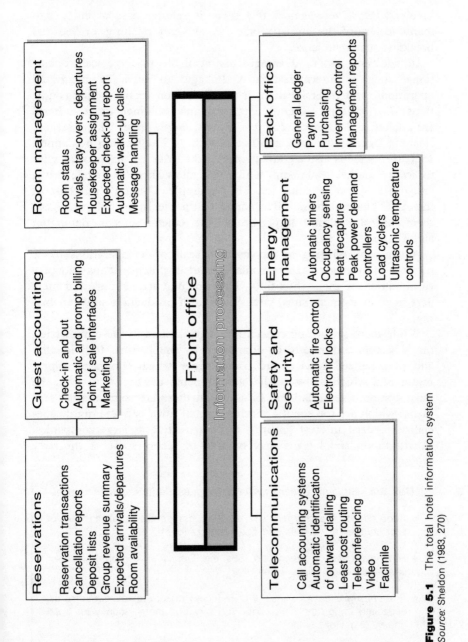

Figure 5.1 The total hotel information system
Source: Sheldon (1983, 270)

Reservations

Reservation transactions
Cancellation reports
Deposit lists
Group revenue summary
Expected arrivals/departures
Room availability

Guest accounting

Check-in and out
Automatic and prompt billing
Point of sale interfaces
Marketing

Room management

Room status
Arrivals, stay-overs, departures
Housekeeper assignment
Expected check-out report
Automatic wake-up calls
Message handling

Front office

Information processing

Telecommunications

Call accounting systems
Automatic identification
of outward dialling
Least cost routing
Teleconferencing
Video
Facimile

Safety and security

Automatic fire control
Electronic locks

Energy management

Automatic timers
Occupancy sensing
Heat recapture
Peak power demand
controllers
Load cyclers
Ultrasonic temperature
controls

Back office

General ledger
Payroll
Purchasing
Inventory control
Management reports

involved. However, against this there is relative ease of entry into many sectors of the industry, such as souvenir retailing, or bed and breakfast accommodation.

In addition, other advantages are available to large-scale operations, such as internalization of linkages in vertically integrated operations, and diversification in the face of uncertain market conditions. For example, Grand Metropolitan's holdings include Berni Inn, Chef and Brewer, Express Foods, Eden Vale, Ski, Cinzano, Foster's lager in the UK, and hotels such as The Carlton in Cannes. Increased scale is also a consequence of the drive by major companies to secure market leadership, which will allow them to dictate prices and other operating conditions. For example, Cannon's purchase of the ABC cinema chain, when added to their existing holdings, gave them control of almost 40 per cent of UK cinema screens (Benington and White 1988, 13).

A company wishing to increase the scale of its operations has a number of strategic choices available, and in practice it may adopt a combination of them (box 5.2). They include acquisitions and mergers, new investment sites, intensification of production and franchising.

While there are strong concentration tendencies in these industries, many sectors continue to be dominated by small firms. Individuality and personalized services are commodities which command a premium and which allow small establishments to survive in even the most competitive situations. In addition, there are some market segments which are too small – serving a small town or some highly specialized tourist interest group – to be attractive to large companies. Furthermore, small firms may be able to secure some of the scale

---

Box 5.2 Strategic options available to tourism and leisure companies

• *Acquisitions and mergers* with existing companies, characteristic of tour companies, airlines and hotel corporations

• *New investment* in green-field sites, e.g. Disney on a global scale, or Granada Lodge hotels within UK

• *Franchising* used as a means of reducing direct capital requirements, especially important in fast food industry and more recently for hotel chains (e.g. Holiday Inn)

• *Intensification of production in situ* via a reorganization of labour processes or addition of new capital

advantages of the corporate chains by forming voluntary groups for marketing or purchasing purposes. One of the most well known examples is the Best Western hotel group, which has successfully developed branding even though the establishments remain in individual ownership.

Internationalization and Transnational Corporations

One particular aspect of the increasing concentration in the leisure and tourism industries is the growth of transnational companies. Some leisure products, such as films, sports wear and video machines, are already highly internationalized. However, there is also growing internationalization of the production of leisure and tourism services.

Taylor and Thrift (1986, 6) suggest that there are at least three levels of transnational corporations: global corporations, multinational corporations and 'small' multinationals. All three are to be found in the tourism and leisure industries. For example, the ITT group, owners of the Sheraton hotels, are a diversified global corporation with a strong presence in 61 countries and in most of the world's largest markets. Trusthouse Forte is an example of a multinational corporation in the hotel sector; while one of the largest chains in the world, its operations are highly regionalized, being concentrated in Europe. An example of a 'small' multinational is Journey's End Corporation of Canada which, in 1990, had 133 hotels but had only recently begun to operate outside of its home country. In the hotel sector, there are few global transnationals, and even the largest corporation tend to concentrate on particular regions. A survey in the late 1970s found that: UK transnationals were most active in Europe, Africa and the Caribbean; American-based transnationals were most active in Asia and Latin America; and Japanese transnationals were most evident in the Pacific Rim region.

There are a number of reasons for the growth of transnationals in tourism and leisure, some of which have already been considered in the discussion of scale in the previous section. Clearly, the international market provides even greater potential for large companies to secure competitive advantages, although these have to be balanced against the increased costs involved in such operations. These tendencies are similar to those which have been observed in the manufacturing sector (see Dicken 1986). Furthermore, there are direct links between the economic sectors; for example, international hotel chains have partly developed in response to the requirements of international business travellers, while some manufacturing corporations, such as ITT, have diversified into tourism.

In addition, there are a number of specific reasons for the internationalization of operations. There is quite simply what Urry (1990, 48) terms 'an international division of tourist sites'. For example, Spain, Austria and the UK, respectively, specialize at the international level in beach, winter sports and heritage-related holidays. Tourism companies wishing to diversify their portfolio of holiday products, or to secure a larger share of their national market must, therefore, internationalize their activities. The role of the transnationals in this is not necessarily passive, for they are one of the agents involved in the social construction of tourism preferences. Another reason for the growth of transnationals is as a strategic response by corporations seeking to lower the costs of production: low labour costs partly underlie the expansion of Mediterranean tourism.

Air travel and hotel chains offer two classic but contrasting examples of transnationalization within the tourism industry. International airlines figure amongst the lists of the world's largest multinational companies. The need to develop comprehensive regional or global networks, so as to attract clients and internalize the revenue from

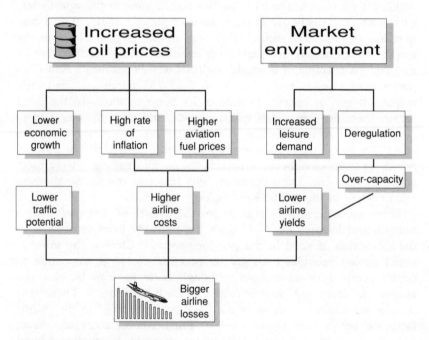

Figure 5.2   International airline economics: the pattern of change
Source: Wheatcroft (1982, 72)

connecting flights, provides a strong logic for the growth of multi-nationals. Yet their operating environment is highly constrained. Wheatcroft (1990, 353) writes that 'Air transport . . . has been shaped in the past by the combined forces of sovereignty, nationalism and protectionism'. Many airlines have been heavily subsidized and protected for nationalistic, economic and prestige reasons. However, the operating environment is changing (see figure 5.2). On the market side, deregulation (especially in the USA, and latterly in Europe) has exposed over-capacity in the industry. The growing proportion of leisure as opposed to business travellers is also pressurizing prices downwards. At the same time, periodic rises in oil prices have put pressure on the operating margins of airlines. Privatization is also changing the competitive environment: more than 30 airlines were privatized during the 1980s, including such market leaders as British Airways and Japan Airways.

The result of this freeing-up of competition has been a major restructuring of the industry. This is most spectacularly evident in the bankruptcy of an airline such as PanAm, which was once a market leader. The other notable response has been the attempt by some leading airlines to become members of the elite group of mega-carriers via a programme of mergers and acquisitions (Wheatcroft 1990). British Airways, for example, acquired British Caledonian in 1988 and has subsequently investigated alliances with both KLM of the Netherlands and United of the USA.

Hotels present a different picture of transnationalization:

Before the Second World War, there were already a few small international hotel groups crossing national frontiers. They were prestigious, family controlled, or personally owned groups of hotels associated, for example, with the names of Ritz or Marquet. These enterprises bore little or no resemblance to the major international hotel chains of today . . . (Fenelon 1990, 97).

There are some major international hotel groups. ITT Sheraton is the most internationalized in that it was represented in 61 countries by 1990, but there are a total of eight chains which operate in more than 30 countries. These could form the bases for the emergence of mega-choice of hotels with 100 000–350 000 rooms distributed globally which will '. . .set the pace through their sheer weight in terms of investment, global positioning, and management talent' (Go et al. 1990, 298). The headquarters of the largest chains are concentrated in the USA and Europe, especially in the UK, France, and Spain, although Japan is also important (see figure 5.3). However, with a

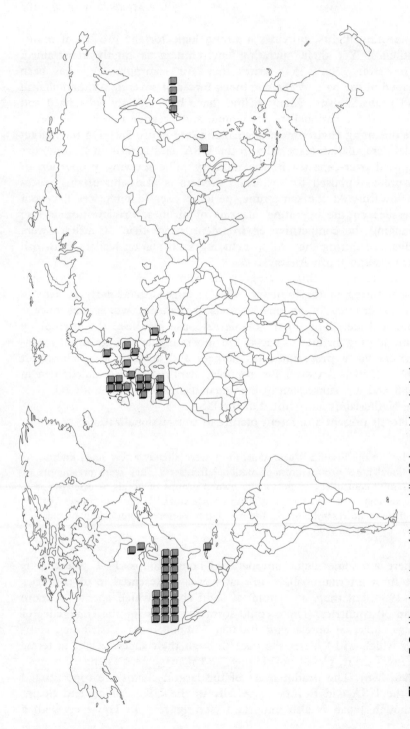

Figure 5.3 Headquarters of the world's 50 largest hotel chains

Source: *Hotels* (1991)

few exceptions, their operations tend to be regionalized, and 80 per cent of the world's hotel rooms are located in Europe and North America alone (Go 1989, 195). This pattern is being modified, however, by the rapid expansion of hotel capacity in the Pacific Rim region.

Dunning and McQueen (1982) provide a systematic theoretical framework for the analysis of multinationals in one tourism sector, the hotel industry. Drawing on Dunning's wider research on the theory of multinationals, they argue that '. . . the propensity of a firm to engage in international production depends on three conditions being satisfied' (p. 79).

First, the firm with headquarters in one country must have net ownership advantages compared to firms of other nationalities operating in that market. These stem from the fact that hotels sell experience goods (already known to the customer) rather than search goods (which can be examined and compared to each other and to advertisements). Hotels sell a package of on-site and off-site services before, during and after a stay at the hotel. Ascher (1985, 37) comments that there is remarkable similarity in the range of services offered by the main hotel groups even though individual corporations have very diverse origins. However, there are differences in the quality and the presentation of these services, and this is the basis for branding. Branding ensures that the services provided or experienced match the client's expectations. The multinational has an advantage over the domestic hotel in that it is familiar with the needs of international travellers and is experienced in providing the package of services they demand. It is, therefore, proprietary rights over a differentiated product that creates the ownership conditions for transnationalism in this sector.

The second main factor is that it must be profitable for the firm to combine its assets with the factor endowments located in foreign countries. In the case of hotels these locational advantages are based on market segmentation. Their appeal to the international traveller is partly based on providing their experience good in most of the major international destinations that he or she is likely to visit. There is therefore a compelling reason to be truly global. However, in practice this is achieved by few hotel corporations. Instead, as observed earlier, hotel corporations have regionalized international markets. Given that most business travellers operate in such regional rather than truly global fields, this is consistent with securing locational advantages.

Finally, it has to be more beneficial for the firm to use these advantages itself rather than to sell them to a foreign firm. In other words, there are internalization advantages to be secured from expanding across international borders. Internalization is explained by Taylor and Thrift (1986, 7) as '. . . a simple term that applies to a simple insight, namely that a whole series of transactions are internalized within the multinational corporation rather than taking place within the market, either to protect against or to exploit market failure'. The most extreme example of this is the ownership of hotels by tour companies or international airlines: for example, Wagons Lits owns 314 Pullman International Hotels, while AIR Nipon airways owns 31 Ana Enterprises hotels (*Hotels* 1991).

Taken together, these three aspects of ownership, location and internalization provide a useful framework for the analysis of transnationals in the hotel sector. However, Dunning and McQueen also highlight a particular feature of international hotel chains; namely, the use of subcontracting. This is based on the division between the buildings required for the hotel, which represent a long-term investment in real estate, and the know-how required to deliver a particular hotel experience. The latter requires a short-term return for a constantly changing product. There is, therefore, a tendency for there to be a separation of ownership of the buildings and the management of the hotels. Increasingly, the large hotel corporations are specializing in providing the know-how under contract to the owners of the hotel building. For example, Hilton International, prior to its takeover by the Ladbroke group, owned 44 hotels, partially owned and operated 14 hotels, and operated another 33 hotels under management contracts (Laws 1991, 219–20).

Given the diverse nature of the tourism industry, it is not surprising that there is considerable diversity in the form of multinationalization. This is evident in the examples provided here of just two subsectors, hotels and aviation. In the next section we examine a third and very distinctive form of transnationalism, the international tour company.

Packaging Paradise: the International Tour Companies

International tour companies play a critical role in the international tourism industry: they link together millions of individual consumers, mostly in the more developed countries, with large numbers of individual enterprises in the travel industry, the accommodation sector and other tourism-related services. These enterprises are often located in less developed economies than the tourists' countries of origin. With the exception of the air travel industry, most of the enterprises are relatively small scale.

Historically, the creation of package holidays is associated with Thomas Cook. Cook's first foreign holiday was arranged only in 1855, but within ten years he had a thriving international business. By 1872 Cook's was able to offer round-the-world holidays. Its main rival in the USA was American Express which, from the 1850s, offered financial and other services to travellers (Feldman 1989). Eventually, other companies entered the market, which was boosted by – as well as contributing to – popular mass tourism. From the 1950s, competition in the industry intensified, as package air tours became feasible for mass tourists. The industry has continued to expand and in the UK, for example, 10 million package tours were sold in 1986, compared to only 6 million in 1980 (Fitch 1987).

Foreign travel can be dominated by, but is rarely monopolized by, tour companies. Alternatively, individuals can make their own direct arrangements with travel companies and hotels, or can purchase these services from travel agents (see figure 5.4). The individual's choice will depend on his or her experience and resources, the difficulty of making arrangements in particular countries, and the attractiveness of the holiday packages offered by the tour company. For example, in the UK 84 per cent of outward tourists to Greece, compared to only 34 per cent of those to France, used tour companies for their holidays (see figure 5.5). In practice, therefore, there is considerable variation between countries with respect to the role played by tour companies. Their role is relatively strong in northern Europe and Japan, and weaker in North America and southern Europe. Germany has the

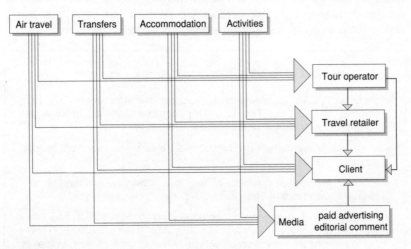

Figure 5.4 Channels of travel distribution
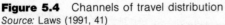
Source: Laws (1991, 41)

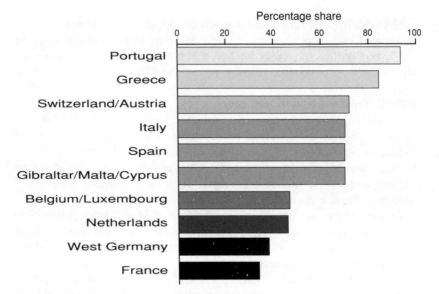

Figure 5.5   The market share of inclusive tours in the main overseas holiday destinations of UK residents, 1985
Source: Fitch (1987, 31)

world's largest tour operator industry, selling 10.9 million packages worth DM 11 billion in 1986 (Drexl and Agel 1987, 29). The UK has Europe's second largest outbound package tour market with about 10 million customers a year in the late 1980s. In contrast, it is estimated that only 27 per cent of US overseas air travellers (but a higher proportion of holiday travellers) are on package tours.

Box 5.3   The economics of tour company operations

- *High productivity and low-cost products*: through generating high volumes of sales; e.g. Thomson (UK) sold over 3 million holidays per annum during the late 1980s

- *Large undifferentiated products*: offer similar bundles of tourism services

- *Efficient marketing systems*: allows tour company to market and charge for bundles of services in advance of their delivery

- *Subcontracting system*: tour companies rarely own travel and other facilities, which means they have very low capital outlays – some companies have more recently established their own charter airlines to internalize an important revenue element

The economics of tour company operations are based on four main elements, as shown in box 5.3. Of these, the system of subcontracting is perhaps open to most variations, in that there is the tendency for some tour companies to set up their own charter airlines so as to internalize one of the most important revenue elements from the sale of holiday packages. This can be observed in the UK, where Thomson own the Britannia charter airline, which is larger than major European carriers such as Swissair and SAS (Urry 1990, 49). The reverse pattern can also be observed, with airlines owning tour companies. For example, Japan Airlines owns Japan Creative Tours, Swissair has a majority holding in TO, Kuoni, the largest Swiss group, and Air France has a 70 per cent interest in Sotair, a major French tour operator. However, most tour companies rely on a pattern of subcontracting, especially for services other than air travel. This can be piecemeal and short-term, based on advance undertakings to fill a certain number of beds in a particular hotel over one or more seasons. Alternatively, as occurs in Germany,

> . . . the main operators also have direct involvement through the setting up of hotel management companies in some foreign hotels such as TUI with Iberotel (35 hotels) and RIU (17 hotels) in Spain. Similar structures exist for NUR with Royaltur and Aldiana Clubs. Mallorca, one of the main destinations in Spain for West German tourists, offers a number of TUI- and NUR-exclusive beds (through its subsidiaries Iberotel and Royaltur) which is larger than the total accommodation capacity of Greece (Drexl and Agel 1987, 37).

The existence of substantial economies of scale in the production (including internalization of vertical linkages) and marketing of package holidays creates the conditions for concentration of ownership. In the USA, for example, in the mid-1970s there were over 1000 tour operators, but 3 per cent of these handled 37 per cent of customers (Sheldon 1988, 53). While the main players remained constant, there was a high rate of instability in the industry as a whole, with large numbers of births and deaths of firms. The German tour industry has a similar structure. Hundreds of small operators offer specialist packages or operate on a regional basis, but 40 per cent of the market is accounted for by just three companies; Touristik Union International, NUR Touristic, and International Tourist Services (see figure 5.6). However, the highest level of concentration is to be found in the UK where, in 1987, the three leading companies – Thomson, International Leisure Group and Horizon – accounted for 60 per cent of the British air tour market (Fitch 1987, 29). Subsequently, Horizon

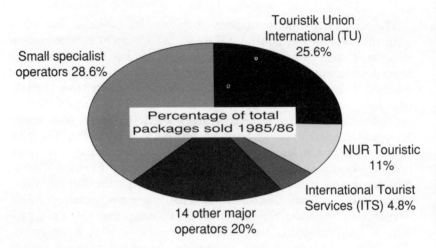

Small specialist
operators 28.6%

Touristik Union
International (TU)
25.6%

Percentage of total
packages sold 1985/86

NUR Touristic
11%

International Tourist
Services (ITS) 4.8%

14 other major
operators 20%

Figure 5.6   The market share of West German tour operators, 1985–6
Source: Drexl and Agel (1987, 34)

has been taken over by Thomson, and International Leisure Group
has become insolvent. Thus, by the 1990s Thomson has secured a
highly dominant market position.

The economic structuring of the tour companies has allowed
them to achieve a major position in the air travel holiday industries
of many developed countries. A number of important consequences
follow from this economic structuring. First, the economies of scale
obtained by the tour companies have allowed them significantly to
lower the cost of foreign holidays. This has been critical in the
growth of mass international tourism (see chapter 9). Second, their
success comes from '. . . maximizing load factors on the travel
portion, and through volume buying to negotiate very low rates
with the accommodation suppliers they use' (Laws 1991, 36). The
large number of mostly small independent operators means that
supply conditions resemble those of perfect competition, whereas
the concentration of ownership amongst tour companies mean that
demand is delivered under oligopolistic conditions. As a result, the
prices paid to local entrepreneurs tend to be depressed. It is particularly notable that UK tour companies, which are characterized
by the highest degree of concentration in Europe, secure some of
the lowest hotel prices in the destination countries. For example, in
39 out of 57 hotels surveyed in Portugal, Greece and Spain, the
lowest price was offered by a British company (quoted in Urry
1990, 48).

Third, tour companies play an important role in the social construction of tourism. Their advertising and, above all, their brochures help to shape the images of what are desirable and achievable holidays in the mass market. One feature of this is the promotion of holiday types, such as 'winter ski' or 'summer sun', which are essentially placeless. The resorts are defined purely in terms of their leisure attributes, and are presented as devoid of nationality, culture or other local context. It follows from this, and from the internationalization of services and architectural styles in these 'identikit' resorts, that virtually the only point of competition is price. This strengthens the bargaining power of the tour companies *vis-à-vis* the independent local operators, and contributes to the depression of prices.

Finally, the tour companies do not market all tour resorts equally. The search for economies of scale and the availability of air links means that they concentrate on a few resorts or regions. This has already been referred to in chapter 2 in the discussion of international tourist movements. As a result, particular resorts or tourist regions tend to become highly dependent on particular market segments. This makes them vulnerable to fluctuations in demand within those markets. This has been a particular problem in the Mediterranean region; for example, the Algarve receives 50 per cent of its visitors from the most fickle of markets, the UK. In some respects, therefore, the geography of tour company operations is also a geography of dependency relationships.

State Intervention

While tourism enterprises are mostly owned by private capital in capitalist societies, the state is usually involved in these sectors. There are a number of reasons for state intervention, and these change over time in response to developments in the political economy of the state and, in the tourism industry, as well as in the larger national and international economy. According to the OECD (1974, 3), there have been three main phases of tourism policies in the developed world since 1945. In the late 1940s and the early 1950s the emphasis was on dismantling health, customs and other regulations which hindered international movements. Subsequently, in the 1950s governments became more involved in promoting tourism as they became aware of its importance as an element of international trade. Finally, in the 1970s and the 1980s, governments became more aware of the environmental, social and regional implications of tourism development (see also Airey 1983).

There are six principal reasons for state interventionism in the tourism industry; national economic goals, political legitimation, equity and social needs, externalities and social investment, regulation and negative controls, and regional development. The prime attraction of tourism for national policy-makers is as an *agent of economic development*. The high ratio of labour to capital in many subsectors, the ease of entry into the market and the rapidity of development – especially compared to most agricultural and manufacturing sectors – make tourism particularly attractive to national policy. The state may therefore intervene directly (for example, as in the publicly owned *parador* hotel chain in Spain) or indirectly (via infrastructural investments or subsidies to private capital) in these industries. The global recession in manufacturing industries in the 1980s and the crisis of overproduction in agriculture has added to the attractiveness of tourism as an object of economic policy.

International tourism offers the added attraction of earning foreign exchange. International tourism trade is growing faster than merchandise trade, and already accounts for more than a quarter of the value of internationally traded services. This can have a considerable impact on a country's balance of trade. In 1987, for example, Spain had net receipts from international tourism of $12.8 billion, while West Germany had a net deficit of $15.8 billion. For Spain this represented approximately one quarter of all its earnings from the export of goods and services (see Williams and Shaw 1991, chapter 2 for further details). For these reasons, most governments have become involved in the promotion of their tourism attractions. There may also be parallel promotion strategies to encourage nationals to take domestic rather than foreign holidays.

Cultural and recreational activities can also become the focus of mega-events. The Olympic Games and the World Cup, for example, not only generate tourism revenue but also attract world attention. This can raise the profile of a country, region or city and enhance its international competitiveness. This is particularly important in the competition between locations for footloose international investments. Such investments – whether in financial services or electronics research – are increasingly attracted by quality of life considerations as much as by labour or transport costs. The development of quality tourism and more generally of leisure facilities – usually focused around a particular event – can therefore be seen as a long-term investment in the future of a city or region: hence the keen competition to host events such as the Olympic Games, or to be designated the European Cultural City. The same sort of competition between localities, and hence policy interest, can also be seen within countries. Arts and garden festivals, for example, are hosted to enhance the

reputation of an area, as well as to improve the leisure facilities available to local populations.

Tourism can be used as an instrument of *political legitimation*.
There are many examples of governments which have used tourism
as one means of improving their international political standing.
Spain (under Franco), and more recently Israel and the Philippines,
have all consciously used tourism in this manner. The reverse position can also be observed and a prohibition on tourism can be used,
on its own or as part of a package of sanctions, to record opposition
to a particular government. For example, for many years the USA
banned travel to China and Cuba, and more recently the same policy
has been applied to Libya (Gunn 1988, 62).

If access to tourism (and leisure) services is allocated by market
mechanisms, thereby reflecting the distribution of income in society,
it will be inherently uneven. In most capitalist societies, the state
intervenes, *reallocating access* in order to bring about greater equity –
if not equality (Gratton and Taylor 1988, 41). The motivation for
this may be the need for the state to legitimate its own role, or it may
be in response to pressures exerted by political parties or interest
groups. The state has, in practice, been particularly important in
helping to provide sports, arts and cultural facilities in recent
decades. In some countries it also provides 'social tourism' (see
chapter 3).

Amin (1983, 142) writes that '. . . the necessity of the capitalist
state arises when the circulation (distribution, exchange and consumption) of commodities is impeded'. This comes about in tourism
when individual groups of capital can not guarantee their own long-
term survival because they cannot meet the general requirements of
production, such as the need for investment in airports, roads or
training. There are *positive externalities* to be obtained by the tourism
industry from such investments. However, these may not be profitable investments for individuals. Social investment by the state may
therefore be required to undertake these key investments. Damette
(1980) terms this the 'devalorization' of capital.

Tourism services can be developed in such as way as to be harmful
to local communities, to consumers or to the long-term interests of
the industry itself. For example, a series of large hotels may be built
to poor standards in a beauty spot. This would destroy the initial
tourism resource, and provide substandard accommodation for the
tourists. The extra traffic generated on the roads could also inconvenience the local community. Therefore, as with most building and
with most consumer goods, the state has to *intervene to regulate the
production and delivery of tourism services and goods*. Regulations may

be introduced to control the location, quality and appearance of facilities, while health and safety regulations apply to their operation, and some attempt is made to regulate quality via consumer laws. In recent years, there has been increasing concern about the environmental impact of tourism and growing calls for more socially responsible provision. However, such regulation may involve short- or long-term costs for the industry, and will also require minimum administrative inputs if it is to be effective. Consequently, regulation is more likely to be found in the developed than in the developing countries.

Tourism development tends to be unevenly distributed spatially both because of differential access and the uneven spread of attractions. While capital city and other forms of urban tourism are important, tourism regions tend to be less developed and more peripheral regions. Indeed, one of their attractions is often their relatively unspoilt nature. Of course, there are exceptions; for example, Florida, one of the primary poles of tourist attraction in the USA, is also a relatively high-income region. However, the generalization does hold and for this reason, therefore, tourism has been used as an *instrument of regional development policy*. This is more plausible in the more developed countries, where even the poorest regions have basic infrastructural provision. However, tourism can also be the object of regional policy in less developed economies. For example, the 1975 master tourism plan for Malaysia attempted to decentralize tourism from the urban areas of the west by developing tourist regions and corridors on the east coast (Pearce 1989, 251).

The actual form of state intervention varies according to the political economy of a country. The most basic divide is that 'institutional frameworks lead to compulsory planning in collective societies and to indicative planning in capitalist economies' (Gunn 1988). However, there are also more subtle differences in accordance with the organization of the state, and the division of responsibilities, resources and powers between the local and the regional state. In the USA, for example, planning is mostly at the local level, and involves physical planning measures such as land-use zoning. In contrast, there is growing local state involvements with tourism in the UK as an instrument of economic policy. At times, the interest of the local state and the central state may conflict. For example, the national aim of expanding tourism to generate international earnings may conflict with the interests of local communities which wish to limit new developments in their areas.

A further level of complexity is added by the increasing involvement of supranational bodies in tourism policy. Foremost amongst these is the European Community which, in 1985, established a policy framework that covered enhanced freedom of movement and protection for EC tourists, improved working conditions for workers in tourism, integrating tourism into the Common Transport Policy, the safeguarding of heritage, and the use of tourism as an instrument of regional policy (Williams and Shaw 1991, chapter 14). As with national policy, considerable contradictions are potentially inherent within this set of aims. Their resolution is dependent on the wider conflicts between interest groups, not all of which are directly concerned with tourism.

SIX

Tourism and Entrepreneurship

Tourism, Economic Development and Entrepreneurial Activity: a Neglected Issue

The growth of the tourism industry and its potential for stimulating economic development has formed an important point in much of the literature on tourism. However, despite considerable debate on the subject (see, for example, Young 1973; de Kadt 1979; Mathieson and Wall 1982) there is still little agreement as to tourism's role in economic development. The overall picture remains clouded, not only by the different assessments of what constitutes economic development (Pearce 1989, 6–10), but also because of tourism's sociocultural and environmental implications (Murphy 1985). Furthermore, within the considerable literature on tourism's economic potential, little attention has been paid to the role of entrepreneurial activity and, in particular, to how tourism enterprises operate in different economies (Shaw and Williams 1990). This omission stands in marked contrast to other areas of economic geography, where the role and characteristics of business organization has been given detailed attention.

This chapter aims to explore the importance of entrepreneurship and to highlight its key position in understanding tourism's impact on economic development. Of necessity, our starting point needs to be a general one, reviewing briefly the study of tourism and economic development, before examining in more detail those studies that have considered entrepreneurial activity.

The general literature on tourism and economic development has focused broadly on two major themes: the economic cost–benefits of tourism, and the measurement of tourism's economic impact. Of course, in many cases these themes overlap, but for the purpose of clarity they will be given separate consideration, with the second theme being discussed in chapter 7. The first approach embraces a considerable range of studies drawn from a number of academic disciplines, although most are grounded in political economy perspectives of tourism and development. Early work was stimulated by the research of Young (1973), Bryden's (1973) study of the Caribbean, and various conferences on tourism's role in developing countries (see, for example, Shiviji 1973). The range of these early studies was such that Kassé (1973) was able to discuss the formulation of a theory of tourism development in under-developed countries. His emphasis was on attempting to understand how tourism could generate capital that, in turn, could be transferred to other economic sectors, as well as measuring the real costs of tourism development. In a geographical context, Bryden (1973) gave early recognition to the fact that tourism took different forms and, more importantly, that its impact was conditioned by the environment within which development took place. Similarly, van Doorn (1979) has argued that tourism development can only be understood within the context of the developmental stages which particular countries have entered.

Unfortunately, there is little consideration of the linkages between these two dimensions of development. Indeed, such an obvious analysis may well be too simplistic, as there is strong evidence that the size of the local economy is also an important consideration Thus, Latimer (1985) demonstrates how larger tourism economies, such as Kenya and Tunisia, have a wider range of entrepreneurial opportunities and locational options compared with some of the mini-economies of the Caribbean.

Within most of the literature, particular attention has been paid to the structure of the tourism industry in developing economies, especially the role played by transnational companies (UN Centre on Transnational Corporations 1982). In Kenya, for example, foreign equity participation accounts for almost 60 per cent of hotel beds, with large transnational hotel groups such as Inter-Continental and Hilton International having major developments (Rosemary 1987). The implications of transnational activities for developing countries are considerable: a loss of control by the host country over its national tourist industry; leakage of foreign earnings (since only between 22 per cent and 50 per cent of the gross revenue remains in the destination country), and the development of isolated tourist enclaves separated from the host population (Lea 1988). Some of these problems have been confirmed in surveys by the World Tourism Organization (1985), which covered 22 developing countries. This research enquired into the countries' attitudes towards transnational tourism, and found that most still considered that the disadvantages outweighed the benefits (table 6.1; see also chapters 2 and 5).

Reliance on international tourism as a strategy for the growth of developing economies has been criticized because it is often associated with a dependency upon external sources of capital and expertise (de Kadt 1979). Such sources tend to be fickle in nature. Choices

Table 6.1   Perceptions of selected developing countries towards transnational tourism

Assertion	True (%)	Partly true (%)	Untrue (%)
Transnational corporations (TNCs) have to some extent influenced the type of tourism activity attracted to developing countries	36	55	9
Lack of bargaining power is the main problem of developing countries in dealing with TNCs	50	41	9
Developing countries are insufficiently informed about the various transnational corporations and forms of their involvement in tourism development	50	27	23
TNCs appear at times reluctant to employ local managers and senior staff	59	32	9
The most significant benefit of TNC involvement is in speeding up the pace of tourism development	45	32	23
The most significant lasting contribution made by TNCs to the developing countries is the transfer of skills, product knowledge, technology and product techniques	27	64	9
The working methods and training schemes of TNCs are not always adapted to the stage of development of the receiving country[a]	45	45	9
Often, TNCs give less emphasis to training local personnel then to meeting production targets and deadlines			

[a]Row adds to 99 due to rounding
Source: World Tourism Organization (1985)

of tourist destinations are highly susceptible to volatile fluctuations, particularly because of economic conditions in the tourists' country of origin or the perception of the situation and status of the holiday destination. There are also significant structural and geographical dimensions of tourism dependency, as shown in Figure 6.1 (Britton 1981; Pearce 1989). In this perspective, the major tourist flows and controls emanate from the developed economies, while in the destination country small resort enclaves are created. For example, Barbados has an area of 430 km^2, but even on this small island the 370 000 visitors who arrived in 1986 were almost entirely concentrated within a narrow coastal strip (Holder 1988). It is through such spatial networks that transnational tourism organizations operate, and unless they are strongly regulated by governments, only limited economic benefits may accrue to the host communities. Such models of tourism development (figure 6.1) have also been couched in terms of core-periphery theory. Hills and Lundgren (1977) argue that there are powerful hierarchical dimensions in the spatial networks, and that these are explained by dependency theory (Britton 1981; see also chapter 2). Moreover, these hierarchical relationships are, according to Lundgren (1972), a clear expression of metropolitan hegemony, being a function of the technological and economic superiority of large urban areas in the developed economies (Pearce 1989, 93-4).

According to many observers, these geographical shifts in activity, and the concentration of tourism resources, also produce structural changes in developing economies. According to Winpenny (1982, 218), '... tourism displaces existing sectors of the economy and makes it more difficult for new ones to develop'. Such sectoral changes operate via competition for labour, and sometimes land, against traditional agriculture (Bryden 1974). However, Latimer (1985) highlights two significant features of such views. First, much of this literature concerning tourism's development role dates from the peak years of international tourism in developing countries, 1960-74, when the pace of change was extremely dramatic. Second, and more importantly, there seems little hard evidence that tourism has been the main cause of agricultural decline in many developing economies. While Brown (1974) noted a 7 per cent decline in the number of agricultural workers in Jamaica between 1960 and 1972, Latimer (1985) has shown that the workforce in Jamaican hotels only rose from a ratio of one job per 50 agricultural workers in 1960, to two jobs per 50 by 1972. This increase only represented one year's net addition to the Jamaican workforce from school leavers. From his review of conditions Latimer (1985, 42), concluded that '. . . from a strictly economic view, if projected benefits outweigh costs, tourism

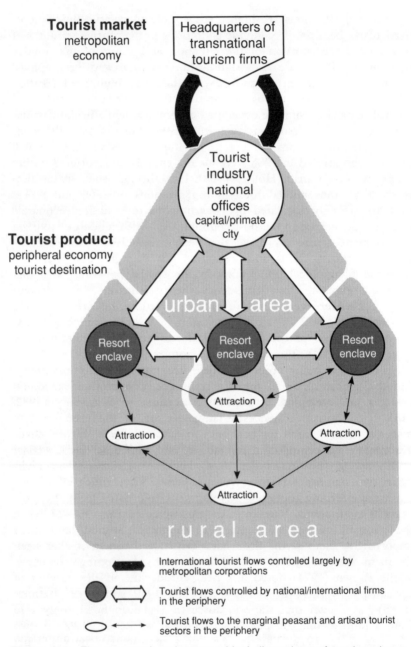

International tourist flows controlled largely by
metropolitan corporations

Tourist flows controlled by national/international firms
in the periphery

Tourist flows to the marginal peasant and artisan tourist
sectors in the periphery

Figure 6.1   The structural and geographical dimensions of tourism dependency
Source: Britton (1981)

ranks with any other export choice'. Of course, such economic possibilities still do not negate the problems associated with the external control of capital and dependency.

These debates on levels of dependency are not limited to developing countries, although much of the early literature would have us believe that this is the case. More recent research has highlighted similar problems associated with the role of tourism in more mature economies. In Austria, for example, foreign tourists account for 76 per cent of all overnight stays, while the equivalent proportion in Spain is 66 per cent (Williams and Shaw 1991, chapter 2). Within the Mediterranean countries, foreign investment is another dimension of the relationship between tourism and economic dependency, and in this there are at least superficial parallels with the developing countries. For example, in Greece the relative importance of foreign investment in tourism peaked at 66 per cent in 1968 (Leontidou 1991). Most of this foreign capital went into hotel complexes in prime coastal locations, creating a phase of speculative development with all the related environmental and sociocultural problems of tourist enclaves.

The Role of Entrepreneurship in Tourism Development

Within the political economy approach discussed in the previous section, only scant attention has been paid to the role of entrepreneurs in the tourism industry. Beyond general discussions of the impact of transnational organizations, the literature is remarkably uninformative on the influence of small or even medium-sized businesses (Harper 1984). However, as Mathieson and Wall (1982, 82) argue '. . . there is little doubt that the tourist industry exhibits backward linkages and that external economies have emerged', yet few researchers have examined the relationship between such linkages and entrepreneurial activity.

One major exception is the work of Lundgren (1973), which examined the characteristics of tourism-based entrepreneurship associated with different forms of hotel development in the Caribbean. Lundgren suggested that a three-stage model of entrepreneurial development could be recognized, based on supply and demand linkages for food by hotels; this was illustrated by the example of an island economy. In stage one a new hotel has no links with its local hinterland, and supplies must be imported from overseas suppliers (figure 6.2). Much of the early hotel development in the Caribbean took the form of large metropolitan complexes which developed closely integrated

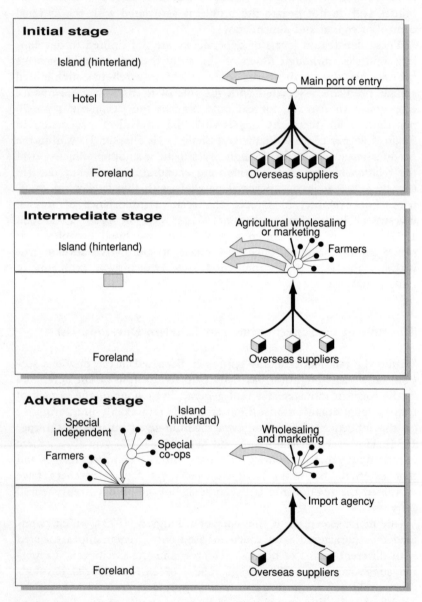

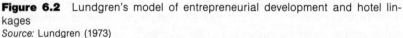

Figure 6.2   Lundgren's model of entrepreneurial development and hotel linkages
Source: Lundgren (1973)

systems with foreign suppliers. This was either because the local agricultural base could not meet the rapid increase in demand, or because the hotel was foreign-owned and had a policy of not using local produce.

The evidence from the developing economies of the Caribbean during the years of fastest tourist growth supports the dominance of such foreign supplies. In Barbados, for example, Gooding (1971) estimated that two-thirds of all food eaten by tourists was imported, with similar figures being recorded by Cazes (1972) for Jamaican hotels. During the early 1970s such high food imports were attributed to the failure of domestic agriculture in countries such as Jamaica (Brown 1974); although Latimer (1985) has argued against such one-sided views, preferring instead to talk about entrepreneurial response being patchy. Indeed, Lundgren (1973), in his study of Jamaica, had found that some large agricultural enterprises had arisen to supply produce, such as pineapples, to hotels over large areas, but that in general most produce came from nearby locations. Other studies have shown difficulties in local entrepreneurs responding to changes in demand, with Latimer (1985) quoting the example of a hotel manager in the Seychelles being unable to obtain locally grown mangoes because no marketing system existed. There is also evidence to support the argument that foreign-owned hotels framed a supply policy around the perceived demands of their guests and showed little interest in local suppliers. Belisle (1983) has examined food production in the Caribbean from this perspective and concluded that six main factors have influenced hotels' links with local entrepreneurs, as shown in box 6.1.

In Lundgren's model local entrepreneurs may develop links with the hotel sector and thereby a marketing channel is opened up

---

Box 6.1 Main factors affecting linkages between local food production and hotels in the Caribbean

- Most tourists are conservative in their tastes, especially those from North America
- Imported food may be cheaper than that locally produced
- Hotels will pay more to ensure high quality and reliable supplies
- Local food may be processed in unhygienic conditions
- Hotel supply managers may be unaware of the possibilities of locally produced food
- Local producers may not know how to contact the hotel trade

Source: modified from Belisle (1983)

between farmers and hotels (the intermediate stage in figure 6.2). The final or advanced stage of entrepreneurial activity sees further expansion of local wholesaling facilities, both in organizational and technological terms, with the latter involving more cold storage capacity. Such changes stimulate agricultural development, improve food processing as well as marketing, and generally reduce the tourism industry's reliance on imported supplies (Mathieson and Wall 1982).

The stage model proposed by Lundgren serves to highlight backward linkages in tourism's demand for food, but similar changes could be explored for other external linkages. Unfortunately, such a progressive change through to the so-called advanced stage has rarely been identified in developing countries. From the limited evidence available, most developing countries seem to be in either the initial or the intermediate stages. Momsen's (1986) work on the small Caribbean islands of St Lucia and Montserrat, for example, shows an improvement in the linkages between the hotel industry and local agriculture over the period 1971–83. In St Lucia, 70 per cent by value of the food consumed by tourists was imported in 1971, compared with 58 per cent in 1983 (Momsen 1986, 17–18). Such a change highlights the fact that better linkages have been established. In the cases of St Lucia and Montserrat, there has been careful government monitoring of local food production and, as Momsen (1986) suggests, tourist tastes in food have also changed. In the early 1970s very few hotels made a feature of local food, whereas by the mid-1980s most hotels served some West Indian food to cater for changing tourist demand.

Clearly, strong linkages between the tourism industry and, in the case of developing countries, local agricultural systems are important if the benefits of tourism are to spread through the local economy. As Mathieson and Wall (1982, 82) argue, 'Although it is attractive to think of a sequence of developmental stages, the exact pattern of entrepreneurial activity is likely to vary from place to place. . .'. Unfortunately, such geographical variations in the development of entrepreneurial activity, which can be conceptualized as local contingencies in their formation and operation, have been little researched. The exception has been the general recognition that linkages between tourism and local business depend on the types of suppliers and producers in operation, the historical development of tourism within the area (only vaguely conceptualized), and the type of tourist development under consideration.

Momsen's (1986) research touches on many of these factors, exploring as it does variations in visitor patterns and tourism development in St Lucia and Montserrat. In the former island, hotel

Table 6.2   Tourist accommodation in St Lucia and Montserrat, 1972–84

| | Number of rooms | | | | | |
| | St Lucia | | | Montserrat | | |
Type	1971	1980	1984	1973	1980	1984
Hotels	555	1043	1080	101	106	100
Apartment-hotels	5	235	312	—	—	—
Apartments	—	—	65	—	25	20
Guesthouses	82	106	71	40	—	—
Villas	—	—	177	10	100	100
Total	642	1384	1705	151	231	220

Source: Momsen (1986)

investment was predominantly British-based (68 per cent of hotel rooms were in British-owned hotels in 1971) and most tourists came from Europe. Montserrat, in contrast, had few European or package tour visitors, while most tourists were from the USA and tended to stay twice as long as the average visitor to St Lucia (just over two weeks compared with 6.8 nights). The pattern of development has produced very different tourist accommodation structures (table 6.2), with villas being more important in Montserrat. These different patterns have influenced the level of entrepreneurial development within local agriculture, with the type of tourist and the structure of hotel development both being important. Indeed, Lundgren (1973) has suggested that the speed of hotel growth is also significant in generating local entrepreneurial activity; with gradual development allowing time for a succession of infrastructural improvements, and creating a gradual increase in demand for local food. The experience of the Caribbean has not followed this pathway, since most growth was rapid and over a short time period (see chapter 9). Many developing countries fall into the second type of development, the so-called metropolitan hotel model. In this case, growth is rapid, creating an instant demand for large amounts of food products. Local entrepreneurs are unable to respond and most food is imported, giving rise to the initial stage of tourism linkages described in figure 6.2.

To date, the limited work on entrepreneurial activity has focused on the linkages between hotel development and local agricultural systems in developing countries. This is not surprising, given the focus of the early debates on tourism's impact on agriculture. However,

Table 6.3 The estimated distribution of tourist expenditure and potential back-ward linkages in Mexico

Type of expenditure	Percentage spend	Potential backward linkages
Food	34	Local agriculture
Hotels/holiday accommodation industries	24	Local construction
Merchandise	14	Small factories and cottage industries
Transportation	14	Local workers in transport
Entertainment and shows	13	Local agents
Other expenses	1	
	100	

Source: modified from Bond and Ladman (1982)

there are two other aspects worthy of consideration. First, we should recognize that there are a range of backward linkages within tourism, and that their utilization depends on entrepreneurial activity. Second, there are also important entrepreneurial issues in the tourist accommodation sector itself, many of which have been neglected in the discussions of tourism in developing countries.

In the case of other backward linkages, Bond and Ladman (1982) have shown that in Mexico strong linkages could exist with the construction industry, while demand for handicrafts can create linkages back to small factories and cottage industries (table 6.3). In addition, external economies can also result from general infrastructural improvements in local transportation networks. While the creation of tourist enclaves (figure 6.1) hinders the establishment of local linkages and limits the wider economic impact of tourism, most evidence suggests that such enclaves tend to break down over time. At this point something of a dichotomy emerges in the literature on tourism development. Many commentators believe that tourism plays its major role during the early stages of a country's economic growth because in the later stages industrialization becomes more widespread (Bond and Ladman 1982; Mathieson and Wall 1982; Lea 1988). However, as we have seen, it is precisely in the early phases that the tourism industry tends to be orientated away from the local economy. One way of counteracting such a shortcoming is for governments in developing economies to examine carefully the forms of tourist growth being proposed, as well as attempting to work more closely with the transnational hotel groups.

In much of the literature there has been a strong tendency to view all transnational development as potentially harmful. Such a perspective is oversimplistic, as was made clear by the UN Centre on Transnational Corporations (1982). This organization argued that '. . . allegations of high import content of transnational-associated hotels have more to do with the "product" which they may produce, that is, luxury or first class hotel accommodation, than with any specific practices of transnational corporations *per se*' (p. 59). The same report went on to highlight how transnational hotels can act as channels of knowledge through their staff training programmes: these not only provide for better hotel staff, but such skills may also gradually spread to other sectors of the tourism industry. Field studies undertaken by the UN project found that, in most countries, the transfer of skill was an important factor in the creation and development of an indigenous hotel sector, with many senior managers having been trained previously by transnational hotels. This process is essential if locally owned hotels are both to develop and compete successfully with foreign-based ones. It is also a factor that conditions the future pattern of growth of tourism in developing economies, and serves to highlight yet another important dimension of entrepreneurial activity.

Tourist entrepreneurs also have another important role which is to

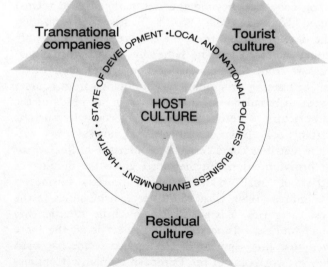

Figure 6.3   Operational forces impacting on host cultures
Source: modified from Jafari (1989)

act – either directly or indirectly – as brokers within the host community. This particular role is obviously conditioned by whether they are drawn from the local community or, if large transnational hotels are dominant, come from outside. According to Jafari (1989), these entrepreneurs operate according to a tourism business culture, and yet they may also be members of the local social system. Given this dual pattern of behaviour between the ordinary and non-ordinary worlds, they can act as brokers between the hosts and guests (figure 6.3). In this perspective the sociocultural impact can be largely determined and shaped by the nature and characteristics of the entrepreneurs themselves. The final section of this chapter is directed at considering the social and economic features of 'the captains of tourism'.

The Nature and Characteristics of Tourism Entrepreneurs

A considerable part of the analysis of the tourism industry is set within aggregate studies of supply and demand. As was shown in chapter 5, the industry itself is a complex network of operations that functions, in many cases, within a framework of some form of state intervention. While this, and the general trends in the role of large-scale enterprises, are well known, very little has been written on the nature of the entrepreneurs themselves. Indeed, it is safe to say that very little is known about the operating characteristics of tourism firms in developing countries, beyond the transnationals and related businesses (United Nations 1982; World Tourism Organization 1985). Within the developing countries, the emphasis has been firmly placed on providing increased training either by the action of transnationals, as we saw from the previous section, or through direct state involvement in training programmes. These range from courses aimed at employees to broader ones that also cover the needs of the managers and proprietors of hotels, in the case of countries such as the Ivory Coast (table 6.4). From official statistics, however, it is difficult to gauge the detailed characteristics of tourism businesses or the dynamics of firm formation. Furthermore, given the dominance in many countries of small, owner-managed tourism businesses (according to Stallinbrass 1980, close to 90 per cent of hotels in the UK fall into these categories) it is surprising how little attention has been paid to small tourism businesses. This neglect is all the more conspicuous given that this segment of the service sector has been identified as a key growth point in the European economy (Commission of the European Communities 1987). Linked with these businesses has been the growing awareness of local cultural systems in

Table 6.4 Government measures taken to improve training standards in holiday accommodation in selected developing countries

Country	Measures
Brazil	Establishment of school for hotel management in State of Rio Grande do Norte
Ivory Coast	Emphasis on training of hotel managers and proprietors; organization of handicraft co-operatives and groups
Jamaica	Attitudinal and skill training programme for hotel workers started in 1982
Philippines	Foreign language courses (German, Japanese, French), mobile training programme focused on rural communities
Thailand	The establishment of a Hotel and Tourism Training Institute

Source: modified from World Tourism Organization (1985)

mediating economic processes such as restructuring. Within developing countries, Jafari (1989) has highlighted the importance of a tourism business culture while, more generally, Cooke (1983) and Massey (1983, 1984) have stressed the role of local cultural systems in economic development.

As was discussed in the previous part of this chapter, such concepts are especially appropriate to understanding the development of tourism. It is not surprising that sociologists have begun to investigate the ways in which cultural features interact with economic changes in tourism (Bagguley, 1987; Urry 1987). Such work has not only focused on 'changes in the cultural practices of tourism and leisure' (Bagguley 1987, 4), but has also highlighted those pertaining to entrepreneurship.

Unfortunately, there have been few studies of firm formation and entrepreneurial skills in tourism research, and all of these have focused on mature economies. Yet, in both traditional tourist regions and in newer areas of tourist development there is a strong need to understand the potential of the local business culture to respond to change. Studies in the UK have identified very diverse business motivations within the dynamics of the hotel industry, and in a case study of Scarborough it was observed that only 33 per cent of hotel owners had any previous experience in tourism (Stallinbrass 1980). Brown's (1987) research on hoteliers in south-east Dorset confirmed this pattern, showing that few owners had any relevant experience or qualifications, and that two-thirds had extremely low turnovers (less than £22 000 in 1985). Two other important features emerge from these studies. The first is that many of the owner–managers had non-economic motives for entering the business. Second, the sources of business capital used to establish firms were extremely varied. Both of these highlight the need to re-evaluate critically many of the conventional economic models (especially those based on multipliers) used in the analysis of the tourism sector.

Within this context, Goffee and Scase's (1983) work on entrepreneurship provides one important lead concerning non-economic decision-making. Their work has drawn attention to the importance of capital structures in understanding general managerial and entrepreneurial skills. As shown in table 6.6, they suggest that four main types of firm characteristics can be identified, ranging from the highly marginalized self-employed category through to owner–director companies, where management and ownership are clearly separated. The few studies of hotel businesses that have been undertaken suggest that many in the UK would fall into either the first or second groups described in table 6.5 (Shaw and Williams 1987).

Research in South West England has focused more closely on the operating characteristics of tourism businesses, as well as widening the range of empirical information in the debate (Shaw et al. 1987; Williams et al. 1989a,b). This research was based on detailed firm-level studies and, unlike previous surveys, it covered most major sectors in the tourism industry, including accommodation (serviced and non-serviced), attractions, retailing and catering. For our purposes we need only consider the accommodation sector to examine the main findings, which highlight three significant characteristics of entrepreneurship in what is a substantial sector of the tourism industry.

Table 6.5 Organizational structures and entreprenurial characteristics

Category	Entrepreneurial characteristics
Self-employed	Use of family labour, little market stability, low levels of capital investment, tendency towards weakly developed management skills
Small employer	Use of family and non-family labour; less economically marginalized but shares other characteristics of self-employed group
Owner–controllers	Use of non-family labour, higher levels of capital investment, often formal system of management control but no separation of ownership and control
Owner–directors	Separation of ownership and management functions, highest levels of capital investment

Source: modified from Goffee and Scase (1983)

The first concerns the levels of experience and expertise of the entrepreneurs, or their social routes to entrepreneurship (Williams et al. 1989). As shown in table 6.6, the dominant route to entrepreneurship is as an ex-employee without any directly relevant job experience. As ex-employees have no obvious access to either management

Table 6.6 Characteristics of businesses within Cornwall's holiday accommodation sectors (per cent of respondents)

	Hotels and guesthouses	Self-catering
Ownership		
Individual	85.6	79.7
Group	6.0	4.1
Limited company	2.4	8.1
PLC	1.2	0.0
Partner	*4.8*	*8.1*
Total	100	100
Age of owner		
20–30	8.6	2.8
31–40	27.2	15.2
41–50	32.1	28.4
51–60	17.3	37.5
61+	13.6	18.1
Non-response	*1.2*	*0.0*
Total	100	100
Birthplace (first five regions)		
Cornwall	16.9	33.8
South West	8.4	9.5
South East	34.9	25.7
Midlands	7.2	8.1
North West	7.2	12.2
Main previous occupations (only top four listed)		
Professional	27.3	23.5
Farming		17.6
Secretarial/clerical	16.9	
Retailing	13.0	13.2
Tourist industry	10.4	11.8
Principal sources of capital		
Personal savings	37.1	37.8
Family savings	15.7	18.0
Bank loan	21.4	19.7
Personal savings and bank loan	11.3	9.8

Source: modified from Shaw and Williams (1987) and Shaw et al. (1987)

skills or capital, this group may well be expected to encounter the greatest obstacles to entrepreneurship. However, within the Cornwall study this was shown to be the most important route in all subsectors of the tourism industry. The accommodation sector would seem to be the one with the lowest entrance barriers, which of course supports the notion that the minimum requirement is the provision of bed and breakfast services from the family home. In this most basic case, investment in personal consumption (the home) is used to underwrite the costs of producing accommodation services. It should be stressed, however, that in the Cornish research most establishments surveyed were considerably larger than this, with 60 per cent having five or more bedrooms available.

The second factor to emerge from the survey concerned sources of business capital. Personal and family savings were the main source of capital, and were found to have been used by more than 50 per cent of the entrepreneurs in the Cornwall study (table 6.6). This, and other research (Williams et al. 1989b), highlights the strong links between sources of capital and the age of the entrepreneur with, for example, older people relying more on personal capital. Given the dominance of ex-employees amongst the tourism entrepreneurs, the reliance on personal or family savings at first appears rather surprising. However, the results are not at odds with research on other economic sectors (Lloyd and Mason 1984), and merely serve to stress the small amounts of capital that are initially required.

The third major element identified relates to business motivations. This is typically a complex combination of motives, aspirations and constraints, although in the Cornwall study it was measured simply by responses to the question of why people established their firms. Significantly, in this particular region, economic motives were matched by the importance given to non-economic reasons, such as 'wanted to live in Cornwall'. Such locational and environmental factors were especially important in the accommodation sectors, where they accounted for almost 33 per cent of all responses. Related to this desire for a 'better way of life' was the fact that a large proportion of entrepreneurs (over 80 per cent) who ran hotels were in-migrants. Indeed, further analysis revealed that many of these had originally come to Cornwall on holiday and had then decided at some time to try their hand in the tourism industry. This has led to the suggestion that such tourism entrepreneurship can be seen as a form of consumption rather than production (Williams et al. 1989b).

All these contingencies and features relating to entrepreneurial characteristics obviously have an impact on the economic health of the tourism industry and of particular local economies. Unfortunately, we have only a few such studies, and it is therefore not possible to examine how such factors vary in their geographical impact. There has been a tendency in both developed and developing countries to over-concentrate research on the role of large national and transnational firms, at the specific expense of smaller businesses. It seems obvious, however, that future research on tourism and economic development will need to examine more closely the relationships between the nature of entrepreneurship, the structural characteristics of the tourism industry and its overall impact on economic change. Certainly on a wider scale, the performance of local entrepreneurs holds the key to strengthening and spreading the benefits from tourism in many developed and developing areas.

SEVEN

Tourism Employment and Labour Markets

Employment in Tourism and Leisure

The tourism and leisure industries constitute a diverse set of economic subsectors, including accommodation services, catering, entertainment, sport and other leisure activities and travel and transport. There are difficulties in locating the boundaries between leisure and tourism and their shared boundaries *vis-à-vis* other sectors. The greater difficulties reside in trying to separate tourism and leisure; leisure facilities and restaurants are used by locals and by tourists, and there is no simple way to distinguish between these two distinct segments. Indeed, in most official statistics, accommodation services are usually the only category which is exclusively dedicated to tourism.

An indication of the complexity of tourism is given in Sessa's (1983) classification of tourism occupations (box 7.1). The list includes construction, maintenance, agriculture suppliers, transport, commercial services such as recreation and retailing, receptive services and administration. The difficulty lies in knowing what proportion of agricultural or construction employment is dependent on tourism. In the absence of official statistics, researchers usually rely on multiplier estimates.

Estimating multipliers requires detailed survey work or statistical estimations. In practice, therefore, there is a tendency for most employment multipliers to be derivative, relying on a small number of original multipliers based on primary data. There are, of course, inherent difficulties in this, because the multiplier effects depend on the size, structure and diversity of the economy in question. Geographical scale is clearly important and, in general, the larger the area of analysis the smaller the leakage effect and the larger the multiplier.

Box 7.1   The principal groups of tourism-related jobs

- Construction of basic infrastructures (e.g. roads, airports, sewage systems and cultural facilities)
- Maintenance of the basic infrastructures
- Agricultural and other primary activities
- Agroprocessing
- Transport
- Commercial and complementary services (e.g. banks, insurance, retailing, sports and cultural services)
- Construction of receptive installations – the tourism superstructure (e.g. accommodation, restaurants, bars and tourist sports installations)
- Operation of receptive services
- Tourism welcoming services
- Public administration

Source: Sessa (1983, 102–3)

This is illustrated by Henderson's (1975) work on income multipliers; he showed that of every £100 spent on tourism in Tayside (UK), £26 was retained in the local economy, but that this figure increased to £32 for the larger region and to £46 for Scotland as a whole. There would be parallel increases in employment with increasing scale. The reliance on multipliers is an attempt to counterbalance the error of underestimating the importance of the tourism industry. However, their widespread use in tourism can lead to the contrasting error of overestimation. There is a tendency to compare multiplier estimates of tourism employment with official statistics of employment in other sectors, such as electronics or car manufacture. However, all economic activities have multiplier effects, and the real comparison is to be made between these.

The error of overestimating jobs in tourism is also to be seen in the global estimates of employment provided by the World Tourism Organization (1984; see figure 7.1). As the report acknowledges, 'The primary data are highly aggregated, which makes it difficult to obtain those most directly related to characteristic tourism activities. They include employment in shops, hotels, restaurants and cafeterias, and sometimes in other services' (p. 81). According to these estimates, the lowest proportion of total employment in tourism is 8 per cent in South Asia and the highest is 20 per cent in the Americas. These figures are considerable overestimations, but they are the only ones available at the global scale.

The figures produced for individual countries are often no more reliable than the global estimates. For example, Johnson and

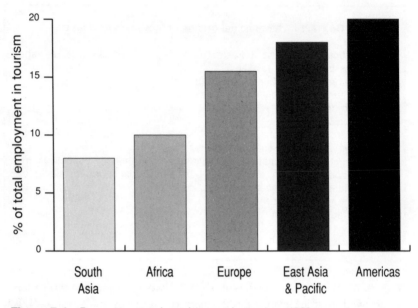

Figure 7.1   Percentage total employment in tourism, 1980
Source: World Tourism Organization (1984, 81)

Thomas' (1990) review of estimates for the UK found that these varied between 1.1 million and 1.7 million jobs (see also Williams and Shaw 1988). However, Champion and Townsend (1990) consider that there is generally a tendency to overestimate tourism employment in the UK. The most common error is to include leisure jobs attributable to day visitors in estimates of tourism employment.

Another problem is the prevalence of the informal economy in tourism and leisure. There are important issues here. The divide between leisure and work is itself blurred. When, for example, does silk screen printing for relatives and friends become work rather than leisure? Or when does operating a steam train cease to be a hobby and become a job? Bishop and Hoggett (1989) provide some guidance in unravelling these complex issues. First, they differentiate three sites in which goods and services are informally produced, exchanged and consumed: entirely within the household, outside of households but within the community, and outside of the household and the community. They also differentiate between two types of exchange relationships and, therefore, two different forms of production and consumption: where production is a means to an end (commonly to earn income), and where it is intrinsically valuable to the producer (such as running a hotel situated in a beautiful location). On this basis they identify three distinctive forms of informal economic systems, and we can apply these to tourism and leisure:

1 An unregulated economy based on outworking and cottage industry. Goods are produced for exchange outside of the community but in an unregulated way. Examples include cooks working at home to supply prepared foods to restaurants, or unregistered bed and breakfast services. The black economy is one version of this but produces mainly for the local community.
2 A communal economy in which goods and services are circulated within the economy and an informal local network, largely through direct exchange unmediated by money. This is often based on a leisure interest such as knitting or carpentry. It also tends to be a system of mutual aid, although it can provide a stepping stone to self-employment or to a cottage industry.
3 The household economy which involves the production and consumption of goods within the home itself. This is linked to Gershuny and Miles' (1983) idea of the 'self-service' economy. Bishop and Hoggett (1989, 160) argue that 'The huge expansion in the production of leisure equipment has meant that more and more people have the means to "do" leisure rather than consume leisure services provided by others'. This also applies, via mobile homes and caravans, to tourism.

As the above analysis makes clear, there are considerable difficulties in estimating employment in tourism and in leisure. However, there is little disagreement that the overall importance of tourism and leisure employment is increasing in most national economies. In a way this is only part of the wider process of the tertiarization of employment, especially in the more developed economies. For example, in the USA between 1977 and 1986 all permanent new jobs – some 17 million – were in services and construction (Champion and Townsend 1990). While employment nationally increased by 20.4 per cent, employment in hotels and retailing increased by more than 29 per cent. The growth of tourism jobs in the UK was even more marked, since between 1981 and 1989 total employment increased by 2.6 per cent, while that in hotels and catering grew by 17.3 per cent. When the broader group of leisure industries in the UK is considered, it becomes clear that there have been diverse trends within the tourism sector. Between 1960 and 1983 employment in cinemas and theatres fell by 18 per cent reflecting the growth of home-based leisure (table 7.1). This is in contrast to a growth of 36 per cent in all leisure services, with employment gains in excess of 50 per cent in

Table 7.1   Employment in leisure services in the UK, 1960–83

	Percentage change in employment		
	Male	Female	Total
Cinemas, theatres and radio	−7	−29	−18
Sport and recreation	+71	+173	+106
Betting and gambling	58	71	64
Hotels etc.	26	12	17
Restaurants	49	8	20
Pubs	32	82	64
Clubs	67	84	79
Catering contracts	110	13	30
All leisure services	37	35	36

Source: Gratton and Taylor (1987, 77)

sports and recreation, betting and gambling, pubs and clubs. As the table makes clear, there are also changes in the gender composition of employment. This, along with other labour-market changes, forms the subject of the following section: the remainder of the chapter focuses more narrowly on tourism.

Labour-force Composition: Internal and External Labour Markets in Tourism

The debate about tourism employment is often highly qualified with references to the quality of the jobs that are generated. A not uncommon stereotype is that the tourism employee is '. . . uneducated, unmotivated, untrained, unskilled and unproductive' (Pizam 1982, 5). This led the Chairman of the English Tourist Board to declare that there are many who believe that '. . . a job in the tourist industry is in some way less than one in a manufacturing industry' (quoted in the *Financial Times* on 16 July 1986). In reality, of course, employment in tourism is as complex and heterogeneous as the different subsectors which together constitute the industry. Furthermore, there is great diversity in the employment within a particular segment, such as accommodation, as is illustrated by Henderson's (1975) study of Tayside. Comparing employment in hotels with bed and breakfast establishments, he found that, respectively, 73 per cent and 18 per cent were full-time jobs, 72 per cent and 11 per cent were permanent jobs, and that 62 per cent and 100 per cent of the employees were women.

While the stereotypes outlined above are oversimplifications, there are several distinctive features of tourism labour markets. These are related to the nature of these services, the role of labour in the delivery of the services, and the temporal and spatial organization of the industry. One of the central features is the weight of labour in the overall costs of producing tourism services. For example, Pine (1987) has estimated that wages represent 20–30 per cent of the pre-tax sales of multiple restaurant chains such as Pizza Express and Berni Inns. Compared to manufacturing, the possibilities for substituting capital for labour in the production of services is fairly limited. This is held by Bell (1974) to be one of the key reasons for the emergence of what he terms 'post-industrial society'.

This is not to say that there is no possibility of substituting capital for labour. Bagguley (1987) argues that in the UK there have been two technological revolutions within catering in recent decades. The first was the introduction of automatic dishwashers in the 1950s and 1960s, which led to a reduction in the number of kitchen assistants' jobs. The second revolution was the introduction of sophisticated methods of pre-preparing foods, such as chill-cook technology and microwaves, in the 1970s and 1980s. This led to a deskilling of kitchens and an increase in the numbers of kitchen assistants at the expense of chefs. Linked to this, there has been enormous growth of fast food outlets based on both new technology and new work practices which, for example, have allowed companies such as McDonalds to reduce their labour costs to, reputedly, no more than 15 per cent of sales.

Technological change is also modifying the face of other segments of the tourism industry. For example, the travel agency industry is being revolutionized by the introduction of new forms of computer reservations systems. These allow for more sophisticated searches of available holiday options, but they also allow for increased labour productivity. The most recent interactive technology enables searches of available holidays, bookings and the issuing of tickets. The combined effects of this are to reduce the customer:employee ratio and to displace jobs from the high street to centralized booking centres. This tendency will be further increased by the growth of tour companies' direct sales to individual customers via interactive videotext methods. The productivity gains from such technological advances can be substantial. In the UK, for example, Portland Holidays were able to increase the number of holidays sold per employee by 21 per cent in 1985 largely through the introduction of an advanced booking system (*Financial Times*, 8 January 1987).

Despite some instances of significant changes in the capital : labour ratio, the potential for such substitution in tourism services tends to be limited compared to, say, agriculture or manufacturing. In the face of this constraint, employers' attempts to reduce labour costs have been firmly focused on labour-market strategies. There is, of course, no universal pattern in this, for labour-market strategies are specific to the particularities of individual labour markets. For example, Sessa (1983, 106) estimates that in the developed countries a 1000-bed medium-category hotel would employ approximately one person per five beds. In contrast, in the less developed countries, where labour was relatively and absolutely cheaper, the ratio was more likely to be one employee per bed.

One of the most common strategies, observable in a number of countries, is the formation of dual labour markets within companies. These can be characterized by core and peripheral workers. Atkinson (1984) is largely responsible for the formalization of the concepts, although there are strong links with Doeringer and Piore's (1971) concept of the internal labour market. Atkinson suggested that core workers were full-time, permanent employees who received job security and high earnings in return for performing a wide range of tasks that cut across traditional skill demarcation lines. He considers that these workers are functionally flexible. Characteristically, they are managerial and professional staff whose skills are in short supply in the external labour market; employers are therefore keen to retain their services.

Several groups of peripheral workers are grouped around these core employees (figure 7.2). There is a secondary labour market made up of full-time employees, but their jobs are less secure, they lack career prospects, and they are often semi-skilled. There is a high rate of labour turnover, which means that their employment offers numerical flexibility to employers. In addition, there are also several other groups of numerically flexible employees. The possibilities include part-time workers, temporary workers (on short-term contracts), training scheme placements, and homeworking. All of these categories offer a high degree of numerical flexibility to employers. They can be hired and fired as the volume of demand rises and falls. Another strategy available to employers is distancing, whereby certain labour tasks are subcontracted to other firms rather than performed in-house.

Atkinson's treatise was largely written as an analysis of the reorganization of modern manufacturing. The empirical evidence for the existence and the growth of the core–periphery structuring of labour in manufacturing is, at best, mixed (Allen 1988). However, there is considerable evidence of such structuring in tourism labour markets.

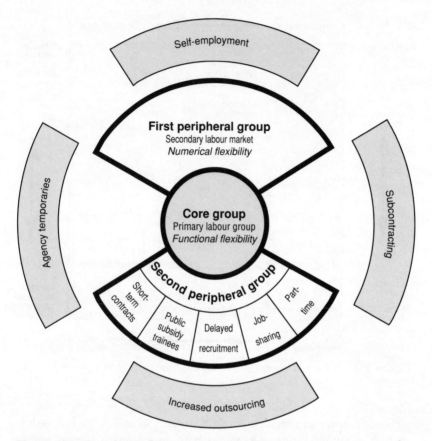

Figure 7.2   Functional and numerical flexibility
Source: Atkinson (1984)

Moreover, there is considerable evidence that this is a long established form of internal labour-market organization in these industries
(Bagguley 1987, 1990; Urry 1990). This stems from the particular
nature of the demand for tourism services. The temporal variation in
demand is far greater than is experienced in any branch of manufacturing. The rhythm of demand varies between seasons, between
working days and weekends/public holidays, and at different times of
the day. The result is that tourism services have to be delivered to
customers in both temporal and spatial clusters.

The response to this rhythm, and to the weight of labour costs in
production, has been the growth of a number of forms of numerical
and functional flexibility in tourism employment (figure 7.3). *Temporary contracts* to cope with seasonal variations in demand have been

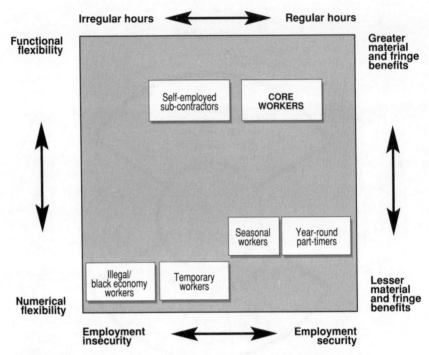

Figure 7.3 Core and peripheral workers in tourism and leisure

a classic feature of employment in tourism. Some tourist industries –
such as in capital cities or locations with an attractive climate all year
– do not have a marked seasonal variation in demand. In Portugal for
example, there is a 30 per cent employment shift between summer
and winter in the highly seasonal Algarve, a 7 per cent employment
shift in Lisbon which has year-round cultural and business tourism,
and only a 2 per cent shift in Madeira with its equable year-round
climate.

Most localities do have a single peak season, flanked by shoulder
seasons. The out-of-season period may be one of reduced activity, or
a total close down. Employers respond to the build-up of demand by
employing labour on seasonal contracts, which tend to become
shorter as the peak of the season is approached. These employees can
clearly be seen as peripheral workers. If the enterprise closes during
the off season, then they may be the only employees even in the peak
period. However, if low-level activity is maintained through the
winter, then a group of core workers may be maintained on permanent year-round contracts. Characteristically, the difference in labour

demands between the peak season and the off season are so great that seasonal workers may be in-migrants. As a result, seasonal workers are often provided with accommodation by their employers, which further weakens their bargaining position.

The impact of seasonal contracts on local labour markets depends largely on whether the workers are local or in-migrants. If they are seasonal migrants, then the off-season unemployment is effectively exported at the end of the peak or shoulder season. If the labour force is local, then potentially there may be high levels of unemployment during the off season. However, this is contingent on the structure of the local economy: seasonal work in tourism can be complementary to seasonality in other local labour markets such as fishing or farming. In the Alps, for example, winter tourism is complementary to the requirements of agriculture, while summer tourism may conflict with these.

Part-time employment is a common response to the uneven distribution of work during the week or the day. Similarly, some staff may be on part-time contracts to work only at weekends, or at other times when demand peaks within the week. These workers are characteristically peripheral employees, who may work alongside core employees such as full-time supervisors, chefs and head waiters. The key to their employment is that the temporal fluctuations in demand are predictable and therefore allow regular employment, albeit on a part-time basis. Depending on the nature of the tourist industry, such jobs may be year-round or seasonal. If the hours of part-time work are fixed and regular, then the tourism job can be combined with other part-time work, whether in tourism, in other paid jobs or in the household. Part-time jobs are more likely to be staffed by locals than full-time jobs.

The tourism industry mostly provides a labour-intensive service at the point of contact with the customer. While demand is rhythmical and largely predictable, there are isolated peaks such as public holidays, a large group booking at a sports centre or a restaurant, or simply an inexplicable rush at the bar one cold and wet Monday evening. These isolated demand peaks can only be met effectively via *temporary increases in labour* at the point of contact. This can be achieved in one of two ways: either via functional flexibility and the diversion of core workers from other tasks in the enterprise, or via numerical flexibility and the temporary hiring of labour. In practice, most small firms will have a pool of friends and family upon whom they can draw to meet such peaks in demand. All firms will also have a reserve of part-time workers or 'regular casuals' who can be drafted in to work a particular weekend or evening. The nature of such peripheral employment makes it likely that such workers will be local. Higher than average payments may be necessary to compensate for the social inconvenience of such unpredictable work.

Many segments of the tourism industry are dominated by *self-employment* or *small family firms*. This applies equally well to farm accommodation as to a shop selling souvenirs in a capital city. The individuals, and their families, provide another response to fluctuations in demand; that is, self-exploitation. Rhythmic fluctuation in demand will be met by a willingness to work very long hours. The small hotel owner will be up early to cook guests' breakfasts and will still be working late at night to prepare food for the next day or to welcome late arrivals.

Initially, it seems surprising that such large numbers of workers are willing to tolerate the rhythmical and the unpredictable variation in work in tourism and leisure. To some extent it is not a function of choice, but the constraint of a lack of alternative jobs in local labour markets. However, there is also a need to look at the total material and psychological income received. The material benefits include wages, accommodation and tips, while the psychological income may include the opportunity to live in an attractive environment either seasonally or permanently. Chalet 'girls' (a term which reflects the gender division of labour), ski instructors, the traditional Butlins' redcoats and the owners of businesses in attractive areas all fit into this model. In addition, Marshall (1986) argues that enterprises such as restaurants are able to retain the loyalty of their peripheral workers despite low wages because these are only one part of the total reward system. Local customers are often friends, the employees spend some of their free time at the restaurant and, in general, the symbolic boundaries between work and leisure are weak.

The core-periphery thesis provides an appealingly simple conceptualization of employment in tourism. However, Urry (1990) stresses the need for caution in accepting this as a model of employment in these sectors. First, he argues that the simple core–periphery divide does not exist. There do seem to be core and peripheral workers, but the former are not always functionally flexible. Kitchen staff and receptionists in hotels, for example, are often functionally inflexible. However, there is evidence of growing pressure on hotels to move to greater functional flexibility. For instance, the Reo Stakis group, which has 33 hotels in the UK, ceased to recognize trades unions in the 1980s and introduced the new grade of 'multiskilled hotel employee'. Second, Urry argues that in hotels and catering, the peripheral workers on temporary contracts often do exactly the same jobs as the core staff. This is because temporary workers are taken on

---

Box 7.2 Structural features of strong and weak internal labour markets

Strong

- Specified living standards
- Single port of entry
- High skill specificity
- Continuous on the job training
- Fixed criteria for promotion and transfer
- Strong workplace customs
- Pay differentials remain fixed over time

Weak

- Unspecified hiring standards
- Multiple ports of entry
- Low skill specificity
- No on the job training
- No fixed criteria for promotion and transfer
- Weak workplace customs
- Pay differentials vary over time

Source: Simms et al. (1988, 6)

---

to replicate the work done by core staff in order to meet fluctuations in demand.

Urry's second point is important, and it may therefore be useful to consider the alternative conceptualization offered by Simms et al. (1988), which suggests that there is a continuum from strong to weak internal labour markets (box 7.2). Weak internal labour markets are relatively open to external labour markets. Their empirical work confirms that tourism is characterized by a weak internal labour market. They found high levels of on-the-job training, small numbers of promotions and transfers, and *ad hoc* management practices. This all fits convincingly with their model of a weak labour market. Such firms fulfil their labour requirements via greater openness to external labour markets: there is recruitment from outside the company, and there is a high degree of labour turnover, with minimal on-the-job training.

The Social Construction of Tourism Labour Markets: Gender and International Migration

In different ways, the works of both Atkinson (1984) and Simms et al. (1988) draw attention to the social composition of external labour markets. This is particularly important for those industries, such as tourism, which have weak internal labour markets. Two features of the social construction of external labour markets are considered here; questions of race and ethnicity in relation to international migration, and the gender division of labour.

In broad terms, women tend to be peripheral rather than core workers, to be in part-time jobs and to receive lower wages than do men (Bagguley 1990). While these stereotypes are largely true, it should be emphasized that there is nothing natural in the gender division of labour (Dex 1985; Beechey 1987). There is strong occupational segregation in most societies, and women tend to undertake tasks such as serving meals, working in kitchens and making beds, which are similar to household tasks. Neither set of jobs is inherently gender-specific: instead, the gender division of labour is socially constructed. Women workers carry into the workplace their subordinate status in society at large. The work of women is often regarded as inferior or unskilled, simply because it is undertaken by women. The definitions of skills may be no more than a social classification based on gender. The same argument applies to part-time jobs. Some jobs in hotels and catering are socially constructed as part-time jobs because they are seen to be women's jobs.

The social expectation that women have 'dual careers', in which they combine paid jobs and domestic responsibilities, contributes to occupational segregation. The traditional delegation to women of the roles of child-rearing or caring for elderly relatives may mean that they are either unavailable for full-time work, or can only take jobs with fixed hours which fit in with their domestic roles. This may exclude them from certain managerial or supervisory posts. Single women are not necessarily constrained in the same way, but do suffer from the general social construction of what constitutes suitable work for women. This brief analysis of women's roles in the labour force serves to remind us that weak internal labour markets do not simply come about as the result of managerial strategies. Instead, they reflect the way in which managers have used the social construction of women's work as one element in the structuring of the internal labour markets in tourism. The tourism industry does not just provide jobs for women; the very existence of a pool of women, and of the social possibility of paying them low wages or keeping them on temporary or part-time contracts, helps to shape the formation of the core–periphery divide in the labour force.

The migrant and ethnic composition is another important dimension of the external labour market which impinges upon the organization of the internal labour market. As tourism, in particular, involves the delivery of services to groups of consumers whom have temporarily been assembled together in particular locations away from home, there is a need to guarantee the availability of labour to fulfil this task. This may be provided by local residents, if the tourism is relatively limited in scale. Alternatively, it may require labour to commute from the surrounding area. However, the demand for labour will frequently exceed its availability in a particular location, thereby requiring inmigration. This may be seasonal or permanent, depending on the nature of the demand. In Portugal, for example, Cavaco (1980) shows that there are two main streams of migrant workers in the Algarve: the first is from villages in the hinterland of the Algarve coast, which lie beyond daily commuting distance; while the second is drawn from the poorer villages of the other regions of Portugal. Potentially, this facilitates the transfer of remittances from one of the more developed to the less developed regions of the country. Migration may also operate at the international scale.

Each of these different labour-market strategies has different economic and cultural impacts both for the tourism area, and for the migrants' home areas (table 7.2). Daily commuters have limited cultural impact and considerable economic impact on their home areas. The same applies to seasonal labour, although workers may have a greater cultural impact on their home areas and the tourist areas. Permanent in-migrants have a considerable economic and some cultural impact on the tourist area. Finally, temporary international migrants have a major cultural impact on both their home and the tourist areas.

International migration is clearly important in tourism labour markets and merits further discussion. While there has only been limited research on international migration specifically in these industries, there has been more widespread research on the role of international migration in the economies of the more developed countries. Worldwide, there may be as many as 16 million international migrants, and

Table 7.2 The impacts of different forms of labour migration

Migration system	On the tourism area		On the migrants' area of origin	
	Economic	Cultural	Economic	Cultural
Daily commuter	Limited	None	Major	None
Seasonal migrant	Limited	Limited	Major	Limited
Permanent in-migrant	Major	Limited/major	Limited	None
International migrant	Limited	Major	Limited	Major

in countries such as Luxembourg and Switzerland they constitute as much as one-third of the total labour force. The main streams are from the poorer countries of the world, and are focused on North America, northern Europe, and the richer Middle East countries. Clout et al. (1989), writing on Europe, stress that 'Very roughly, we may say that 1 in 10 workers in the EC are cross-national migrants and about 1 in 10 of the workers in the main Mediterranean sending countries . . . earns his living in industrial Europe'. Their motives are mostly economic, although some are primarily politically inspired. Interestingly, the streams of male and female economic migrants from the poorer to the richer countries run counter to the tourist movements from the richer to the poorer countries.

International migrants fill critical labour shortages in many developed countries. Most research (e.g. Castles et al. 1984) shows that unskilled migrants tend to occupy poorly paid, insecure, unpleasant and/or boring jobs. Tourism and leisure often figure large as potential employers. The weak organization of internal labour markets in these industries makes them relatively easy to enter. At the same time, the continuous supply of low-cost labour in external labour markets provided by international migration may encourage the perpetuation of such weak internal markets. Such migrants invariably tend to occupy peripheral jobs, and sometimes their illegal status serves to reinforce their insecurity. The importance of this reserve army of low-cost, unorganized industry is immense, and underpins the tourist industries of many areas, including several of the world's major capital cities, such as London, Paris, Sydney and New York.

However, it would be wrong to assume that international migrants are permanently condemned to subordinate positions in the tourism industry. Böhning (1972) argues that there are four stages in international migration: the first stage mainly involves short stay young, male workers; the second stage sees more older and married male migrants involved; in the third stage more families are involved and the duration of migration increases; and, finally, the migrant community 'matures' and becomes self-feeding through generating its own demand for services. Migrants may develop businesses as shops, restaurants and travel agencies to provide specialist goods and services to their own communities. Peneff (1981), for example, records such experiences amongst Algerians in France, while Anderson and Higgs (1976) record a similar process amongst the Portuguese communities in Canada. Migrants may also, or alternatively, be able to market their ethnic distinctiveness. Examples include Chinese restaurants and shops in London or Vancouver, and Indonesian restaurants in the Netherlands. This is both part of the internationalization of culture and supported by this specific process.

International migration to work – in, amongst others, the tourist and leisure industries – within the more developed countries also has consequences for the migrants' home countries. They usually remit a high proportion of their savings; King (1986, 24) estimates that about 20 per cent is common amongst southern European migrants. This represents a significant international transfer of resources in many cases, and makes a major contribution to the current account in several countries (King 1986).

Temporary emigrants eventually return to their home countries. Most studies of returnees have found that their first priority is to invest in better housing conditions for their families. Only a small proportion of emigrants establish businesses on their return, but those that do invest most frequently in restaurants, hotels or other commercial establishments (Lewis and Williams 1986; Unger 1986). King (1986, 21) comments that '. . . going to Germany seems to convert peasants into petty traders'. There are several case studies of return migrants' diversification into the tourism industry. In southern Italy, a region which offers only limited opportunities for successful investment in manufacturing, running small restaurants has attracted many returnees (King et al. 1985). In Nazaré, in Portugal, a quarter of returnees had invested some of their savings in tourism establishments as part of their economic coping strategies (Mendonsa 1983).

Tourism therefore potentially provides jobs and income for the workers of less developed countries in one of two ways: in the home countries, providing services for tourists; or as international migrants working in tourism industries abroad. However, the economic and cultural implications of these two different models are very different. The relationship between tourism and labour markets is therefore a complex one. Furthermore, while the concept of internal and external labour markets is useful for analysing these industries, it is important to remember that the latter stretch across international boundaries, with diverse economic and cultural effects.

PART IV

Tourism Environments

EIGHT

Tourism and Leisure Environments

Typologies of Tourism and Leisure Environments

Much of the discussion so far has focused on the functional processes operating within the broad areas of tourism and leisure. We have examined not only the structure of these industries but also the nature of consumer behaviour patterns and their social consequences. It should also be recognized that tourism and leisure take place in a diverse range of environments, although most have in common one or all of the following elements: a landscape to observe and enjoy, activities to participate in, and experiences to anticipate or remember. Attempts to classify or to come to terms with the nature and characteristics of these different environments (Gunn 1980) have been fragmented along a number of thematic lines. Lew (1987), in a wide-ranging review of the literature on tourist attractions, has attempted to overcome such fragmentation, and has identified three broad approaches towards developing typologies that encompass ideographic, organizational and cognitive perspectives. The first and perhaps most important of these frameworks, that based on the ideographic approach, focuses on the concrete uniqueness of 'environment' and, as such, stresses the differences between nature-orientated and human-orientated attractions (Perry 1975). In contrast, typologies based on organizational perspectives focus on the spatial characteristics of size and scale (Gunn 1980), carrying capacity, and the temporal nature of attractions (Lew 1987, 359). Finally, cognitive approaches stress classifications relating to tourist perceptions and experiences. These can be either at very general levels, as suggested by Pearce (1982) who defined a tourist environment as any place that fostered the feeling of being a tourist, or through such feelings of 'outsiderness' and 'insiderness' as discussed by Relph (1976) in a humanistic perspective.

Each of these three main bases of classification reveals important characteristics of tourism and leisure environments, which in turn can contribute to understanding of developments and their impacts. In all three cases, Lew (1987) attempted to provide composite typologies based on past studies, and by using different classifica-

Table 8.1   An ideographic typology of tourist and leisure environments

Nature	Nature–human interface	Human
General environments		
Panoramas	Observational	Settlement infrastructure
Mountains	Rural/agriculture	Utility types
Sea coast	Scientific gardens	Settlement morphology
Plain	Animals (zoos)	Settlement functions
Arid	Plants	Commerce
Island	Rocks and archaeology	Retail
		Finance
		Institutions
		Government
		Education and science
		Religion
		People
		Way of life
		Ethnicity
Specific features		
Landmarks	Leisure nature	Tourist infrastructure
Geological	Trails	Forms of access
Biological	Parks	To and from a destination
Flora	Beach	Destination tour routes
Fauna	Urban	Information and receptivity
Hydrological	Other	Basic needs
	Resorts	Accommodation
		Meals
Inclusive environments		
Ecological	Participatory	Leisure superstructure
Climate	Mountain activities	Recreation entertainment
Sanctuaries	Summer	Performances
National parks	Winter	Sporting events
Nature reserves	Water activities	Amusements
	Other outdoor activities	Culture, history and art
		Museums and monuments
		Performances
		Festivals
		Cuisine

Source: Lew (1987)

tory criteria. In the ideographic approach (table 8.1), we can recognize a range of environments, from natural through to those comprising the nature–human interface and purely human-orientated ones. Within each of these, attractions can also be arranged according to their general environment characteristics, specific features and levels of inclusivity (table 8.1). Using such a framework, it is possible to classify the whole range of tourism and leisure environments in any one of nine major categories. For example, 'general environments' are, as Lew (1987, 557) explains, 'broad in scope and often large in scale', requiring little or no tourist involvement for them to exist. In contrast, 'specific environments' tend to be smaller and often have clear links with tourism and leisure. 'Inclusive environments' are the main attractions drawing tourists to a particular destination, with the inclusivity deriving from the fact that tourists are completely involved in the leisure experience. Clearly, the nature of tourist involvement varies considerably between the different environmental types, although leisure superstructures intrude into a range of tourism and leisure settings. These overlaps lead to consideration of the two additional composite typologies derived by Lew (1987). The organizational one stresses scale and levels of participation, while the cognitive one focuses on activities, attraction characteristics and tourist experiences.

In addition to such broad-based typologies, there have also been attempts to develop specific classifications of resorts and resort development. Most of these are based on structural and spatial variations relating to a limited set of examples drawn from particular local or regional environments. However, despite such backgrounds, they all tend to have five main features in common: the resource being developed, the context of development, its spatial organization, the way in which development occurs, and finally the characteristics of the developer (Pearce 1987, 13). As shown in table 8.2, these typologies range from those concerned specifically with forms of coastal developments (Barbaza 1970; Peck and Lepie 1977), Alpine environments (Préau 1970) and broader-based classifications of resort development processes (Miossec 1976; Pearce 1978; Gormsen 1981). Barbaza's (1970) typology, based on surveys of the Mediterranean and Black Sea coasts, identified three main types of development, while Peck and Lepie's (1977) work relates to small coastal resorts in North Carolina. Studies of Alpine environments have identified two main types of resort development which are characterized in Préau's work (1968, 1970) as the so-called Chamonix and Les Belleville models (table 8.2). This approach has subsequently been extended by Pearce (1978, 1987), who attempted to recognize development

Table 8.2   Main typologies of tourist resort developments

Environment	Author(s)	Major findings
Coastal	Barbaza (1970)	Three main types of development; spontaneous resorts (e.g. Côte d'Azur, Costa Brava), planned and localized development (e.g. Black Sea littoral of Romania and Bulgaria), extensive planned developments (e.g. Languedoc, Roussillon coast of France)
	Peck and Lepie (1977)	Three main criteria identified with which to assess development; i.e. speed of development, power basis in terms of local/non-local control, and impact of development on host communities
Alpine	Préau (1968, 1970)	Stresses three factors; state of local community at onset of development, rhythm of development, and characteristics of site. Identifies two types: (i) *Chamonix* model – outside influences are only gradual and complementary; (ii) *Les Belleville* model – development conceived by outside promotors based on technical and constructional criteria for ski development
Mixed	Pearce (1978, 1987)	Recognition of two main development processes: (i) integrated development involving a single promotor, e.g. ski resorts such as La Plagne (France); (ii) catalytic development – initial activities of a single promoter act as a catalyst for other complementary developments, e.g. ski resort of Vars

processes that could be applied to a range of environments, using the concepts of integrated and catalytic types of resort growth (table 8.2). In both cases, single promoters are involved, although within the catalytic type the process of development also becomes strongly related to a number of secondary developers. According to Pearce (1987, 19), both processes produce differing resorts, with catalytic developments usually being grafted on to existing settlements (see also chapter 9).

Of greater significance than Pearce's attempts to produce a general typology of resorts are the resort models presented by Miossec (1976) and Gormsen (1981). These stress a far greater number of variables, as well as being grounded in a wider range of case studies. Miossec's (1976) model stresses the spatial dynamics of tourism development through a consideration of four main elements: resorts, transportation, tourist behaviour and the attitudes of tourist brokers in the local community. Within this framework, Miossec highlights the relationships between phases of tourism development and changes in each of the four main elements. The model postulates that resort areas pass through four major phases of development. Phase one sees the establishment of a pioneer resort based on very limited transport networks, and used by tourists with global perceptions of tourism opportunities. This is followed in the next phase by a multiplication of resorts, increased transport linkages and a greater tourist awareness of the place. By phase three there exists the beginnings of a resort hierarchy and some resorts begin to specialize, while excursion circuits also develop, as does host–guest segregation. Finally, in phase four, the resort hierarchy is complete, as is the specialization of functions. Resorts become saturated under conditions of full mass tourism, which also sees the development of maximum transport connectivity. The significance of this approach lies not in its sophistication, for the model is somewhat basic in format, but rather in its attempt to draw together such a range of variables within a spatial framework (Pearce 1987c).

In contrast, Gormsen (1981) has presented a spatial-evolutionary model that describes seaside resort development at an international level. The model specifically focuses on three factors; the nature of holiday accommodation, levels of local and non-local participation in tourism development, and the social structure of tourists. The model is rooted in the historical evolution of European tourism and recognizes four major types of resort regions, which Gormsen terms 'tourism peripheries'. Periphery one covers Channel and Baltic coast resorts; periphery two, Mediterranean Europe; the third periphery includes the North African coast; and the fourth periphery covers more distant resorts in West Africa, the Caribbean, South America and the Pacific. Each periphery passes through a sequence, the early stages of which are characterized by external developers, elite tourists and mainly hotel accommodation. Later development stages show more local involvement, a greater diversity of holiday accommodation and a wide range of social classes using the resorts. Such a development sequence has been reached in periphery one since the 1960s, while periphery four is still within the early stages of the model. As Pearce (1987c) points out, this model corresponds broadly with the earlier work of Lundgren (1972) and Britton (1980) who also, in a less formalized fashion, stressed the structural characteristics of resort development.

Like most of the other researchers who have attempted to provide some form of resort environment model, Gormsen (1981) based his work on one specific region, in his case Western Europe. However, we could use his ideas within very different regional contexts, which would obviously change the nature of the resort peripheries. For example, if the model is switched to focus on North America (periphery one) then the Caribbean would shift out of periphery four and into periphery three. Such re-positioning draws attention to two main factors concerning such models. The first is that most models are fairly specific and should only be taken out of their environmental context with great care. Second, none of the models is really general enough to provide what Pearce (1987c, 19) terms a 'comprehensive, all-embracing model of tourism'. Indeed, one would question whether such a model could even be derived or be at all worthwhile, given the complex and dynamic nature of tourism environments.

Finally, it is important to recognize that there are many different forms of tourism, and that each has distinctive regional implications which do not necessarily conform to any simple centre–periphery model. For example, two of the most polarized forms of tourism are international conference and exhibition activities, and mass winter holiday tourism, but they have very different regional implications. Thus, mass winter tourism is essentially located in the more peripheral regions of those states in, or bordering on, the Alps. In contrast, international conference tourism, as well as international cultural tourism, is essentially a capital or major city activity. As an illustration, in the UK only Birmingham seriously challenges London as a venue for international exhibitions and conferences, and two-thirds of all top-class exhibition space in the UK is located in these two cities (Law 1985a). Table 8.3 provides a first attempt to summarize some of the most salient regional features of these different forms of tourism. Moreover, they also have different implications in terms of their contributions to centre–periphery patterns of regional development. Mass summer tourism is more likely than short-break tourism to favour peripheral regions, if only because of the accessibility and time constraints on the latter type of holiday. The typology in table 8.3 is obviously very tentative, and much research is still required to establish the precise regional implications of different forms of tourism.

Table 8.3   A typology of the regional implications of tourism developments

Type of tourism	Locational bias		Selective regions			
	Core	Periphery	Capital	Urban	Rural	Coastal
International cultural	*		*			
Industrial heritage		*		*	?	
International conference and exhibitions	*		*			
Conference	*	*	*	*		*
Exhibition	*	*	*	*	*	?
Business general	*		*			
'Events'	*	*	*	*	*	*
Mass holiday (summer)		*			*	*
Mass holiday (winter)		*			*	
Short break (summer)	*				*	*
Short break (winter)	*		*	*		

Source: Williams and Shaw (1990)

There is also a need to establish a temporal dimension to the typology, which is the seasonality characteristics of each of the main products. Such clarifications could aid considerably in the refinement of tourism models, and must surely form a critical issue in the geography of tourism.

Resort Cycles and Changes in Tourist Environments

Tourist environments tend to be extremely dynamic, influenced as they are by the changing tastes of holidaymakers and the often fickle nature of the tourist industry. The notion of life-cycle change in tourist destination areas has already been touched upon at several points within this book. Various authors have sought to conceptualize these changes, drawing on the general ideas surrounding the product

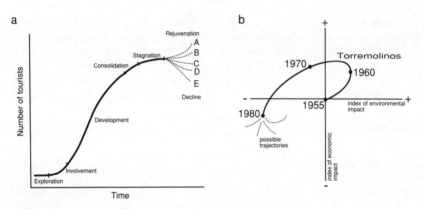

Figure 8.1 Resort life-cycle models
Sources: (a) Butler (1980); (b) Wolfe (1983)

life-cycle. The earliest of such attempts was that made by Butler (1980), who popularized the idea of a resort life-cycle to explain the growth and decline of resorts. Butler (1980) suggested a six-stage cycle of the evolution of tourist destination areas, expressed in terms of changes in the numbers of visitors over time (see figure 8.1a):

- *Exploration*: small numbers of visitors attracted by natural beauty or cultural characteristics – numbers are limited and few tourist facilities exist.
- *Involvement*: limited involvement by local residents to provide some facilities for tourists – recognizable tourist seasons and market areas begin to emerge.
- *Development*: Large numbers of tourists arrive, control passes to external organizations and there is increased tension between locals and tourists.
- *Consolidation*: tourism has become a major – if not the main part – of the local economy, although rates of visitor growth have started to level off and some older facilities are seen as second-rate.
- *Stagnation*: peak numbers of tourists have been reached, although the resort is no longer considered fashionable and turnover of business properties tends to be high.
- *Decline*: attractiveness continues to decline, visitors are lost to other resorts, and the resort becomes more dependent on day visitors and weekend recreationalists from a limited geographical area – long-term decline will continue unless action is taken to rejuvenate the area.

This is not the only life-cycle model of changes in tourist destination areas, since Wolfe (1983) offers a similar approach that more explicitly takes environmental changes into account (figure 8.1b). In this respect, it provides some linkages with the more general evolutionary model proposed by Miossec, which was discussed previously in this chapter. Wolfe's perspective is that, in the early stages, tourism can have positive economic and environmental effects. However, with increasing numbers of tourists, the balance of environmental effects tends to become negative. Finally, the economic benefits may also become negative due to the leakage of revenue to organizations outside the local economy and rising operational costs within the resort. This pessimistic trajectory is known as the Ellis curve.

The model proposed by Butler has attracted criticism, particularly for failing to take into account changes in the demand and supply sides. Cooper (1990) argues that the life-cycle concept is extremely dependent on supply side factors, such as the rate of development, tourist access, government policy and competing resort areas, as well as demand factors. Debbage (1990) argues that Butler's model has focused on the internal dynamics of specific resorts, thereby ignoring both the structure of the tourism industry and the competition from other resorts. He therefore draws on Markusen's (1985) theoretical work on the profit cycle as '. . . it allows the exigencies of industrial organization and oligopoly to be explicitly introduced in a discussion of the cyclical theory of resort development' (Debbage 1990, 520–1). In some resorts, large companies may exercise oligopolitistic powers in order to protect market shares and profit levels in the latter part of the resort cycle. However, this may lead to a long-term loss of competitivity and innovation. These arguments are backed up by a case study of the oligopolistic powers of Resorts International in Paradise Island (Bahamas).

The exact shape of the Butler curve has also been criticized, as has the notion that all resorts have to pass sequentially through the six different stages of the life-cycle. Identification of such stages and of specific turning points between each stage is also problematic, with both Haywood (1986) and Cooper (1990) providing critiques of the difficulties of operationalizing the model. Haywood, for example, suggests that there are six major conceptual and measurement decisions concerning the definition of: the areal unit of analysis, the relevant market areas, the shape of the curve, the resort's stage in the life-cycle, the unit of measurement (i.e. numbers of tourists, visitors, overnights, spend etc.), and finding the relevant timeframe. He argues that until such issues are fully resolved the model's applicability to strategy and forecasting is questionable.

It should also be stressed that all these definitional problems are relevant to geographical research and form a critical issue for further progress. Thus, the definition of the resort area touches on questions of spatial diffusion as well as the nature of functional areas. For example, when does tourism growth in an area adjoining an established resort represent the early stages of a new, quite different cycle of resort development as opposed to the rejuvenation of the existing area? The definition of the temporal framework is also problematic. In this respect, does a downturn in the tourism curve represent a temporary fluctuation or a long-term shift into the decline stage of the model? Another criticism is that the resort cycle model assumes a false universalism, and that this is maintained only by failing to take into account differences in the competitive positions or resources of different resorts.

Despite these criticisms, the resort model has been tested in a variety of situations, although with varying degrees of success. Meyer-Arendt (1987) has, for example, attempted to correlate resort morphology and environmental impacts with stages of tourism development in the Gulf of Mexico. He argues that the model provides a useful conceptual framework within which to study various forms of land-use intensification and environmental improvement or degradation. However, he rightly concludes that the resort cycle model is culturally and politically specific and, for example, seems inappropriate for application to developing countries. As with all such models – and we saw examples of this in the earlier part of this chapter – there is a danger in using them as anything other than descriptive devices that are relevant to the development of resorts in particular places and time periods. Newly emerging resorts face very different markets and trading conditions to those experienced by older resorts in earlier time periods. Furthermore, the model seeks to describe a process of change but, as Massey (1984) has shown, in economic geography process and structure are strongly linked. For example, previous rounds of investment have created a set of structures in particular resorts. In turn, these subsequently condition the possibilities for further investments within these resorts or perhaps in new areas. The view that the model is too deterministic is underlined by van Duijn's (1983) work on the product cycle. He argues that decline is not predictable, because the cycle can be predicted in one of three ways: substitution of a new product; extension of the life-cycle by updating the product; or changes in technology which make a product more competitive. All three possibilities could apply to a tourism resort.

Other workers, notably Haywood (1986), have attempted to shift the resort model away from its somewhat deterministic stance.

Having recognized that the original model as expressed by Butler is destination specific, Haywood attempts to present a range of possible resort cycles for different types of destination areas. These include evolutionary curves for purpose-built resort complexes, through to those representing resorts strongly conditioned by external events. In this way, a certain degree of flexibility is introduced to the model, although these new perspectives still suffer from many of the criticisms directed at the original work. Perhaps a potentially more valuable contribution is made by Haywood (1986), through his introduction to viewing resort development via the process of natural selection. Such perspectives have been applied to forms of institutional change, particularly retailing (Alchain 1950), but these ideas remain undeveloped within tourism research. Haywood views the tourist destination area as the 'organism' fighting for survival, and in doing so he draws attention to three significant points. The first is that, according to the theory of natural selection, whenever there is strong competition, specialization confers advantages on those resorts that focus on particular forms of tourism. Second, the theory draws attention to the fact that environmental changes establish new conditions that in turn determine the suitability of resort survival. This also raises a third point, that highly specialized resorts adapted to one specific set of environmental conditions tend to be the ones that are less capable of adjusting to sudden changes in tourist demand, compared to less specialized areas. In this respect, resort areas directed at narrow market segments would tend to have much shorter life-cycles than those resorts aimed at more broadly based markets.

Such a perspective gives therefore a more realistic as well as a flexible approach to the study of resort development, and opens the way for more empirically based studies to examine these notions. The limited evidence that we have from studies of resorts suggests that, in addition to levels of specialization, size also plays an important part. In England, for example, on average the country's six largest resorts draw one million or more staying visitors per annum, and have sufficient market volume to organize their own programmes of regeneration (English Tourist Board 1991a). By contrast, the 60 or so smaller resorts, which have lost at least one-half of their market since 1970, have little scope for arresting their decline and shifting their life-cycle curve.

The Falsification of Place and Time

A great deal of leisure consumption, especially that related to tourism, is about myths and fantasies. The creation of unreal images is essential for many tourists seeking to escape the blandness of their home and work routines. Early tourists, with large amounts of time and money, sought such differences in the romantic authenticity of the 'Grand Tour', through an examination of ancient cultures. Indeed, the present-day equivalents of this group still search for holiday experiences that bring them into contact with 'original' cultures and societies untouched by the modern world. In contrast, we can also represent a very different set of tourist environments which have deliberately set out to attract visitors by falsifying both place and time. Such developments have increased dramatically over the past 20 years, and have attracted growing attention from a diverse range of academics. Urry (1990, 104) views these tourist sites within a threefold dichotomous classification based on whether sites are authentic or unauthentic, historical or modern, and whether they are subjected to the romantic or collective tourist gaze. Thus, many theme parks may be classified as unauthentic, modern and the object of the 'collective gaze'.

For Urry (1990), the growth of this form of leisure setting is bound up with the rise of postmodernism, which in turn involves the dissolution of boundaries '. . . not only between high and low cultures, but also between different cultural forms' (Urry, 1990, 82). At this point, we are less interested in overall causal processes then in the characteristics of the resultant environments. Indeed, we can recognize a number of different tourism products associated with the process of falsification; ranging from the semi-tropical artificial environments of Center Parc type developments found in England, Holland and northern Germany (Shaw and Williams 1991b), to large theme parks and shopping/leisure malls, and developments associated with the so-called heritage industry (Hewison 1987).

Much has been written about the rise of the heritage industry, as well as its associated problems of historical falsification and cultural commodification (Shaw 1992). The debate has been brought sharply into focus in countries such as the UK and the USA due to the increased economic importance of heritage-based tourism. Much of this is based around the redefined idea of a museum which, according to Lumley (1988, 2), is not used in the '. . . narrow sense of a particular building or institution, but as a potent social metaphor and as a means whereby societies represent their relationships to their own history and to that of other cultures'. In basic economic terms, the shift is towards the open-air museum and the commercialization of the past. Morton (1988) sees this as part of increased competition within the leisure sector: the greater the success of shopping malls and theme parks, the greater has been the pressure on museums to mount expensive, innovative displays.

Inevitably, such trends in heritage development have raised some strong criticisms from commentators who view the whole process as one whereby the tourist industry produces a history-making business. Lumley (1988) has summarized the concern over these trends under three broad headings: the commercialization of history, the pursuit of realism, and the impact of the media. The first two theories echo the earlier and broader debates discussed in chapter 4, regarding tourism's impact on culture, although Lumley singles out developments in the UK as being driven by the cultural marketplace, with the museum addressing the 'consumer' rather than the 'citizen'. It is perhaps the third element, the impact of the media, that adds a new dimension to the debate, since its influence has given rise to a new generation of multimedia museums. This commodification or, as some would argue, falsification, of the past has spawned important tourism environments supported by both private and public investments (Shaw 1992).

While heritage centres have received substantial comment from historians and industrial archaeologists concerning the commodification of history, geographers have been relatively neglectful of those tourist sites involved in the falsification of place. Of particular importance is the development of theme parks, the main aim of which is to create a wonderland. The visitor is immersed in a fantasy which provides '. . . entertainment and excitement, with reassuringly clean and attractive surroundings' (Smith 1980, 46). Walt Disney is credited with the original notion of the theme park, with the creation of Disneyland (California), opened in 1955. Originally, this contained just 18 attractions in five theme areas, but its success was immediate– attracting 3.8 million visitors during its first year. It was followed in 1963 by Walt Disney World in Florida, based on the 'Magic Kingdom', that essentially duplicated the successful formula of the original Disneyland. This has now been extended into Europe, with the opening of Euro-Disney in 1992 near Paris.

In the case of all the 'Disneylands' and similar, if somewhat smaller, theme parks, the main focus of the theming tends to be geographical. Disneyland, for example, has Bear Country (the Rocky Mountains), Frontierland (the Mississippi and the Wild West), New Orleans Square, Main Street USA (typical small town America), and Adventureland (Africa and the Pacific) (Smith 1980, 51). This repackaging of geographical areas onto one tourist site, together with numerous funfair rides, appears to provide an important element in the success of the theme park. Interestingly, the diffusion of such ideas to Europe has proved relatively easy using the same formula, a strong testament to the universality of theme parks.

There appear to be at least two major reasons for the appeal of theme parks. The first, and most easy to identify, is associated with the fact that they offer the visitor a safe, controlled and clean recreational environment. Second, they present an easy to comprehend view of very different geographical environments that can be readily labelled and consumed by visitors. As Urry (1990, 146) argues, the '. . . scenes are in a sense more real than the original, hyper-real in other words', or in the words of *Eco* (1986, 44), '. . . Disneyland tells us that faked nature corresponds much more to our daydream demands'.

The ideas of the theme park have also been developed in other leisure environments, especially the newer shopping malls that combine retail and leisure elements (Jansen-Verbeke 1990). Many of these have now been built, although much of the literature has focused on the largest development to date; the West Edmonton Mall in Canada, which has over 800 shops, and 10 per cent of its floorspace given over to leisure facilities. It has been planned to break away from the image of 'elsewhereness' in an attempt to create both a shopping experience and to attract tourists (Jackson 1991). This has been achieved through falsifying place '. . . creating an appropriately entitled but spatially restricted Fantasyland' (Butler 1991, 291). Within the West Edmonton Mall, as in Disneyland, the focus is on geographical places, although in the shopping mall the emphasis is on 'selling an ambience of foreignness rather than specific locations' (Butler 1991, 291; see also Hopkins 1990). The visitor can be in France, England, Asia or West Coast America – all within Fantasyland (table 8.4). In the UK, smaller examples of the West Edmonton exist at the Metro Centre, Gateshead and Meadowhall near Sheffield, both of which are themed.

The whole concept of the themed environment is to a great extent based around the use of 'place', with the ideas reaching out into the development of World Fairs (Ley and Olds 1988) and Garden Festivals (Holden 1989). Thus, the 1988 Expo fair in Brisbane was organized around a number of different national displays, with over 50 themed environments based on different national stereotypes, such as the British pub, the German beer garden and South Sea Island exotic dancing (Urry 1990, 152). These fairs, shopping malls and theme parks represent a very different perspective on tourism, making it possible to experience the world's geography in a representative fashion (Harvey 1989).

As we have previously discussed, the importance of 'themed'

Table 8.4   The falsification of place in West Edmonton Mall, Canada

Place	Representations in the mall
Europe	
England	Crown jewels
France	Versailles Fountains
Italy	Roman room (theme room), Caesar's statue
North America	
Canada	Via Rial (theme room)
United States	Las Vegas (Caesar's Palace bingo), New Orleans (Bourbon Street), Miami (Water Park), California (Pebble Beach mini golf), Grand Canyon (rafting), Hollywood (theme room), truck room (theme room)
Asia	
China	Ming vases, rickshaws
Japan	Pagoda
Middle East	Arabian Room (theme room)
Oceania	Polynesia (theme room)
Ocean	Dolphin show, aquaria, submarines, *Santa Maria*

Source: Butler (1991)

attractions from the tourist's point of view is that they are both locationally and perceptually convenient. The latter point operates through the system of labelling, often using highly recognizable symbols or features to tell the visitor that what they are viewing is 'old England' or 'small town America'. Of course, image creation is obviously important in tourism, especially when associated with the notion of 'themed' environments. The whole concept of image-making is at the heart of much of the tourism industry, and occupies a good deal of the effort of various tourist boards – both nationally and locally. In this respect, regions are labelled and sold to tourists on the basis of single themes acquired through history, novels or television (Pocock 1992). We can recognize attempts to theme and sell images of England and Wales in this way, as shown by figure 8.2. Thus, the Yorkshire Dales become 'Emmerdale Farm Country' from a popular and long-running television 'soap opera', while parts of East Anglia can be marketed as 'Hereward the Wake Country', seeking links with Anglo-Saxon history.

Figure 8.2 A tourist image of England and Wales
Source: The Guardian, 11 November 1990

The idea of constructing tourism environments is obviously noth-ing new, for some of the older traditional seaside resorts quickly acquired funfairs and piers to sell tourism. What is new, however, is the scale, nature and diversity of these concepts. The ideas of them-ing – which may involve falsification of both 'place' and 'time' – are strongly commercial forces within the modern tourism and leisure industries. Moreover, such ideas, and their associated developments, cut across much of the more traditional typologies of 'tourist environments'. The theme park, shopping mall and heritage centre are as likely to be found in rural areas as in urban ones. This also means that it is increasingly difficult to talk about tourist environments or tourist resorts, since tourism touches almost every type of place.

NINE

Mass Tourism

The Origins of Mass Tourism and Leisure

As noted in chapter 1, there are several definitions of leisure: the main ones are based on free time, function (non-work) and on the pleasure or satisfaction derived from an activity. There has been an increase in the free time available in modern societies (Shivers 1981), and this has opened up the possibility of mass leisure. However, there are criticisms of this argument: Kando (1975, 43) for example, states that '. . . the oft heralded leisure boom and the growth of a multibillion dollar leisure market are merely more mass consumption' as opposed to genuine leisure. An increase in free time is not necessarily translated into leisure; instead, it may be translated into 'dual work', whether in the black economy or in household production such as cooking, gardening or do-it-yourself activities (Rojek 1985). Despite these definitional difficulties, at an empirical level it is possible to show that there has been an increase in both free time and the enjoyment of leisure activities in most developed countries.

During the twentieth century one of the most spectacular growth sectors in leisure activities has been tourism. In the developed countries, there is a widespread perception that tourism is an essential feature of modern life. 'Not to go away' is like not possessing a car or a 'nice' house. It is a marker of status in modern societies and is also thought to be necessary to health' (Urry 1990, 4). Tourism has become mass tourism in such countries. Mass tourism is now deeply embedded in the organization of life in the more developed world. Over time, the objects of what Urry terms the 'tourism gaze' have changed: winter sports have been added to coastal holidays, and the field of mass tourism has become increasingly internationalized. As we saw in chapter 8, new attractions have been added, such as industrial heritage and theme parks. Despite this diversity, mass tourism has a character and impact which is distinctive compared to most other forms of more selective tourism. This stems from it being a form of mass consumption. It is also potentially an agent of profound economic and cultural change (see chapter 4).

The origins of mass leisure lie in the reorganization of production during the nineteenth and the twentieth centuries. This has been driven by the logic of capital accumulation, although not in any simplistic way; technology has played a partly autonomous role, while there has also been a continuous struggle between capital and labour over the distribution of the material and non-material rewards of production, including free time. The experience of leisure, and the ability to enjoy leisure, is of course differentiated for social groups (de Grazia 1964). The employed and the unemployed, men and women, different income groups and different age groups all have differential access to leisure (chapter 3).

The modern growth of mass leisure is less impressive when seen in longer historical perspective. Wilensky (1960) estimated that the skilled urban worker of the mid-twentieth century had only just regained the leisure he or she would have enjoyed in the thirteenth century in Europe. Leisure – seen as a rest from work – was well-established in the medieval period when approximately one in three days was a holiday of some kind. In Europe these conditions were decisively lost during the industrialization and urbanization of the eighteenth and nineteenth centuries. It was only in the twentieth century that the moral and legal right to leisure time was re-established in the developed world.

Shivers (1981) has traced the growth of mass leisure in the USA, where there has been a decline in the hours of work; the average factory worker worked for 35 hours a week in 1980 compared to 60 hours a week in the 1920s. This trend is reflected globally, at least in the formal economy if not in the black or informal economy. The World Tourism Organization (1984) estimated that between 1960 and 1980 the proportion of countries in which the average working week exceeded 40 hours fell from 75 per cent to 56 per cent. There has also been an increase in those who are excluded from the formal economy; for example, there are more people of retirement age able to enjoy leisure. In the developed countries, legislation has also excluded children from workplaces. The position is different in the less developed countries, and they will not necessarily follow the same course.

One form of mass leisure is mass tourism. The emergence of mass tourism was conditional not only on the growth of leisure time but

Table 9.1   The structure of free time

Distribution of free time	Potential for
Daily	Local leisure
Weekly	Short-break tourism
Annually/lifetime	Longer holidays and mass tourism

also on the structure of free time and on the economics of the tourism industry. Free time is distributed within days, weeks, years and lifetimes (table 9.1). Changes in the length of the working day necessarily have only a limited impact on tourism. This was also true of the length of the working week; whether or not Saturday and Sunday were free days did not directly affect traditional long-stay holidays, although latterly it has been an important precondition for the growth of short-break holidays. Instead, the distribution of free time within the year, and especially of paid holidays, was critical in the growth of mass tourism in the twentieth century. The World Tourism Organization estimated in 1983 that there were 645 million workers globally who received paid holidays from work. Their global distribution was, of course very uneven (see figure 9.1). The lifetime distribution of free time has also been an important influence on mass tourism. The aging of the population and the growth of active groups with disposable income has added significantly to the demand for tourism. Perez (1987) estimates that in Europe the proportion of tourism demand coming from the 65+ group increased from 15 per cent to 25 per cent between the mid-1960s and the mid-1980s.

Sessa (1983) summarizes the social mega-trends which underlie the increase in mass tourism, at least until the 1990s: demographic transition, social progress, international peace, broader tourism consciousness and higher incomes. The demand for tourism is also fuelled by the image-makers who effectively create tourist attractions. This is a diverse industry and includes designers of hotels and attractions, as well as media and travel writers. Together they generate what Krippendorf (1987, 10) terms 'the promises of the paradise sellers'.

The economics of the tourism industry are also important in the emergence of mass tourism. This is discussed in chapter 5 and only the most salient points are repeated here. Changes in transport technology – by air and by land – have accelerated travel and reduced costs. This has encouraged an increase in demand which, in turn, has

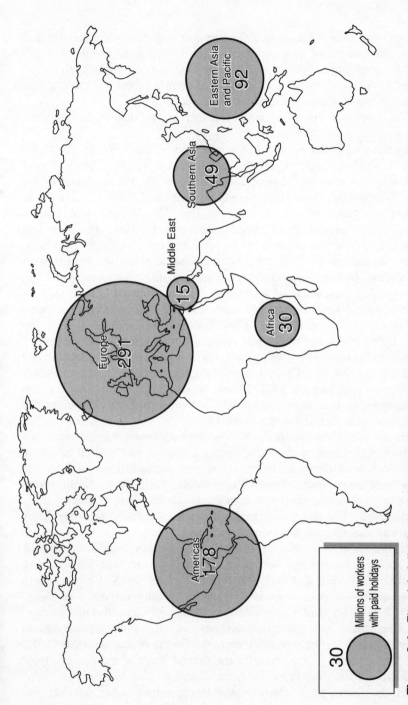

Figure 9.1 The global distribution of leisure time, 1982
Source: World Tourism Organization (1984)

led to economies of scale and further cost reductions. There has also been the growth of tour companies able to sell large numbers of all-inclusive package holidays at relatively low cost. As a result, there has been a 'virtuous circle' – at least in economic terms – of falling real costs, rising demand and economies of scale.

The 'virtuous circle' of mass tourism in the developed countries has had five main phases.

In the *first phase* mass tourism emerged in the USA in the 1920s and the 1930s. The two critical conditions were the spread of paid holidays and the extension of car ownership. By the outbreak of the first World War, there were already an estimated 2 million cars in the USA, compared to only 132 000 in the UK (Burkart and Medlik 1981, 28). The growth of motel chains also provided the necessary accommodation infrastructure for the emerging tourism industry. The destinations of most tourists were coastal areas, spa resorts such as Yellow Springs and Saratoga Springs, and 'the great American outdoors'. Later, artificial attractions became popular. Places such as Coney Island became national attractions as well as recreation areas for nearby cities, in this case New York (Gunn 1988, 111). Comparable living standards in Canada and the development of an integrated transport system also meant that the two countries became locked together in the world's first significant international tourism market (Cosgrove and Jackson 1972). There was some working-class tourism in Europe at this time, but it was less universal, reliant on public transport and directed at the coastal areas.

In the *second phase*, in the 1950s, domestic mass tourism emerged in Europe, fuelled by the same preconditions as had existed earlier in the USA – in terms of leisure time and accessibility – and by the economic boom that followed the Second World War. Public transport was still important, although car ownership was becoming more widespread. The coast was the main destination, although rural tourism was also important in some countries.

In the *third phase*, the late 1950s and the 1960s, mass tourism took on another dimension, becoming increasingly internationalized (see Burkart and Medlik 1981). Between 1950 and 1988 the number of international tourists increased from 25 to 389 million (see figure 9.2). The USA and Canada led the way, for in addition to travel between these two countries, Europe was the main destination of North American international tourists. Cosgrove and Jackson (1972, 74) wrote that '. . . traditionally the Grand Tour of Europe occupied at least half the time spent by Americans travelling abroad'.

In the *fourth phase* there was a Europeanization of international tourism from the 1960s. According to the World Tourism Organiza-

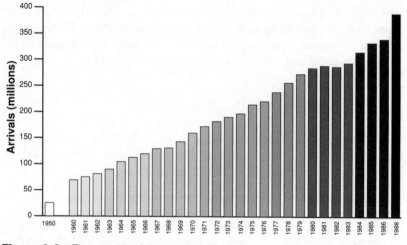

Figure 9.2   The growth of international tourism
Source: World Tourism Organization (1989a)

tion, globally there were 405 million international tourists in 1989, and the destinations for 64 per cent of these were in Europe, being mainly movements within that continent. This remarkable distribution is conditioned by the nature of national boundaries so that even relatively short trips – by North American standards – become international trips in Europe. The growth of mass tourism has been facilitated by the easing of travel regulations and by the growth of the international air travel industry. The financial, legal and practical barriers to foreign travel within Europe have been significantly reduced. The development of all-inclusive tours by air was critical in this, and made Western Europe an integrated macro-region for mass tourism. Between 1965 and 1970 alone, the number of air package holidays sold in the UK increased from one to two million (Burkart and Medlik 1981, 32). Mass car ownership in Western Europe was also an important precondition of mass international travel, replicating the North American experience of 40 years earlier.

In the *fifth phase*, in the late twentieth century, there has been a globalization of the tourism industry: the two main nodes have been linked. There had been a strong flow of tourists from the USA to Europe throughout the twentieth century. However, the level of trans-Atlantic movement in *both* directions soared in the 1970s as keen competition reduced the real price of travel. At the same time, there was genuine globalization as more and more countries became locked into international travel: tourists from Japan, Europe, North America and Australia/New Zealand have become increasingly internationalized. The use of Japanese tourism is particularly notable (see chapter 2). At the same time, the range of destinations of mass tourism has increased, and now encompasses virtually all countries in the developed and many of those in the developing world.

The Characteristics of Mass Tourism

Mass tourism is a distinctive form of tourism. This stems from its character as a form of Fordist mass consumption. Urry (1990, 14) summarizes the features of mass consumption as:

> purchase of commodities produced under conditions of mass production; a high and growing rate of expenditure on consumer products; individual producers tending to dominate particular industrial markets; producer rather than consumer as dominant; commodities little differentiated from each other by fashion, season, and specific market segments; relatively limited market choice – what there is tends to reflect producer interests, either publicly or privately owned.

Both domestic and international mass tourism would seem to fit this model of mass consumption, given the characteristics shown in box 9.1.

Box 9.1   The main characteristics of mass tourism

- The sheer numbers involved mean that the tourism product has to be offered under conditions of mass production

- There is a growing level of expenditure on consumer goods associated with tourism, i.e. surf boards for the beach holiday and skis and skiing accessories for the winter holiday

- A few producers dominate particular markets; Disney in the world of theme parks, and travel companies such as Thomson and Neckermann in the world of package holidays in Europe

- Producers take the lead in developing new tourism attractions, whether opening up new mass destinations such as Thailand, the Gambia and Turkey, or in designing new theme parks such as Euro-Disney

- By and large, mass tourism products are little differentiated: the Mediterranean beach holiday offers much the same mix of architecture, facilities, food and drink and entertainment whether it is located in Turkey, Greece or Spain

---

The nature of mass tourism as a form of mass consumption also gives rise to a number of basic characteristics which have important economic and social implications. Some of the latter have been explored in chapter 4. Mass tourism tends to be highly *spatially polarized*. This is partly to do with the way in which the tourist gaze is constructed. Urry (1990, 47) argues that 'The contemporary tourist gaze is increasingly signposted. There are markers which distinguish the things and places worthy of our gaze. Such signposting identifies a relatively small number of tourist nodes'. In the latter half of the twentieth century the tourist image creators in North America and Europe have mainly promoted beach and ski holidays and, to a lesser extent, 'rural idylls' such as National Parks, as the rightful objects of the tourist gaze (see chapter 8). Although there is some flexibility in the definition of such attractions, there are constraints on their supply. As a result, most tourists are concentrated into a small number of areas. In Spain, for example, there are 47 bed places per square kilometre in the Balearic islands compared to less than two per square kilometre km in the country as a whole (Alvarez 1988). In addition, the economies of scale in developing airports and other infrastructure, and in providing charter flights, holiday accommodation, entertainments and services, are also conducive to the spatial concentration of mass tourists. Agglomeration economies thereafter reinforce the development of other complementary tourism services. Eventually, diseconomies of scale arising from spatial polarization may lead to the decline of particular resorts, although not of the generic type of tourism attraction. The most obvious manifestation of this spatial polarization is tourism urbanization. Mullins (1991, 326) writes that 'Tourist cities represent a new and extraordinary form of urbanization because they are cities built solely for consumption. Whereas Western urbanization emerged in the nineteenth century generally for reasons of production and commerce, tourist cities evolved during the late twentieth century as sites for consumption'.

Mass tourist destinations also tend to have *segmented markets*. This is determined by both national differences in the construction of the tourist gaze and by the economics of mass tourism. As minimizing costs is a paramount objective – unlike in elite tourism – there is an historical tendency for there to be high levels of movements between adjoining places (Williams and Zelinsky 1970). Thus, in the UK in the early twentieth century, Southend developed as the resort for East London, Blackpool as the resort for industrial Lancashire, and Skegness as the resort for the East Midlands. At the international scale, there are several examples of similar processes; Germans constitute two-thirds of the tourists in Austria (Zimmermann), while

Japanese tourists are dominant in South East Asia, and North Americans in Mexico (table 9.2). However, proximity is not the only consideration and, for example, 50 per cent of the tourists in the Algarve come from the UK (Lewis and Williams 1988). This is to be explained by the way in which the Algarve has been marketed in the UK, and the fact that British tour companies have established sufficient business volume so as to secure significant cost reductions. Therefore, the level of market segmentation is scale specific: it tends to increase with decreases in spatial scale; that is, from country to region to resort to individual hotels.

Dependency on particular market segments brings certain economic relationships. Destinations become more vulnerable to external influences, whether political (Richter 1983) or economic. This is most marked with respect to international tourism. Small changes in one or two markets can have major effects. For example, fears of terrorism have led to dramatic fluctuations in the numbers of American visitors to Europe, particularly in cities such as London, Paris and Rome. Within Europe, domestic political turmoil can easily deter international visitors. It took Portugal four years to recover the tour-

Table 9.2 Segmentation and dependency in selected major tourism markets, 1987

Destination country	Major source of tourists	Percentage of all foreign tourists/visitors
Bahamas	USA	88
Botswana	South Africa	57[a]
Canada	USA	93
Czechoslavakia	East Germany	43[a]
Cyprus	UK	29[a]
France	Germany	24
Korea, Republic of	Japan	48[a]
Malta	UK	60
Martinique	France	47
Mexico	USA	85
New Zealand	Australia	35[a]
Pakistan	India	45
Paraguay	Argentina	38
Portugal	Spain	46
Spain	France	23[a]
Thailand	Malaysia	22
Tunisia	France	26

[a]Visitors, not tourists
Source: World Tourism Organization (1989b)

ists numbers lost following the 1974 military coup. More dramatically, the nationalist conflicts in the former Yugoslavia in the 1990s effectively wiped out several years of foreign tourist arrivals. Less extreme, but also important, is the dependency on economic conditions in external markets. The Algarve, for example, with its high degree of dependency, is highly susceptible to changing levels of prosperity in the UK market (Lewis and Williams 1988). The numbers of American tourists in the international market have also fluctuated from year to year, as the dollar has risen and fallen dramatically in value since fixed international exchange rates were abandoned in the early 1970s. The position is exacerbated by the role of the international tour companies. They rarely own facilities in particular countries, instead preferring to lease these on short- or medium-term contracts. It is therefore relatively easy for them to shift their interests between different resorts or countries in response to changes in costs or fashion.

Mass tourism involves the movement of large numbers of tourists with relatively little surplus income. High gross income is yielded from relatively low expenditure per capita. Mass tourists are seeking more and more exotic (if comfortably packaged) holiday destinations. Given the income constraints, these can only be provided at relatively minimal levels of services and facilities. In addition, the construction of the tourism gaze is related to the nature of tourism motivation. Krippendorf (1987, 29) writes that 'Where the journey leads is not so important, the main thing is to get away from the routine, to switch off, change the scene. To this extent travel destinations are altogether interchangeable'. This means that there is intense competition between largely undifferentiated tourist products which have been constructed along the lines of 'identitikit resorts'. Given they have the same combination of attractions (beach, hotel and entertainments), *their main point of competition is usually price.* There is therefore strong downward pressure on price levels – both for the tour companies and for the local operators (Guitart 1982). This is confirmed by Truett and Truett (1987) who estimated, empirically, the tourism demand functions for Spain, Greece and Mexico; they found that the quantity of tourism services demanded is highly elastic with respect to both income and price.

Mass tourism is necessarily highly seasonal. The tourists are purchasing access to particular seasonal environments or 'space–time' packages'. There are two principal reasons for this: '. . . there is an institutionalised and a natural *seasonality* which both affect tourism' (Hartmann 1986, 25). First, the main objects of the mass tourist gaze – snow or sunny beaches – are temporal attractions. While snow exists in high mountain ranges all year round and some coastal areas are warm or hot all year, there are usually seasons in which conditions are optimum. A few destinations are able to develop year-round tourism. Florida provides winter sun for North Americans and cheap summer sunshine for Europeans. Some resorts in the Alps and the North American mountains have a double seasonal peak; skiing in winter and driving/walking through scenic mountains in the summer. However, most mass tourist resorts typically have an attraction which is seasonally specific and characteristically of short duration. Seasonality is underlined by a second factor: namely, the construction of free time. In the developed world paid holidays tend to be seasonally specific. There is a season – usually the summer – during which it is expected that long holidays will be taken. Companies' work programmes and school vacations are both organized around this assumption. This is reflected in the temporal concentration of holiday-taking: in Italy, Belgium and Portugal more than 70 per cent of main holidays are taken in July or August (Romeril 1989, 207). Baron (1975) argues that seasonality has the effects of reducing holiday enjoyment because of overcrowding, under-utilization of fixed capital in hotels and so on, seasonal employment and reduced profitability.

It should also be noted that *temporal polarization has the effect of reinforcing spatial polarization.* Mass tourism is already concentrated in space, and time adds another dimension to this: the dual concentration of tourists in time and space gives rise to saturation tourism, arguably a potent threat to the environment. Again, this is socially constructed because of the way in which society organizes free time. The shoulder season often offers good holiday conditions, but this period is not available to most mass tourists. In this case, the economics of tourism run counter to polarization. Hotels and companies charge higher prices in the peak season not because costs are higher but because the market will bear them at this time of the year. This does little to deter tourism demand and it is the tourists who have to bear the higher costs.

Mass tourism by assembling large numbers of tourists in small areas creates intense *environmental pressures.* There are the normal urbanization pressures of air, water and terrestrial pollution. However, these are accentuated by the temporal polarization of mass tourism. Infrastructures are required to cope with the throughput of a large volume of consumers in a short period of time, yet they will be underutilized during much of the remainder of the year. Therefore, the per capita (per tourist) costs of infrastructure provision can be formidable, and may well lag behind need. In addition, tourism pressures are different from those of normal urbanization in that they bring particularly acute pressures to bear on very limited zones such as mountain slopes or coasts, which also tend to be ecologically sensitive. Freedom from the norms of conventional social behaviour may also affect tourist behaviour, leading to increased noise or litter pollution. Attempts have been made to relate the environmental impact of tourism to the carrying capacity of an area for environmentally sound development. However, '. . . while the theory may be easy to conceptualize, the practical reality leaves much to be desired' (Romeril 1989, 205). But there is an alternative and more positive view of tourism. Hartmann (1986, 31–2) argues that '. . . dead seasons are the only chance for a social and ecological environment to recover fully'.

MacCannell (1973, 1976) sees the tourist as searching for an 'authenticity' that he or she cannot find in everyday life. However, the arrival of mass tourism in an area is necessarily intrusive to the lives of local people. The latter respond by organizing tourism spaces on the basis of 'staged authenticity', as was discussed in Chapter 4. Mass tourists therefore experience culture via a formidable social and commercial filter. Arguably, *staged authenticity* is an inevitable consequence of the logic of mass consumption and the requirements of capital accumulation. Temporal and spatial polarization mean that the demand far exceeds the supply of authentic cultural events, while increased numbers of folk events have to be staged in order to extract more money from the tourists. Authenticity cannot survive in this context. The result of this, and of the demands for familiar comforts, is the creation in the tourist resort of '. . . a small monotonous world that everywhere shows us our own image' so that '. . . the pursuit of the exotic and diverse ends in uniformity' (Turner and Ash 1975, 292).

The characteristics of mass tourism discussed here are, of course, only tendencies and their precise form is highly variable (Smith 1977b; see also Urry 1990, 57–60). The degree of spatial polarization, market segmentation, dependency and control, price depression, seasonal polarization, environmental pollution and cultural sterility is contingent on local and national conditions, including:

- the volume of tourists
- the form of market segmentation
- the specific nature of the seasonality
- the tourist activities
- the organization of the tourism industry
- the nature of the local society and economy

These and other dimensions of mass tourism are explored in the following section.

Mass Tourism: Contrasting Case Studies

There are many different forms of mass tourism, but the most common are sunshine/seaside tourism and winter sports tourism. In the USA, 'the great recreational outdoors' is also an object of mass tourism. However, as the effects are less polarized and there is a separate chapter on rural tourism, this topic is not considered here in any detail. Sex tourism in Thailand, and mass tourism at cultural sites such as Paris and London, are also excluded here but discussed in chapters 4 and 10 respectively. So are mega-events such as the Olympic Games and the World Cup; the Los Angeles games in 1984, for example, attracted over 400 000 tourists (Pyo et al. 1988). Instead, we concentrate on the two archetypical mass tourism products.

While coastal resorts had been popular in the earlier period of elite tourism, only in the late nineteenth and early twentieth centuries did they become the focus of mass tourism. There were several reasons for this, including the emergence of paid holidays, the arrival of mass transport via the railways, and the desire to escape the harsh living conditions of urban–industrial capitalism. The attraction was sea and sand and the contrast to home provided by the absence of industry. In the early twentieth century, the arrival of mass car ownership modified this pattern. In North America improved accessibility rein-forced the attraction of 'the great outdoors'. In Europe, while it gave some boost to rural tourism, it mainly led to a dispersion of tourism along the coast rather than away from the coast. Cosgrove and Jack-son (1972, 39) summarize the changing spatial dynamics arising from the spread of car ownership: this '. . . enabled the coastline to be uti-lized more in accordance with its linear resource base than by the point pattern of exploitation associated with the railway-based resorts'. In Europe this incipient domestic coastal mass tourism reached a peak in the 1950s. Rising real incomes and transport improvements led to a massive increase in seasonal tourist migrations to the coast.

As was discussed earlier in this chapter, from the 1960s mass coastal tourism in Europe underwent a further change. Inter-nationalization was facilitated by changes in the technology and the costs of air transport, in the construction of the tourist gaze, and in the falling real costs of foreign holidays at a time of rising real incomes. International coastal mass tourism has subsequently devel-oped into a major industry. Europe is the principal focus of this, although by no means the only one. The beaches of Australia,

Mexico, the Caribbean and the Black Sea, amongst others, have also been attractive to mass tourists from many countries. However, the Mediterranean represents the most highly developed form of mass coastal tourism. In figure 9.3a are shown the main international tourism flows in Europe, and this confirms that they are essentially movements from the north of Europe to the Mediterranean countries, especially Italy and Spain.

The growth of Mediterranean tourism has been underpinned by

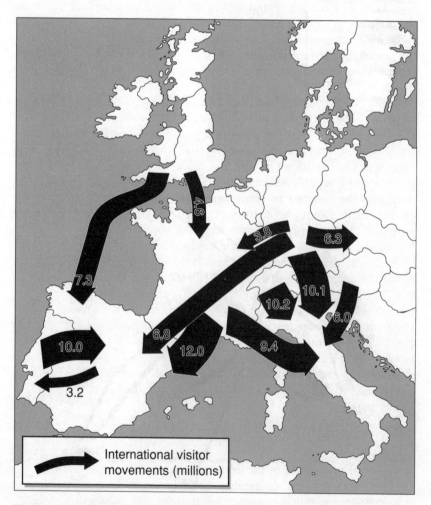

Figure 9.3a Mass tourism in Western Europe: international visitor movements, 1988–9
Source: OECD (1990)

the development of all-inclusive tour holidays, or package tours. While these were popularized by Thomas Cook in the nineteenth century, the first package holiday *by air* – from the UK to Corsica – was launched only in 1950. Thereafter, growth was so rapid that by 1970 the volume of charter traffic within Europe surpassed the volume of scheduled traffic (Pearce 1987b, 183). The comparative cost advantages of package holidays stem from selling a bundle of

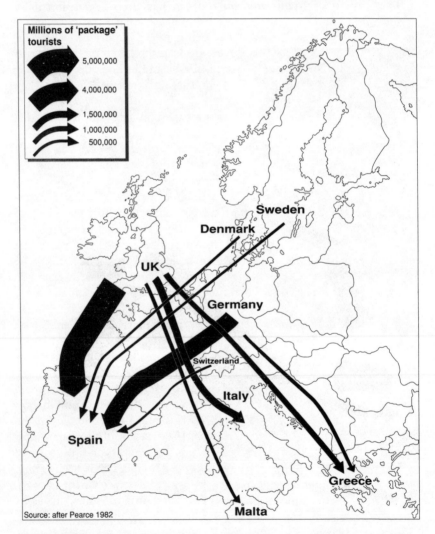

Figure 9.3b   Mass tourism in Western Europe: major package holiday flows in Europe, 1980
Source: after Pearce (1982)

services – air and ground transport, hotel, insurance and so on – and from the use of charter aircraft. Reduced levels of services on these airplanes, combined with high passenger load levels, give them significant cost advantages over scheduled flights.

Pearce (1987a,b) has analysed the origins and destinations of air package holidays in Europe (figure 9.3b), showing that Spain is the main destination of these flights. The UK–Spain and the Germany–Spain routes alone accounted for 35 per cent of all intra-European package flights. Over time the pattern has changed, with countries such as Greece and Portugal becoming more important, while the Spanish share has fallen. However, package holidays by air are only one element of the picture: France, for example, does not feature in figure 9.3b, because most of its international tourists rely on their own cars for transport.

Such data only presents the aggregate picture, and further dis-aggregation reveals more complex and more polarized relationships between destinations and origins. Thus, Pearce (1987a) has shown that there is a high degree of regional segmentation. In Spain, for example, Malaga, Gerona, Alicante and Menorca are relatively important destinations for British tourists compared to other foreigners. Similarly, Mallorca is particularly important for the German mass market. Within national markets there is further segmentation. Particular tour companies tend to specialize in serving particular resort areas, and again economies of scale tend to dictate this. The UK's largest tour company, Thomson, provides a classic example. The major Mediterranean resort areas in which Thomson delivered more than 30 per cent of all UK package holiday tourists in 1987 are shown in figure 9.4. The company is particularly strong in Spain, Italy and Greece. Furthermore, this high degree of market control gives the major European tour companies considerable influence over the presentation of these resorts, and their price levels.

Spain is one of the most important examples of international coastal mass tourism in the Mediterranean region. The combination of the social construction of the tourist gaze and the economics of the industry result in a very high degree of polarization of tourism within Spain (figure 9.5). Alvarez (1988) estimates that four-fifths of the country's tourists are concentrated within provinces that occupy just one-fifth of the land area of the country. Domestic tourism is more evenly distributed spatially than is foreign tourism. Thus, in 41 of the country's 50 provinces national tourism predominates, accounting for up to 90 per cent of the total. In contrast, some regions – notably the Balearic (85 per cent) and Canary Islands (71 per cent) – are dominated by foreign tourists (Valenzuela 1991, 44).

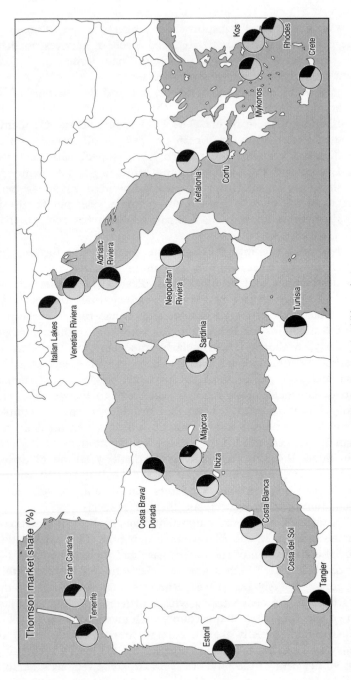

Figure 9.4 Tour company market domination: Thomson and the UK market
Source: Monopolies and Mergers Commission

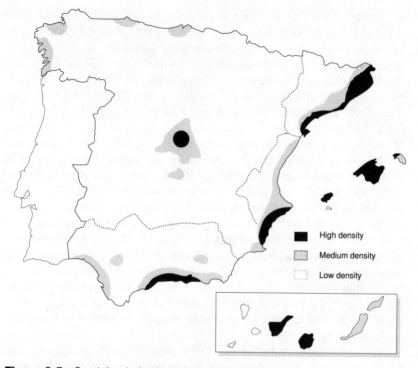

Figure 9.5   Spatial polarization of tourism in Spain
Source: Alvarez (1988, 72)

Variations in the tourism attraction (especially climate) and in the organization of the industry result in considerable regional differences in the degree of temporal polarization. This influences occupancy rates, which vary from 21 per cent in Gerona to 62 per cent in the Canaries, costs and rates of profit. There are also differences in the economic structures of the regions. Tourism in Catalonia is located in a more developed region which does not lag far behind the levels of living in the more prosperous parts of the EC. There is therefore less of a cultural divide between the local populace and the tourists, a large proportion of whom are from adjoining regions in France. In contrast, tourism in the Balearic and Canary Islands is located in what were some of Spain's and Europe's poorest regions. Tourism has had a far more profound effect in these regions, culturally, economically and environmentally. Another important difference between the regions is the strength and organization of local capital. Whereas there were well-developed sources of capital in Catalonia, these were relatively weak in the Islands where, consequently, external capital played a more important role. As the islands are also more dependent on package tours than the mainland (where individual car-borne travellers are an important market segment), they tend to be more dependent on particular markets (Valenzuela 1991, 46).

The Economist Intelligence Unit (1988) estimates that there is strong leakage of income from tourism in the Balearic Islands. Furthermore, 'Hotel profit margins have been steadily cut as pressure from the tour operators has risen' (p. 26). There is also a high degree of dependence on the British and German markets, which accounted for 80 per cent of all foreign tourists in the 1980s. In addition, UK tourists are relatively low spenders (6476 pesetas per day) compared to the Germans (7175) and the Swiss (more than 9000). The overall assessment is that there has been overdevelopment to cope with mass tourism, and the result has been poor quality, a loss of amenity and neglect of the traditional economy. Llinas (1991, 20) comments that 'Tourism has consumed the landscape of Majorca as industry has consumed the reserves of coal or of minerals of the old Europe'. Spain therefore provides an example of the diversity which exists within mass tourism, and indeed the regions can be conceptualized as lying at different ends of a continuum of mass tourism characteristics, as shown in figure 9.6.

Early mass tourism in the USA occurred in the North East region, where there was a combination of major population centres and relatively cool coastal summer temperatures. For example, the linking of Atlantic City to Philadelphia by railway assured the development of the former as a middle-class resort. Winter sunshine resorts in Florida and California had also emerged by the end of the century. The detailed forms of the new tourist destinations revealed the influence

Dimensions of mass tourism

Greater   **Lesser**

Market segmentation

Spatial polarisation

Cultural sterility

Environmental pressures
from foreign tourists

External control

Figure 9.6 Mass tourism in Spain: regional contrasts

of human agencies. In Florida, for example, Henry Flaglet built a series of luxury hotels down the east coast, including the Royal Palm in Miami (Lavery and van Doren 1990).

Mass tourism reached the take-off stage in the USA in the early part of the twentieth century. The economic boom that followed the First World War boosted leisure and tourism, while growth in car ownership rates, the commercial bus network and motels provided the means for increased mobility. This boom in mass tourism continued after the Second World War, fostered by further growth in incomes, leisure time and individual mobility: 'The society has truly reached a period of travel democratization, the flowering of mass travel' (Lavery and van Doren 1990, 30–31). In figure 9.7 is shown the distribution of all major resorts in the USA by the mid-1980s, with the most notable clusters being in the North East, Southern California/Las Vegas and Florida. The top performing resorts – measured by sales per room in leading resort hotels – are also mostly clustered in Florida and Hawaii (table 9.3).

Despite these healthy financial returns in some of the principal resorts, some of the older destinations have suffered from declining markets since the 1950s, due to domestic and international competition. The more successful resorts not only offer quality products but are also attuned to catering for particular market segments, for example sport-based resorts (especially tennis, watersports, golf and casinos), or adult education and conference provision.

Turning to mass winter sports tourism, the first point to emphasize is that this originated in Europe. Traditionally, the Alps had been an area of summer tourism, and the attractions were climbing, walking and viewing the scenery. The first major expansion was in the nineteenth century. Writers and other image creators brought the Alps into the tourist gaze, while the railroads, together with Thomas Cook's tours, made them an economically feasible objective of middle-class tourism. Early in the twentieth century, the first ski course was opened at Arlberg, while the holding of the first winter Olympics at Chamonix in 1924 greatly boosted the growth of winter sports tourism. However, mass international winter tourism only developed in the 1950s and 1960s (Barker 1982). The ingredients were similar to those for international mass coastal tourism: the reconstruction of the tourist gaze, rising real incomes and car ownership levels, and falling real costs allied to increased tour company activity. As with coastal tourism, the industry is characterized by a high degree of spatial polarization, external control and environmental pressures. There is also a high degree of temporal polarization, although some resorts have developed a sig-

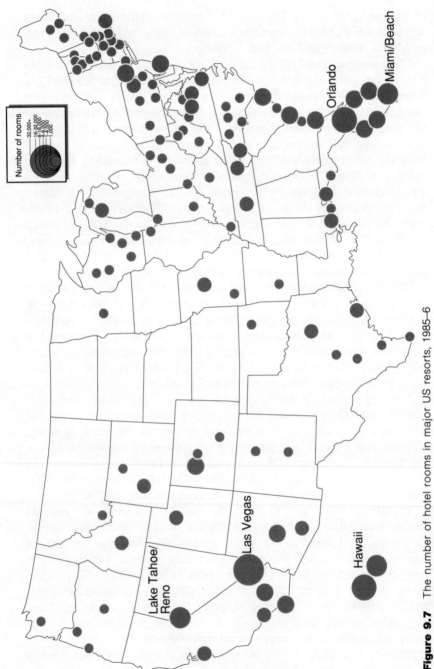

Figure 9.7 The number of hotel rooms in major US resorts, 1985–6
Source: Lavery and van Doren (1990)

Table 9.3 The top ten performing US resorts, 1987

Resort	Number of guest rooms	Average occupancy (%)	Sales per room (%)
1. Turnberry Isle (Miama Beach)	118	56	154 966
2. Holiday Isle and Marina (Islamorado, Florida)	71	84	141 831
3. Hotel Hana (Mani, Hawaii)	61	70	139 344
4. Caneel Bay (St John, Virgin Islands)	171	77	118 591
5. Kona Village Resort (Kailua-Kona, Hawaii)	100	76	117 880
6. Pier House (Key West, Florida)	120	87	112 500
7. Holekulam Hotel (Honolulu, Hawaii)	456	83	109 649
8. Boulders Resort (Carefree, Arizona)	120	75	109 525
9. Ilakas Hotel (Honolulu, Hawaii)	798	83	102 632
10. Trump Plaza Hotel (Atlantic City)	586	91	99 555

Source: Lodging Hospitality, August 1988

nificant summer season based on warm-weather pursuits or high-altitude skiing.

The character of the mass winter tourism resorts is as variable as that of the summer coastal resorts. They can also be arranged along economic, social and cultural continua. Barker (1982), for example, compares the resorts of the Eastern and Western Alps. The former have been developed at lower altitudes and are more integrated with the economic and cultural lives of the indigenous communities than are the high-altitude resorts of the Western Alps. They can be dichotomized, in a simplified fashion, as lying at the two extremes of a continuum of resorts (table 9.4).

Although they generate different types of environmental pressures, both types can threaten the ecosystems and the landscapes of their surrounding regions. Both are also characterized by temporal polar-

Table 9.4   The continuum of characteristics in Alpine resorts

Low altitude	High altitude
Integrated settlement	New settlement
Local capital	External capital
Local labour	External labour
Cultural exchanges	Cultural islands
Environmental pressures	Environmental pressures
Temporal polarization	Temporal polarization

ization, although there are differences in the extent to which they can attract summer visitors. Neither of these ideal types is static and the tourist resorts are in process of continual change. One of the more pessimistic aspects of Baker's analysis is that the initially more positive experiences of the more integrated developments of the Eastern Alps can be temporary. She writes (p. 409) that after the initial stages '. . . the intensity and the volume of tourism in peak season, however, result in an overcommitment of financial resources to tourist accommodations and infrastructure as well as in congestion, suburban-like sprawl, pollution, and loss of traditional ways of life'.

Europe is the principal winter skiing focus, with some 26 million skiers (Cockerell 1988) but there are also important mass winter tourism markets in North America (12 million skiers) and Japan (also 12 million). A recent survey has estimated that, in the USA alone,

Table 9.5   North American ski resorts: regional contrasts, 1989–90

Resort area	Features of average resorts			
	Gross fixed assets ($)	Number of beds at base	Average skier visits (000's)	Average revenue per skier visit ($)
New England	19 586	1 453	271	24.74
East	10 308	529	158	23.64
MidWest	2 895	123	69	18.57
Central Rockies	23 339	3 812	358	24.18
Northern Rockies	11 302	886	181	22.82
California and Nevada	20 229	437	282	32.00
Pacific Northwest	10 676	146	185	16.62
Western Canada	16 789	840	231	24.81

Source: Goeldner et al. (1991)

there were approximately 50 million skier visits in 1989–90 (Goeldner et al. 1991). They are highly seasonal and, on average, resorts
operated for only 117 days during the year. However, there are
important regional variations (table 9.5) and differences of scale; for
example, the average number of beds per ski resort is only 123 in the
Mid-West compared to 3812 in the Central Rockies. In addition,
there are also seasonal differences, with Western Canada managing
136 days of operation compared to only 101 in the Eastern region.
This contributes to considerable variations in the economic efficiency
of the resorts. The revenue extracted per skier visit ranges between
$16.62 in the Pacific Northwest to almost double this, at $32.00, in
California and Nevada.

Changes in Mass Tourism and Leisure: the Challenge of Postmodernism

Mass tourism is one form of mass leisure. The amount of leisure time
available in developed countries has been increasing steadily during
the course of the twentieth century. Gershuny and Jones (1987) have
traced the major changes in the UK during 1961–84 (see figure 9.8):
the amount of time taken by paid work has increased, domestic work
has been largely static, personal care has declined and leisure, both in
and out of the home, has increased. There are considerable differences between social groups according to income/unemployment, age
and gender. In general, while the leisure patterns of men and women
have converged, the former remain relatively privileged (see chapter
3).

As well as an increase in overall leisure time, there have also been
changes in the content of leisure. Gershuny and Jones' (1987)
empirical analysis of UK trends, for example, found that the amount
of time devoted to walking and sports had increased, while passive
leisure (listening to music, watching TV and so on) had decreased.
'Going for a ride', or excursions *per se* as a form of leisure had also
declined in importance, leading the authors to conclude that
'Domesticating the means of production of transport services, seems
to have robbed travel (or at least, local travel) of something of its
previous romance'.

Roberts (1989) provides a more general analysis of changes in leisure in the UK, and identifies four main trends. First, there is
greater *home centredness* as a result of long-term privatization of leisure. This is linked to the decline of community, greater individual
mobility and the expansion of the leisure market in sound and vision
equipment, computers and technology. Second, there is greater *out-*

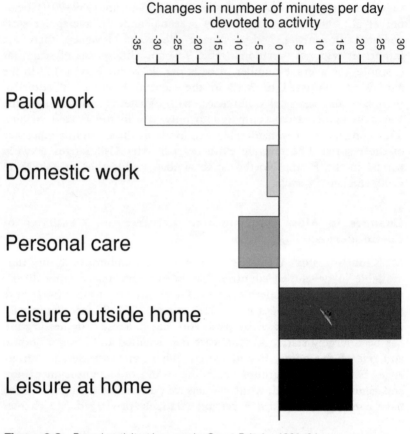

Figure 9.8   Broad activity changes in Great Britain, 1961–84
Source: Gershuny and Jones (1987, 20)

of-home recreation as sports participation, visits to historic sites and theme parks, tourism and second homes become more important. This is linked to a growing preference for active rather than passive leisure. Third, *connoisseur leisure* is on the increase, with more specialist minority interests spawning specialist magazines and shops, although these usually require relatively high disposable incomes. Fourth, there is the *threat of the mob* linked to rising unemployment and poverty: young people socialize on the streets and sometimes their behaviour spills over into lawlessness or even riots.

These four trends all affect tourism. Home centredness and individuality lead to a greater preference for self-catering and villa holidays. Out-of-home recreation interests lead to a demand for more active recreation while on holiday. Connoisseur leisure creates a demand for specialized holidays, while unemployment and the threat of the mob means that there is an increasingly polarized group who do not have access to tourism in an increasingly tourism-conscious society (see chapter 3). Tyrell (1982) notes another trend in modern society, that there is a blurring of the distinction between work, education and leisure. Educational courses are followed as a form of leisure, while some forms of domestic tasks such as gardening or do-it-yourself have a dual function as work and leisure. Given these societal pressures, the continued growth of disposable income amongst those in work, and further advances on the supply side of the tourism industry, it is not surprising that there have been changes in mass tourism.

In mass tourism, the tourist gaze is focused on the extraordinary as a reaction to the 'miserable' conditions of the urban–industrial localities in which the bulk of the working and lower middle classes live. The extraordinary has mainly been presented as sunshine and sand, or ski slopes. However, the conditions of mass tourism have been changing, and there is now the challenge of what Urry (1990) terms 'postmodernism'. The essence of the mass tourist gaze had been distinctive phenomena – such as beaches and sunshine – which occurred at specific time periods and distinctive places located away from the localities in which people lived. However, postmodernism has led to the dissolution of the boundaries between high and low culture, and between different cultural forms such as art, architecture, shopping and tourism. As a result, the tourism gaze has become indistinguishable from other social and cultural practices:

> Pleasure was associated with being away from the place in which one worked and from the boring and monotonous pain of work, especially of industrial production. Now, however, such a division is much less clear-cut. Pleasures can be enjoyed in very many places, not all concentrated at the seaside. There has been a proliferation of objects on which to gaze, including the media. What now is tourism and what is more generally culture is relatively unclear. Pleasures and pain are everywhere, not spatially concentrated in particular sites (Urry 1990, 102).

Urry uses this argument to explain, in part, the decline of the traditional British seaside resort. These are no longer perceived as being so extraordinary; there is better accommodation available in towns and cities, while leisure centres can simulate beach conditions. There are also new attractions in the forms of theme parks, heritage museums and other centres of recreation, so that almost everywhere has become 'a centre of spectacle' (see chapter 8). While domestic seaside resorts in northern Europe – such as Blackpool or Scheveningen – have suffered from this trend, there are also signs of decline in foreign destinations such as Spain, at least in those resorts which have become more familiar to the mass tourist and therefore cease to be 'centres of spectacle'. This is not to say that tourism *per se*, or mass tourism, is in terminal decline; far from it, since large parts of the populations of less developed countries have yet to enjoy any holiday tourism. In the developed countries, second and third holidays are spreading from the middle classes to the working classes, or at least to those with disposable income. There is, therefore, likely to be a continued increase in mass tourism, but the tourists will seek out new venues and new kinds of objects to gaze upon. This will mean that resorts will grow and decline more rapidly, and their cultural content and built form will also change. However, the essential features of mass tourism – spatial and temporal polarization, dependency and external control, and intense environmental pressures – will remain little changed.

TEN

Urban Tourism

The Dimensions of Urban Tourism and Leisure

Urban areas of all types act as tourism destinations, attracting domestic and international visitors, including holidaymakers, as well as those on business and conference trips. This is not surprising as towns and cities offer a wide range of attractions, which tend to be highly concentrated spatially. Moreover, tourism in these environments is an extremely diverse phenomena in at least three different ways. The first concerns the very heterogeneous nature of urban areas themselves, distinguished as they are by size, location, function and age. The other two dimensions are associated with the sheer variety of facilities offered, i.e. their multifunctional nature, together with the fact that such facilities are very rarely solely produced for, or consumed by, tourists but by a whole range of users (Ashworth and Tunbridge 1990, 52). Such users, and the facilities to supply their needs, define a whole range of different 'types of city'. Thus we can talk about the 'tourist city', the 'shopping city', the 'culture city' and the 'historic city', all of which may exist within a particular urban area (Burtenshaw et al. 1991, 165; see also figure 10.3).

For most commentators it is this very diversity that has led to urban tourism being difficult to describe (Law 1985, 2). Consequently, until relatively recently, it has been misunderstood as a social, economic and geographical force, and much underestimated in its importance (Vandermey 1984, 123; Blank and Petkovich 1987, 165; Ashworth, 1989). However, such criticisms have become less relevant since the late 1980s, as increasing political and academic attention has been focused on the significance of urban tourism as a spur to economic and environmental regeneration.

Urban tourism is also characterized by the fact that cities very often exist within distinctive spatial networks, which function at two different levels. One of these, as Ashworth and Tunbridge (1990, 51–2) point out, sees urban areas operating regardless of their regional and national contexts, with particular cities forming parts of important tourism circuits. At a West European level, Paris, London and Rome may operate as part of an international tourism network. At a national level, within the UK, the overseas visitor circuit encompasses London (which accounts for almost 59 per cent of all overseas visitors to the UK), Edinburgh, Bath, Stratford and York; all of which are linked by strong historical and cultural factors. At a second spatial level, the tourism activities of cities, especially from the viewpoint of domestic tourists and local visitors, exist within a strong regional framework. In this context, cities act as important focal points for a region's tourism industry. Once again, this apparent dichotomy of spatial functions highlights the complex nature of urban tourism, together with the difficulties in isolating how facilities are perceived and used by different types of visitors.

One way in which to consider the different dimensions of tourism in cities is to view the urban environment itself as a 'leisure product', which also has many common elements with the idea of an urban tourism product (Jansen-Verbeke 1986, 85–88). For example, both are based on the spatial concentration of a variety of facilities, together with characteristic environmental features. As shown in figure 10.1, these dimensions can be identified in terms of an 'activity place', which defines the supply of facilities, and an overall 'leisure setting', thus covering both physical as well as sociocultural facilities. In this perspective, three main elements, or levels of facilities, may be recognized; primary elements covering major tourist attractions, which in turn are supported by retail and catering facilities (secondary elements), and a general tourist infrastructure (conditional elements).

While such an approach allows a systematic consideration of the supply side of urban tourism, it is not without its difficulties. For example, in many cities the so-called secondary elements of shops and restaurants may well be the main attractions for certain groups of visitors. Similarly, as we shall see later in this chapter, the importance of the 'leisure product' in an urban setting is also open to debate when discussing the factors that act as motives for sightseeing tourism (Jansen-Verbeke 1986, 87).

The supply-side elements identified in figure 10.1 tend to have distinctive geographies within urban areas, a fact recognized by the numerous attempts to provide a spatial model of the so-called tourist city (for general overviews, see Ashworth and Tunbridge 1990;

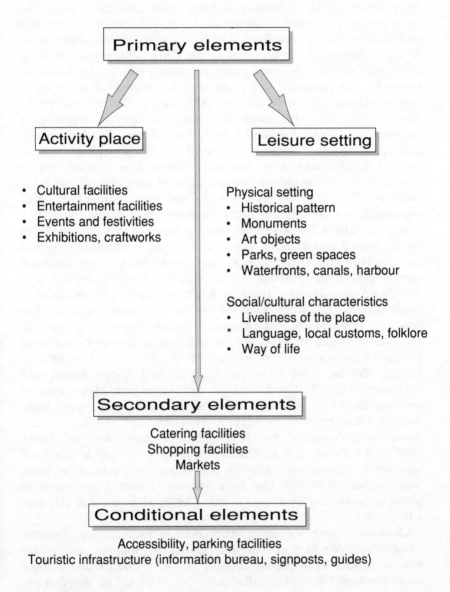

Figure 10.1   Urban tourism and leisure settings
Source: Jansen-Verbeke (1986)

Pearce 1987c). These attempts range from studies that have placed tourism and leisure facilities within the overall framework of classical concentric land-use models (Yokeno 1968), through to those that have sought to define a 'recreational business district' (Stansfield and Rickert 1970), or a 'central tourist district' (Burtenshaw et al. 1991) by extending the concepts of the CBD. In many other cases, the spatial models have been based on specific supply-side variables, especially the locational distribution of hotels and other forms of tourist accommodation (Gutiérrez 1977; Vetter 1985; Pearce 1987c; Knoll 1988). In some cases these studies take an evolutionary approach that shows the early development of hotel locations in certain cities, and the spatial development of such groupings. Indeed, Knoll's (1988) study shows the early imprint that tourism and its related facilities has had on the structure of central Köln, with the majority of today's tourist areas being well established by the mid-eighteenth century (figure 10.2). Drawing on a range of studies, Ashworth (1989) has suggested that six types of hotel location can be recognized within cities, and that these are controlled by factors such as land values, accessibility, environmental amenity, historical inertia and, in the postwar period, planning controls. In box 10.1 are shown the six main types of locational clusters resulting from these factors, to which may be added a seventh category that describes those hotels located close to major tourist attractions. In the case of Köln, for example, the influence of the city's cathedral on hotel locations is clearly highlighted in figure 10.2. The different factors affecting hotel locations obviously vary geographically and over time. Thus, in North America and Australasia, higher rates of car ownership have produced more motels located along major highways; a factor stressed by Mayo's (1974) findings of the influences determining American motorists' choice of motel and by Pearce (1987c). In places such as London, a primary determinant of hotel location in the postwar period is that of planning control, as many local authorities in the city have restricted hotel development to preserve residential land use (Eversley 1977; Horwath and Horwath Ltd 1986).

Of course, there are many other tourism facilities found within cities which also have recognizable spatial distributions, one of the most numerous of which are catering and specialized tourism-orientated retailers. Once again, distinctive forms of urban development are influential. Thus Smith (1983) has highlighted some of the different spatial associations and emphasized the marked linear distributional pattern of catering establishments in many Canadian cities. Work in Paris by Bonnain-Moerdyk (1975) has also served to show

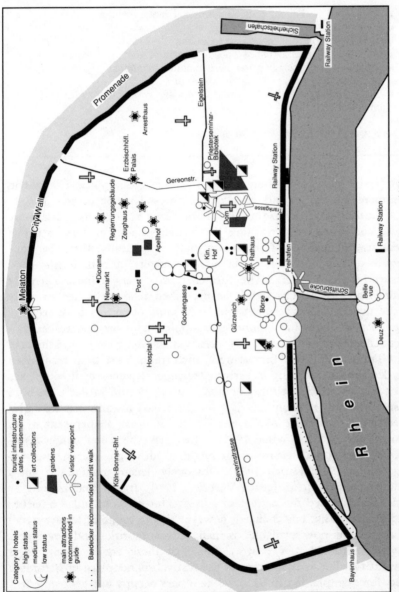

Figure 10.2 Tourism facilities and related facilities in nineteenth-century Köln

Source: Knoll (1988)

Box 10.1   The main types of hotel clusters found in urban areas

• Traditional market/city gate locations in historic centres
• Major tourist attraction locations
• Railway station/road approach locations
• Main access road locations outside of central areas
• Medium-sized hotels in good environmental locations
• Large modern hotels in zone in transition
• Large modern hotels in urban periphery on motorway or airport interchanges

Source: modified from Ashworth (1989)

---

how restaurants have often had to move as geographical changes in commercial activities and entertainment areas have occurred.

A further very diverse group of functions relating to tourism are those concerned with retailing. Both tourists and visitors to urban areas use all manner of shops but, more specifically, they also contribute to the formation of distinctive clusters of both tourist- and leisure-related retailers. The former term covers a more narrowly defined area of activity, while leisure-based retailing is just as likely to be used by local residents. Indeed, some observers have recently argued that a growing number of shopping trips are leisure-based, a fact reflected in the growth of specialized shopping centres (Ashworth and Tunbridge 1990). Increasingly, such trends have been recognized by developers, resulting in early redeveloped leisure–retail complexes such as Covent Garden in London, and the Forum in Paris. In both cases the retail environment is strongly biased towards leisure activities, and in the case of Covent Garden at least 33 per cent of all visitors are tourists (Wood 1981). There have been few detailed studies of tourist and leisure-based retailing, although interest is growing (Kuhn 1979; Jansen 1989). Obviously, leisure retailing is not a new phenomenon, as Jansen-Verbeke (1990) argues that as long as cities have existed the pattern of going to town has included a leisure experience. What has changed, however, is the range of leisure–retail environments now available, as many city authorities and developers have constructed new centres. Some of these are in town, as at Covent Garden in London or at the festival marketplace in Baltimore (see, for example, figure 10.7), while others occupy out-of-town/edge-of-town locations. In both cases we can speak of theme park shopping centres, as discussed in chapter 8, which cater for a leisure-based experience and are directed at the middle class. Such centres range in scale from the very large West Edmonton Mall in Canada, which combines distinctive leisure-based components (10 per cent of floorspace), 800 shops and a 'Fantasyland' Hotel, and the Metro-Centre in the UK, through to smaller so-called 'free-time' shopping centres in Germany. Such developments blur the distinctions between so-called primary and secondary leisure products, as tourists become increasingly attracted to these stage-managed shopping experiences.

It is clear from the discussion so far that tourism facilities have distinctive and diverse spatial distributions within urban areas. Moreover, when taken together with major attractions and cultural facilities, such activities provide fundamental components in the character of urban environments. As Pearce (1987c, 189) argues, the geography of urban tourist attractions and related facilities are best considered via networks of '. . . nodes, clusters of nodes, and [the] routes linking them'. In New York, for example, Broadway and Fifth Avenue have dominated the city as its major thoroughfares since the early twentieth century (Jakle 1985, 268–9). In terms of tourist demand, such an urban geography is often described by the many tourist circuits that feature in guides to particular cities. Where these are formalized through organized bus or coach tours, geographers have been able to map such circuits (Burnet and Valeix 1967). The critical nodes within these spatial circuits are viewing points which allow visitors to gain a general perspective of the city. Such tourist nodes and pathways can also be defined by the location of major tourist attractions and functional districts, enabling the tourist city to be geographically identified.

The Tourist in the City

All tourists and visitors approach cities with definite expectations of its sights and attractions (Jakle 1985, 246). Such expectations are formed not only by a variety of social experiences and information sources which produce distinct images of urban areas, but they also vary with the type of visitor. Within the somewhat limited literature on visitor activity in urban areas, two main perspectives can be identified. One concerns types of users and visitor motivation, while the other, with an even smaller research base, examines visitor behaviour within the city.

In terms of identifying visitor types and their motivations, problems centre on devising a meaningful classification of visitors. Jansen-Verbeke (1986, 88) notes, for example, that urban tourists can be distinguished '. . . from other visitors by two criteria, "their place of residence", situated outside the urban hinterland, and "their motives for visiting" '. Within this particular view tourists are identified by length of travel, being people drawn from outside the city region. This is a somewhat simplistic, if practical, approach that is very often used in surveys of urban visitor behaviour undertaken by local authorities (Blank and Petkovich 1987). It is obviously dependent on discovering visitor motivations through questionnaire methods. For this reason the work to date is still fragmented along the lines of individual city case studies. In North America some cities have received detailed attention over a number of years (Blank and Petkovich 1979), while in Europe, Jansen-Verbeke (1986) has researched Dutch towns, Ashworth and Tunbridge (1990) Norwich, and Buckley and Witt (1985) Glasgow. Beyond these published results lies a wealth of local authority sponsored reports (for English examples see Shaw et al. 1990 on Plymouth; ETB 1984 on Chester).

Most of these studies, together with nationally based surveys, provide general information on the purpose of visit. In large British towns (those with populations over 100 000), short- and long-stay holidaymakers account for around 44 per cent of all bed-nights, and those visiting friends and relatives 24 per cent, with business and conference tourism a further 20 per cent (English Tourist Board 1981). In table 10.1 is shown similar tourist-based information for selected US cities, which highlights the variation in tourist usage of different urban areas. Obviously, tourists are only one set of urban visitors (see figure 10.3). Indeed, much of the detailed research at the individual city level has attempted to focus on the different motivations between tourists and other urban visitors. In Holland, Jansen-

Table 10.1   Types of trips to selected US cities

Purpose	Percentage of trips		
	Orlando	Indianapolis	Portland
Visit friends and relatives	18	38	29
Business/conference	12	30	30
Outdoor recreation	6	3	3
Entertainment/sightseeing	53	8	13
Personal reasons	5	13	17
Shopping	1	0	3
Others	5	8	5
Totals	100	100	100

Sources: US Census of Travel (1977), Blank and Petkovich (1987)

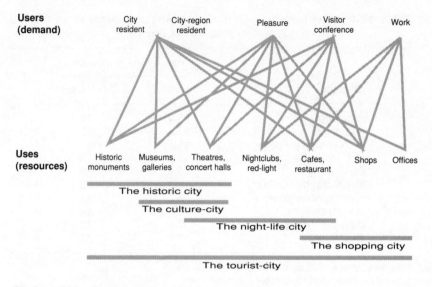

Figure 10.3   Functional areas in the 'tourist city'
Source: Burtenshaw et al. (1991)

Verbeke (1986) has shown that the obvious motivational differences between tourists and day visitors (drawn from the local area) concern the priority given to 'having a day out' and 'sightseeing' by tourists, compared with 'shopping' and 'visiting restaurants' by day visitors (table 10.2). Some, but not all, of these differences have been borne out in British cities. For example in Chester, 21 per cent of day visitors, compared with only 4 per cent of the tourists, came because of the shops, although detailed comparisons are difficult because of differing methodologies (English Tourist Board 1984, 13).

To date, much of our knowledge of urban tourism has come from the study of tourist facilities and their locational distributions. However, as was emphasized in the previous section, many of the components of the 'tourist city' can only be fully understood through more detailed research on visitor behaviour. Two important research questions are the following: How closely do visitor motivations match their actual use of facilities? And how do visitors use the various nodes and routeways that seemingly make up the 'central tourist district'?

Neither of these critical issues has been pursued closely in the research literature. Ashworth and de Haan (1986) have undertaken limited work on Norwich, comparing the motivations of visitors with their actual use of facilities in the city, while Jansen-Verbeke (1986) has examined visitor activity patterns in three Dutch towns. The

Table 10.2   Main reasons given by tourists and day visitors for visiting city centres: Dutch cities, 1985

	Percentage responses	
Reasons	Tourists	Day visitors
A day out	29.3	3.0
Shopping	13.6	30.0
Professional purposes	12.7	6.2
Visit family/friends	10.4	1.8
Sightseeing	9.1	0.5
Visit restaurant/pub/bar	6.9	14.3
Walking around	3.2	3.4
Visit market	2.9	5.0
Daily purchases	2.7	12.3
Visit museum	1.1	2.0

Note: sample sizes; 375 tourists and 762 day visitors
Source: modified from Jansen-Verbeke (1986)

main points to emerge from these studies are that the vast majority of trips are of a multifunctional nature and that visitors who are attracted to one particular facility in a city invariably make use of many others. In Norwich, for example, while 18.9 per cent of holiday-makers came primarily to visit the castle and cathedral, 35 per cent also used the city's restaurants and department stores (Ashworth and Tunbridge 1990, 121–3). Studies in America of Minneapolis–St Paul have shown that people visiting friends and relatives in the city also generate large volumes of retail sales (Blank and Petkovich 1987, 166). One of the most detailed studies of visitor behaviour is that by Tuynte and Dietvorst (1988), who have examined visitor linkages between museums in Nijmegen (Holland) and the town's other facilities. From this research a number of key functional linkages were identified, including a 'museum and shops' combination which covered 26 per cent of the visitors, and a 'museum–general sightseeing' cluster encompassing 22 per cent of visitors.

These functional linkages also produce particular spatial patterns, although geographers have rarely considered the activity space of urban tourists. Notable exceptions are Murphy (1980), working on Victoria in Canada, and Chadefaud (1981), who has presented detailed maps of Lourdes (France) showing the activity space of both organized groups of tourists and those travelling independently. The former had much more concentrated zones of activity compared with the relatively dispersed patterns of independent tourists. In both

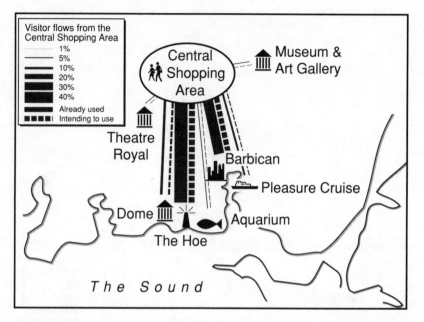

Figure 10.4   Visitor movements within Plymouth, 1992

these studies pedestrian flows were the prime source of information and, to a large extent, functional linkages had to be inferred. A more detailed and accurate method of examining the activity space of tourists is to ask visitors which urban facilities they used and in what order. In this way functional linkages can be placed in a spatial framework. Such a study has been undertaken in Plymouth (Shaw et al. 1990). Visitors to the city were asked which tourist attractions they had visited before shopping in the central retail area, and which they intended to use after shopping. Some of the results from this survey (of over 4000 visitors) are shown in figure 10.4, which highlights the strong linkages between the historic part of Plymouth (the Barbican), the Hoe (a major tourist area) and the central retail area.

The information presented for Plymouth (figure 10.4) provides details of the routeways and nodes that comprise the city's 'central tourist district', which in this case is relatively concentrated. In much larger urban tourist environments, such as London, the action space – and hence the routeways and nodes – of tourists are obviously more complicated, as illustrated in figure 10.5. In London the information is based purely on the main sites visited by overseas tourists and therefore does not give the same detailed linkages as the Plymouth

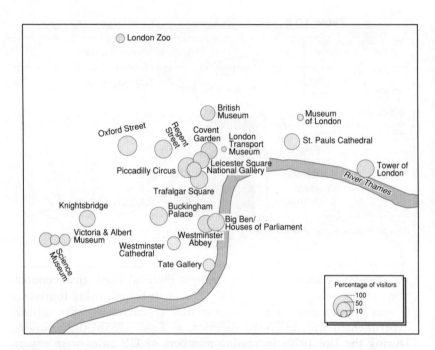

Figure 10.5   Major patterns of tourist visits in Central London, 1989

study, although in both cases we can obtain impressions of the spatial complexity of tourist behaviour.

Tourism and Urban Regeneration

Tourism in large and historic cities is not a new trend; for example, Paris, London, Rome and New York all have long-standing tourism industries. Unfortunately, it is difficult to document the scale and importance of urban tourism in a comparative context, since few statistics exist; those that do suggest that, at an international level, European cities are dominant (table 10.3). At a national level, in English cities such as York and Bath, it has been estimated that tourism contributed around £53 million and £45 million per annum, respectively, during the mid- to late 1980s.

While tourism was traditionally recognized in historic towns, within large cities and industrial centres the significance of tourism had been neglected until the 1980s; since then it has been perceived as having important roles in economic and environmental improvements (see Law 1992). The issue of tourism's role in urban regenera-

Table 10.3 International visitor nights in large cities

City	Millions of visitor nights
London	c.20
Paris	16
Rome	5.6
Madrid	5.5
Athens	4.7
Vienna	4.6
Munich	2.6
Amsterdam	2.5
Brussels	2.4
Copenhagen	2.1

Source: modified from Ashworth and Tunbridge (1990)

tion has had strong international dimensions (Falk 1987) concerning the transfer of ideas, and even stronger political ideological connotations in countries such as the UK. The ideas behind using tourism as a spur to economic and environmental regeneration were initially experimented with in North America, as Law (1985b) demonstrates. During the late 1970s increasing numbers of US cities were experiencing decline of their central cores, sapping the strength of their economic base. Political and business interests combined to shape a new set of policies aimed at office development, tourism and gentrification (Fainstein 1983), although tourism was seen as the prime motivator of change (Judd and Collins 1979). Tourism was selected because it was a growth industry, provided jobs and could lead to environmental improvements. At the heart of this strategy is the idea that visitors will be attracted to the city, thus generating income and jobs. Furthermore, as tourism develops, new facilities will help create a better urban environment, some of the benefits of which will be passed on to local residents, and there will be a general improvement in the image of the city to would-be investors (Law 1991a, and see figure 10.6).

An important example of the initiation of this tourism-based strategy is the city of Baltimore, which commissioned a plan for revitalizing its run-down inner harbour area in 1964. The overall plan was based on people having direct access to the shoreline and so the first step was to return this area to public ownership, with the city buying land, clearing derelict sites and laying out a waterside park. As the plan developed, tourism took a more prominent role, especially with the completion of the Convention Centre in 1979 and the Harborplace festival shopping centre in 1980 (figure 10.7). In addition, a

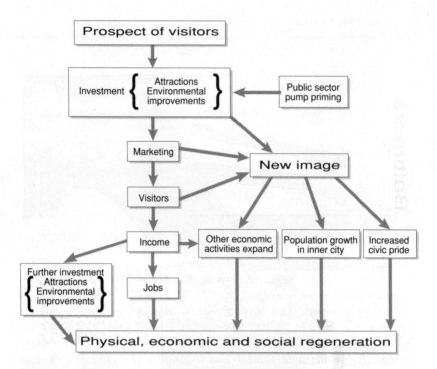

Figure 10.6   The processes of tourism-based urban regeneration
Source: Law (1992)

World Trade Center was completed in 1977, together with a science museum and 12 new hotels opened between 1984 and 1987 (Law 1985b, 21).

These developments in Baltimore have certainly been successful in economically and environmentally improving a part of the downtown area, as well as developing a significant tourism and convention trade. Limited data are available on the scale of change, although survey data in the early 1980s showed that the volume of visitors increased from 2.25 million in 1980 to 6.8 million by 1985. Over the same time period, visitor expenditure grew from $125 million to $400 million, and a fifth of all visitors came from outside of the region (Law 1985b, 24). In addition, the Baltimore Office of Promotion and Tourism estimated that, in 1981, tourism accounted for 16 000 jobs, a figure which increased to 20 000 by 1988.

The apparent success of Baltimore appears to have been based on two critical factors. The first was that the city was in receipt of large Federal Government grants, gaining more money under the Urban Development Action Grant (UDAG) scheme than any other US city.

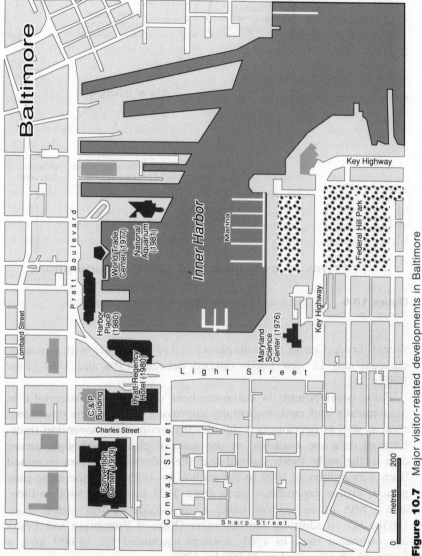

Figure 10.7 Major visitor-related developments in Baltimore

This was particularly significant for some of the large-scale projects; for example, the inner-city hotel development was stimulated in 1981 by a $10 million UDAG (Law 1985b, 18–21). The second factor was strong and stable political leadership which was able to carry through long-term, ambitious plans.

We have dwelt on the Baltimore case because it has been used as a template by other cities, especially in the UK where the British government and agencies such as the English Tourist Board have stimulated the take-up of these ideas. As in the USA, tourism in the UK was a growth industry during the 1980s at a time when other sectors of the economy were stagnant. During 1985 tourism's economic role was promoted in three key reports, The Banks Report (Banks 1985), the Confederation of British Industries (1985) report and, most influentially, the Young report (1985). These stressed three key elements of tourism; its labour-intensive nature, its strong local economic multiplier effects and the low capital cost of job creation (less than one-half of that in other economic sectors). Such promotional material was not lost on city authorities suffering massive economic restructuring, especially when grants were also available from the English Tourist Board.

The focus of national authorities such as the English Tourist Board was on using tourism to revitalize the inner-city areas of depressed industrial environments (English Tourist Board 1981). Local city authorities responded quickly and enthusiastically, so much so that by the mid-1980s a number of cities had started either to introduce or to strengthen tourism. As can be seen from table 10.4, a wide range of tourism developments was initiated, with conference and business tourism providing a strong component (Law 1987), together with industrial heritage sites. In 1982 Manchester, for example, created the Castlefield Urban Heritage Park, which included using an old warehouse as a new museum of science, together with other purpose-built visitor attractions (including the Granada TV studios) and restored Roman sites (Law 1991b, 14). Since the mid-1980s tourism projects have proliferated in the city, with the former Central Station being converted into a large exhibition centre (GMEX); significantly, a 'Tourism and Leisure Association' was formed in 1980. This latter organization has the specific aim of bringing together the public and private sectors, the marriage of which has formed a central theme in the state's approach to inner-city renewal (Law 1988).

Much of the development of 'new' forms of urban tourism is associated with effective marketing strategies. Cities have created new marketing organizations and have developed key slogans to present a positive image to potential visitors. Glasgow has led the way in this

Table 10.4 Tourism development in selected UK cities

City	Population	Visitor characteristics	Economic impact
Birmingham	1 million	91% business and conference tourism (I million + visitors)	£170 million (1983) 34 000 jobs (1985)
Glasgow	765 000	Mixed, day visitors and 40% overseas tourists	£57.6 million (1982) 5 000 jobs (1982)
Liverpool	510 000	Mixed, many day visitors	£58 million (1982) 10 000 jobs[a] (1982)
Bradford	460 000	Specialized trips and packages (30 000+); 500 000 visits to National Museum of Photography	£4.5 million
Nottingham	271 000	Mixed, but 58% business tourism in hotels	£16 million (1980)
Cardiff	200 000	Mixed market, mainly day visitors (439 000)	

[a]Impact figures based on Merseyside data
Source: Law (1985c)

respect with its 'Glasgow's miles better' campaign, which has proved a potent marketing force. Perhaps one of the most significant and unique blends of image creation has been by Bradford in industrial West Yorkshire. Bradford was quick to market itself for special interest holidays and to develop short-break holiday packages, based on cultural tourism (the Brontë sisters), an industrial heritage tour, television themes and the National Museum of Photography, Film and Television (Buckley and Witt 1985, 207).

The faith in tourism to regenerate urban areas was reaffirmed in 1989 with the English Tourist Board's launch of their five-year 'Vision for Cities' campaign. This formalized links with central government's 'Action for Cities' programme, as well as introducing four key elements for urban tourism development (box 10.2). As in the earlier case of Baltimore (which figured prominently in the campaign's launch), great emphasis was given to the partnership of public and private enterprise. The process was focused on five inner-city areas in Cleveland (North East England), the Black Country (Midlands), Sheffield, Manchester and London, which were to act as models to inspire other urban areas. In addition, a number of Tourism Development Action

---

Box 10.2 Key elements in the English Tourist Board's 'Vision for Cities'

- Bring together partnerships of key public and private personalities
- Prepare an agreed comprehensive development framework
- Bring forward key development projects within the agreed framework
- Undertake a concerted and coordinated action programme of environmental and infrastructure improvements

---

Programmes (TDAPs) were established, which are partnerships between national agencies (tourist boards) local authorities and the private sector with the purpose of promoting tourism development. The whole aim of the programme is to '. . . dispel the myth that tourism is a fringe activity' and 'by the early 1990s. . . to see private and public sector investment in tourism and leisure projects rise to £3–4 million' (English Tourist Board 1989, 2).

At this stage it is worthwhile reiterating the perceived benefits of tourism to urban regeneration in order to obtain a clear picture of just what the various government-led initiatives are attempting to achieve. In basic terms the potential benefits of inner-city tourism developments are threefold. The first, and the most important in the policy documents, concerns economic benefits, especially the creation of new jobs. For example, within the five-year ETB programme, the desired target is to create 250 000 new jobs. Second, there are physical and environmental improvements to the inner-city area. In the promotional material for the 'Vision for Cities' campaign, the role of tourism was to create a 'positive image' (English Tourist Board 1989, 2), while in physical terms '. . . views, squares, streetscapes and waterfronts should be preserved and opened-up' for visitors (Collinge 1989, 2). Such a view recognizes, in policy terms, the main elements of what geographers have termed the 'central tourism district', which in many of the industrialized cities, such as Manchester, corresponds to parts of the inner city. The third and final benefit is that tourism developments can bring improvements and better access to the leisure facilities of local residents. This is based on the presumption that most of these developments are multifunctional, incorporating new hotels, tourist attractions and conference facilities, together with retail and leisure components.

Tourism has been seen by policy-makers at all levels as a major catalyst for urban regeneration. However, what is not clear is tourism's ability to meet such ideals. The final section of this chapter will examine these issues within the context of the three major benefits supposedly offered by urban tourism schemes.

Selling the City: Who Benefits?

The restructuring of inner cities around the development of new tourism and leisure facilities raises questions over the wisdom of such projects. In effect, we can recognize two central issues or areas of debate. One concerns sustainability, and addresses the economic question of whether urban tourism projects can lead to sustained economic growth. The second debate is primarily social, and concerns the distribution of who benefits from these developments. In addition, both of these overlapping debates are strongly linked by the significant geographical issue of how these socio-economic and environmental benefits spread out spatially within the urban area.

Underlying these debates is the problem of how to combine public and private funding, since each tends to have a very different set of goals. Some of the most obvious differences are highlighted by the financial incompatibility of many schemes. Private-sector investment often aims to develop national and international conference facilities, festival marketplaces and international hotels, seemingly with little regard for the leisure needs of local people. Similarly, public and private interest have created land-use conflicts as new tourism schemes have commodified recreational land and created facilities for non-local residents (Spink 1989).

Such perspectives assume that all policy-making surrounding urban tourism projects is led by the demands of private investment. Clearly, this is not always the case, since there are a number of possible outcomes from mixed public and private tourism ventures (box 10.3). However, what appears to be happening is a shift towards urban tourism and leisure schemes becoming more institutionalized as they become strongly linked with economic policy. In a review of the structuring of leisure policies in Dutch cities, Mommaas and van der Poel (1989) identify the increasing dominance of private investment as dating from the 1980s. From this period, urban leisure policy changed from being local authority driven and funded (often linked

---

Box 10.3   Possible outcomes of privately and publicly funded inner-city tourism projects

- Private success, public success (best outcome) – may be good benefits to local residents
- Private success, public failure – no real benefits to local residents
- Private failure, public failure (most unlikely outcome)

in the 1970s to the needs of the unemployed), to a situation in which public and private partnerships developed to service the 'pleasures of the well-to-do' rather than reintegrating disadvantaged groups (Mommaas and van der Poel 1989, 263). The thrust of the new policy, as illustrated by the building of the World Trade Centre in Rotterdam, was to attract a larger share of the middle-class job market. Such trends, which are also clearly identifiable in British cities, relate to the institutionalized nature of capital accumulation as central government has reduced financial support but increased the costs of local authorities. The outcome has been that urban areas have been forced to compete with each other to attract new invest-ment. Increasingly, having a positive image, which can be secured through good tourism and leisure facilities, has become a major factor dominating all other forms of leisure policy-making.

The selling of urban areas through such image creation has led some observers to question the whole *raison d'être* of tourism and lei-sure developments. Bramham et al. (1989, 4) asks '. . . is the city a product to be sold on the tourism market', or 'is a city a place to live, where people can express themselves?' From this perspective the new initiatives in urban tourism are seen as divisive, as they target the affluent members of society who have lifestyles based on sophisticated commodity aesthetics and conspicuous patterns of consumption. Such patterns of development ignore or at best neutralize local ways of life merely by reproducing the leisure interests of the wealthy (Bramham et al. 1989, 296).

Running counter to these arguments are those which claim that tourism brings prosperity and jobs to inner-city areas, as well as high-profile environmental improvements. Evidence to support all these claims is often sadly lacking since, as Law (1992) emphasizes, few studies have assessed the impact of tourism. In Baltimore, for example, where the processes have had longest to run, Sawicki (1989) argues that many of the new jobs associated with retailing represent a geographical shift in employment within the CBD. Similarly, the creation of new opportunities for local businesses was somewhat lim-ited. Indeed, the evidence from long-established tourism cities in the UK, such as Bath, suggests that while tourism has strong multipliers, there is also considerable leakage from the local economy (Bath City Council 1987). Other studies of specific inner-city projects show that job creation varies greatly between different projects, with hotels creating few off-site jobs compared with museums, retail develop-ments and marinas (table 10.5). Furthermore, as Vaughan (1990, 24) argues, while tourism may not be providing the highest paid or skil-led jobs, it is '. . . providing jobs relevant to many of the [skills of]

Table 10.5 Estimates of job creation by selected inner-city tourism developments

Jobs created	Types of development		
	Museum/shop	Hotel	Marina
On site	460	80	14
Off site	285	6	26
Totals	745	86	40

Source: Vaughan (1990)

unemployed resident of the inner city'. This somewhat negative approach is the pragmatic one accepted by many policy-makers.

Even if the numbers and quality of jobs are debatable, supporters of inner-city tourism point to its role in helping to refurbish the urban environment. Once again hard evidence is scant. However, Sawicki (1989) agrees that tourism schemes in Baltimore brought rapid improvements to the immediate inner harbour area, although there was little evidence that such environmental upgrading had spread to other parts of the inner city. Set against these limitations, however, is the fact that tourism schemes tend to produce a rapid change in the physical environment, albeit in relatively small areas.

Finally, we can return to the critical issue of whether tourism offers a viable and sustainable industry for depressed urban economies. Law (1991) has highlighted two features relating to such issues; one concerns the types of visitors, while the other examines trends in visitor numbers. In the case of Manchester day visitors were dominant, as they represented 75 per cent of all visitors. Furthermore, of those visiting from an overnight stay, only half were staying in hotels, with the rest visiting friends and relatives. Day visitors bring fewer economic benefits than staying tourists, as illustrated in a survey of Plymouth in Devon, where the average spend by a day visitor was £17.3 compared with £22.5 by staying tourists (Shaw et al. 1990). However, as table 10.5 showed, not all urban tourism projects are based on leisure visits, as an increasing number of cities are competing in the business, conference and exhibition market. This is an important, growing market (Exhibition Industries Federation 1990), but it is also extremely competitive. In the USA, major conference meetings have increased from just under 843 000 in 1981 to well over 1 million by 1987; while in the UK it has been estimated that there were some 700 000 conferences (including smaller ones) in 1990 (Law

Table 10.6   Average expenditure patterns of conference delegates

	Percentage of expenditure	
Items	European cities	US cities
Accommodation	44.8	43.5
Meals in hotels	7.7	10.7
Meals out	14.8	16.0
Entertainment	13.4	5.1
Shopping	14.6	9.8
Local tours/transport	4.7	6.8
Other	0.0	8.1
Totals	100.0	100.0

Source: modified from Lawson (I982)

1992). Unlike leisure visits, business and conference tourism generates income around hotels and, as table 10.6 shows, meals out, together with shopping. More importantly, on average, visitors to conferences spend between two and two and a half times per day more than the typical tourist (Smith 1989; Law 1992).

The other issues to emerge from Law's work are that tourist demand is extremely variable, and highly dependent on offering new products. In other words, the implementation of an urban tourism policy is not a one-off investment. Tourist attractions and infrastructure must be constantly updated, a fact which also applies just as strongly to the conference and exhibition market. Tourism can therefore only be a viable economic policy if city authorities recognize the need for such long-term strategies. Failure to realize this, or indeed the very dynamic nature of tourist demand, could leave some cities in a similar position to many of the older coastal resorts – short on visitors and with few new jobs.

ELEVEN

Rural Tourism

Nature as Playground and the Filter of Social Access

Rural areas have long played an important role in tourism and leisure within the developed world. For example, it is estimated that in 1990 three-quarters of the population of England visited the countryside at least once (Countryside Commission 1991). Similarly, Cordell et al. (1980) consider that much of rural America has appeal to drivers and walkers. Rural areas are perceived variously; as idylls to which to escape from the pressures of modern urban–industrial society, as untamed wildernesses which can rekindle the human spirit, or simply as large reserves of open areas suitable for space-intensive recreational pursuits. Harrison (1991, 11) catches something of the importance of rural areas when she writes '. . . visits to the countryside can be regarded as the actualization of deeply-felt needs, especially those relating to the high quality of life associated with the countryside'. Williams (1975), in his seminal work *The country and the city*, similarly emphasizes that the country has come to be defined in terms of qualities which are absent from urban life. In short, the notions of urbanity and rurality are cultural definitions.

The previous argument can be extended to rural recreation and tourism. There is nothing that is inherent in any part of the countryside that makes it a recreational resource. Patmore (1983, 122) writes that 'There is no sharp discontinuity between urban and rural resources for recreation, but rather a complete continuum from local park to remote mountain peak.' He rightly emphasizes the substitutability of some locales for recreation, although not necessarily for tourism. However, the argument is more complex than this, because 'the countryside' has its own special appeal over and above its actual physical attributes (see chapter 8). That is to say, the countryside is socially defined as a premier area of leisure and tourism in modern societies; and visiting the countryside is a socially valued end in its own right.

While rural areas are highly esteemed as locales for leisure and tourism, their use is heavily contingent. The main contingencies are social access and the politics of countryside ownership. The remainder of this section considers the first of these contingencies as it pertains to the twentieth-century traditions of rural tourism and recreation in the developed world. Three concepts are critical here; the rural opportunity continuum, accessibility and time–space budgets.

There is a *rural opportunity continuum* in the countryside as the location of a wide range of outdoor leisure and tourist activities, although over time the composition of these has changed. The Countryside Commission surveys for the UK in 1977 and 1984 (reported in Harrison 1991) emphasize just how quickly the use of rural areas may change. Drives, outings and picnics were the most popular activities in 1977, followed by walks over two miles. By 1984 walks had been significantly overtaken in popularity by visiting unspoilt countryside and by visiting historic buildings. Obviously, rural recreation is segregated within the countryside, since different areas provide settings for different types of leisure activities.

Spatial variation in the use of the countryside is also a question of *accessibility*. In the simplest terms, Clawson and Knetsch (1966, 36–8) consider that there are three types of rural recreation zones. There are accessible user-oriented areas, resource-based areas with relatively scarce but often inaccessible physical attributes, and intermediate areas between these two types. Sidaway and Duffield (1984) provide empirical information on variations in activities at different rural sites (figure 11.1). Many outdoor recreation activities are of similar relative importance in all rural zones, but others vary with distance from the city. In the urban fringe, visiting zoos or watching sport are relatively important; in the countryside near towns walking and visiting historic settlements are relatively important; and in the intermediate and distant countryside driving or outings are particularly important.

On its own, the rural opportunity spectrum does not explain the varied use of different parts of the countryside. Access depends on more than simple distance, and expressed demand is not the same as latent demand, let alone need. Indeed, accessibility is socially conditioned. It depends on access to transport, either public or private. Research in the UK by the Countryside Commission (1991) confirms that there is a socio-economic basis to the use of the countryside. Frequent users tend to be young professional households with one or two cars; occasional users tend to be clerical and skilled manual

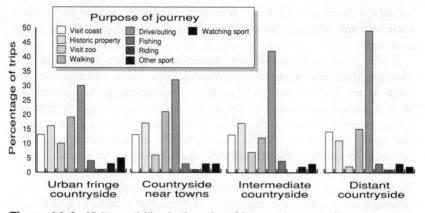

Figure 11.1 Visitor activities in the urban fringe and countryside
Source: Sidaway and Duffield (1984, 792)

households with one car; and rare users tend to be low-income, unskilled, unemployed, elderly or ethnic minority households without a car. There is an underclass in terms of access to rural tourism and leisure, just as there is in the general construction of developed societies (see chapter 3). This is not simply a question of household car ownership, for there are transport-poor individuals in both high- and low-income households. The accessibility of children and of disabled persons may be constrained by lack of access to a car. In one-car households, one spouse will inevitably have inferior access to transport. There is, therefore, a strong social filter on the accessibility of the countryside to individuals.

Another social filter on countryside recreation and tourism stems from the fact that the distances involved, and the nature of some of the activities, impose particular *space–time budget constraints*. Large blocks of time are required in order to be able to enjoy some types of rural activity, such as long-distance walking. As a result there are distinctive daily, weekly and annual rhythms to recreation and tourism in different parts of the countryside. This can be represented in terms of a simple model relating the consumer's available leisure time to travel time (figure 11.2). During the working day leisure time is limited to a few hours at best, so that most recreation for the urban dweller will occur within the city. If a full day is available then the nearby countryside becomes a possibility for recreation. If a weekend is available then short-break rural tourism is feasible. Finally, if a long holiday is available then longer-distance travel to more remote areas becomes possible. This is, of course, only a model of possibilities, and there is no automatic conversion of leisure time into parti-

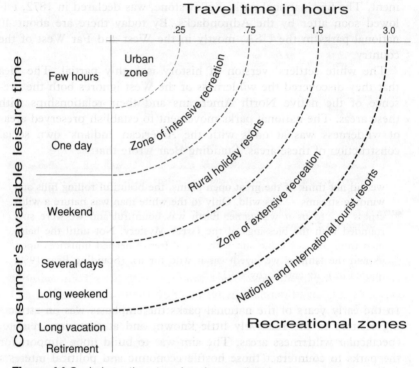

Figure 11.2   Leisure time, travel and recreational zones
Source: Pigram (1983, 35)

cular activities in particular rural zones. This is because of the inter-vening social filter of accessibility, as well as of competing leisure and tourism opportunities, interests and perceptions.

The Changing Social Construction of Rural Tourism

The classic case of the social construction of rurality is white Amer-icans' relationship with 'the West', and the changing role ascribed to the American national parks. The early white settlers feared the rugged and mountainous areas of the West as areas which were beyond human control (Hartmann and Hennig 1989). In the mid- and late nineteenth century, the image of the social parks was con-structed more positively. The 'wilderness' of the frontier areas came to be seen as a public good, for they were considered to offer restora-tive and psychological benefits and to be a balm to the stresses of urban–industrial life. This contributed to the National Parks movement. The first national park, Yellowstone, was declared in 1872, followed soon after by the Adirondacks. By today there are about 40 national parks in the USA, mostly in the West and Far West of the country.

The white settlers' version of history is highly partial. The idea that they discovered the wilderness of the West ignores both the presence of the native North Americans and their relationships with these areas. The national parks movement to establish preserved areas of wilderness was at odds with the American Indians' own social construction of these areas. Standing Bear wrote that:

> we did not think of the great open plains, the beautiful rolling hills and winding streams . . . as wild. Only to the white man was nature a wilderness . . . to us it was tame. Earth was bountiful and we were surrounded with the blessings of the Great Mystery. Not until the hairy man from the east came and with brutal frenzy heaped injustices upon us and the families we loved was it wild for us. (Standing Bear 1989; quoted in Katz and Kirby 1991).

In the early years of the national parks the emphasis was on attracting visitors to the relatively little known, and at that time remote, spectacular wilderness areas. The aim was to build upon support for the parks to counteract those hostile economic and political interests who were fundamentally opposed to their establishment. The opposition included the settlers who had been encouraged by government to develop these areas, but now saw large parts of the resources of the West locked away within national park boundaries. However, by the end of the century there was an expanding American middle class with available leisure time and income. The railways, and later the automobile, made the national parks far more accessible to them. Places such as the Rocky Mountains national park rapidly grew in popularity; '. . . once experienced, the cool, dry climate of Colorado's mountains became addictive for Americans seeking refuge from the hot summers of the East and Midwest' (Buchholtz 1983, 117). By 1915 wilderness was to be cherished rather than conquered.

After 1945 the growth of population, disposable incomes and individual mobility contributed to a further social reconstruction of the national parks. They were now seen as national playgrounds and the park authorities responded by expanding the facilities offered to visitors. By the 1960s the social climate of opinion was again in transition as public concern mounted over the exploitation of the wilderness. As Buchholtz (1983, 212) writes 'Observers wondered whether park planners had curried too much favour with concrete and Cadillacs'. The emphasis shifted to preserving and, if necessary, recreating the natural. Public access to the most congested places was reduced, and the 1964 Wilderness Act set aside large expanses to be preserved in their 'primitive' state. These roadless areas within the national parks, mostly in the West (figure 11.3), were to be visited but not remained in. In no way has this reduced the attractiveness of the national parks, and visitor numbers doubled to an estimated 282 million between 1972 and 1986. Indeed, the designation of wilderness areas was very much in sympathy with the growth of the consumer movement in the USA and the demands for quality consumption, whether in terms of goods or leisure time.

The wilderness emphasis was an attempt to preserve the 'natural' element within the national parks. However, as Katz and Kirby

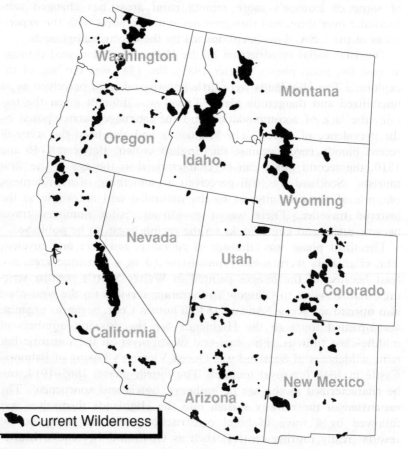

Figure 11.3 The US national wilderness preservation system

(1991, 266) forcefully argue, the national parks are simulacra (copies without originals) of primordial nature: 'Yosemite . . . is as much a construction as Disneyland, and perhaps more insidious in that its construction is concealed within a supposedly external nature'. As such, the present social construction of the national parks cannot be taken as fixed, and may well shift again as the social construction of rural tourism and leisure changes.

The European experience of rural tourism and leisure is somewhat different from that of the USA, not least because wilderness has hardly existed in Europe in recent centuries, or even decades. Hence, European national parks are mostly attempts to preserve cultural landscapes 'raw' and are very different from those found in the USA, Canada, Australia and Africa, many of which seek to preserve little changed primordial landscapes. Nevertheless, the social construction of some of Europe's more remote rural areas has changed substantially over time, and this provides some parallels with the experiences of the USA. This is epitomized by the Scottish Highlands.

Tourists' social construction of the Highlands has passed through at least five main phases (Butler 1985). Pre-1745 was the 'age of the explorer'. The Highlands were little known and were perceived as an uncivilized and dangerous place. Travel was difficult given the terrain, the lack of accommodation and the language barrier posed by the prevalence of Gaelic. The Highlands had also been the scene of recent bloody revolt against the English crown. Between 1746 and 1810, the second phase can be characterized as the age of the 'first tourists'. Scotland was still perceived as something of a wilderness, but one of growing interest to the naturalist and accessible to the intrepid traveller. There was a growth in visitor numbers, travel became easier and guide books on the region began to be published.

The third phase was 'the age of romance, red deer and royalty'. The Highlands were socially reconstructed as a romantic area, not least because of the images painted in Walter Scott's popular writings. Rail services to Glasgow and steamer services up the west coast also opened up access. And in 1846 Thomas Cook began to organize accompanied tours to the Highlands for the growing numbers of middle-class tourists. The final seal of approval on the romantic but tame wilderness of Scotland was Queen Victoria's leasing of Balmoral Castle in 1848 for royal tourism. The fourth phase, 1865–1914, can be characterized as the age of 'railways, hotels and sportsmen'. The expansion of the railway system into the Highlands themselves was followed by a wave of hotel construction, and the emergence of resorts (really touring centres) such as Oban and Inverness. Individual travel for active tourists, such as hunters, and landscape consumers had now become highly accessible for the middle classes. Finally, in the twentieth century, in the age of the automobile, the Highlands have become 'a popular playground for the car owner'. This has brought about intense environmental pressures and cultural challenges as the number of tourists and in-migrant families has increased.

There are parallels between the Scottish and the American experiences. A change in social construction led to and accompanied a growth in tourist numbers. Images of tranquillity and natural beauty attracted large numbers of visitors but, in turn, these threatened to undermine the social constructs which had given appeal to the areas. However, there is a fundamental difference between the areas in that the Highlands were essentially a cultural landscape with a few areas of wilderness. It has therefore not been feasible to return them to even a simulacra of primordial nature. Furthermore, any attempt to freeze the existing cultural landscape would have conflicted with the aspirations and needs of the communities which lived in these areas.

In the late twentieth century the growth of incomes, leisure time and mobility, amongst all except the underclass, has led to more intense demands being made on rural areas as locales for recreation and tourism. At the same time, the social construction of rural areas in the developed world has undergone further, often subtle changes. As a result, the conflicts over the use of the wilderness and national park areas are being replicated more widely throughout the developed world. The middle classes, in particular, have given greater centrality to 'true' countryside in their systems of values. Urry (1990) argues that this is linked to postmodernism and the disillusionment with the effects of modernism, such as regimented and massive architecture. This is also associated with the demand for 'real' holidays, away from the mass tourists and large-scale tour organizations (see chapter 12). Not surprisingly, rural areas – and the opportunities that they provide for more individualized tourism and recreation – have figured prominently in these new forms of consumption.

Both Urry (1990) and Thrift (1989) believe that the service class has been particularly influential in the new movements. The service class is '. . . a powerful . . . social grouping which has begun to impose its framework upon much of wider society, and hence its distinctions of taste have become highly significant for other classes and social groups' (Urry 1988, 41). The service class has taken both the countryside and heritage into its value systems. This is reflected in the more than 500 per cent increase, between 1971 and 1987, in the memberships of organizations such as the National Trust and the Royal Society for the Protection of Birds (Thrift 1989). Further evidence of this movement is provided by the Countryside Commission (1991) which found that frequent users of the countryside tend to be young professionals, who are mobile and wealthy enough to be able to maximize their use of the countryside.

All of this has a strong impact on rural communities, and is also leading to growing pressures to open up access to private and publicly owned land in the countryside. It also contributes to the demands for preservation of the 'traditional' countryside, and for stronger controls on modern agriculture and other economic uses of the countryside. Harrison (1991, 157–8) writes that '. . . the pastoral idyll of the post-enclosure landscape is revered – the countryside aesthetic – but scant attention is paid to the conditions of rural society which support it'. In other words, the service class demands are for the countryside to be constituted principally as a zone of tourism, leisure and consumption, rather than as a zone of production. This and related themes are pursued in the following section.

Trouble in Paradise: Competition and Conflict in Rural Tourism and Leisure

The construction of the countryside as a zone of consumption necessarily results in a number of sharp contradictions. The first of these is the reality that, in most developed countries, the vast majority of rural lands are in private ownership, which severely constrains accessibility. Second, there are many social constructions of rural areas – as pastoral idylls, as areas of recreation and as production zones. All or some of these may come into conflict with each other. There is the potential for host–guest conflicts, which is given a special twist in developed societies by the prevalence and continuing growth of second-home ownership. Finally, there is the question of the rural residents' own access to recreation.

Space is critical to outdoor recreation, and this is particularly true if it possesses certain attributes such as water resources, beautiful landscapes or, for example, areas suitable for mountaineering or hang gliding. Such factors incorporate both the main leisure functions of rural areas: as a setting for space-extensive activities and as an attractive landscape, the visiting of which is an object in itself. Yet, in practice access to rural areas is often circumscribed by the system of capitalist landownership. This is particularly the case in agricultural lowland areas, where the immediate pressures for recreation are often intense. In the UK, for example, less than 2 per cent of the population control and farm more than 70 per cent of the land surface, while the bulk of the population live on just 11 per cent of the land. The latter's demands for recreation are likely to bring them into conflict with farmers whose main interest is the productive capacity of the land. This is particularly acute in countries with high population densities, such as the UK and Netherlands. In the USA, Canada and Australia the conflict over land ownership is less intense, as there are large areas which are still relatively little used, and where access is open despite the existence of nominal private ownership. The conflicts are also less in Sweden where there is a tradition of allowing recreation on private land, so that this has now become a part of public expectations. This contrasts with the UK where public access to the countryside has had to be contested. In the 1930s the Ramblers Association and other groups campaigned to gain access to upland areas such as Kinder Scout; in the 1960s and 1970s there were campaigns to open up access to publicly owned countryside areas such as reservoirs and Forestry Commission land; and in the 1980s and 1990s attention has focused on the maintenance of the traditional network of rights-of-way footpaths.

One way in which to resolve the conflict between ownership and use of the countryside is for the state to intervene via purchasing land to be set aside for recreational use. This is the system in much of the USA, and it is also employed in some European countries such as Spain. However, it is not the approach adopted in the UK, where the national parks were constituted as areas of privately owned lands with some additional means of development control. This is linked with the fact that they were preserving cultural landscapes rather than wildernesses: apart from anything else, the cost of outright state purchase was greater than the government of the day was willing to contemplate. In terms of active outdoor recreation, this offered some prospects of greater control over the landscapes in the parks, but it did not confer any new rights of access on the public (Patmore 1983, 175).

Even where there is outright purchase or nationalization of land for enclosure in national parks or other reserve areas, this does not obviate the conflict with private capital. The objective of developing parks either as wildernesses or as recreation zones may generate conflicts with the owners of adjoining private lands. For example, in Spain the Coto Donana has been set aside as a publicly owned national park which is an internationally important ecological area. However, the attempt to conserve the sensitive ecosystem in the delta area, which is home to large numbers of over-wintering birds, is under threat from changes occurring just outside the park. More intensive agriculture and the demands of coastal tourism are both affecting the water table in the Coto Donana. In this case, there is the added twist that mass tourism is adversely affecting eco-tourism.

The limited supply of available rural recreational spaces inevitably leads to their multiple use. Pigram (1983, 43) writes with respect to outdoor recreation that 'Pressure on capacity . . . may stimulate multiple use of space over time for varied activities, day and evening, week and weekend and year round rather than seasonal'. An upland area may face competing demands from long-distance walkers, short-distance strollers, climbers, car-borne tourers, horse riders, skiers and campers. Each of these groups makes demands on the use of the rural space. While they may vary somewhat in their temporal rhythm, there are also time periods and some zones in which they tend to coincide (see figure 11.4).

Some of these recreational uses may be complementary, or at least non-conflicting, but others are in direct competition and may generate negative externalities for other activities. The interests of walkers and hunters may coincide if they require simultaneous use of the same space, say at weekends in 'the season'. Skiers and mountain walkers may not appear to conflict directly in that they make claims on the same recreational space in different seasons. However, the skiers' activities and associated infrastructure may scar the mountain slopes and detract from their value as a setting for mountain walking.

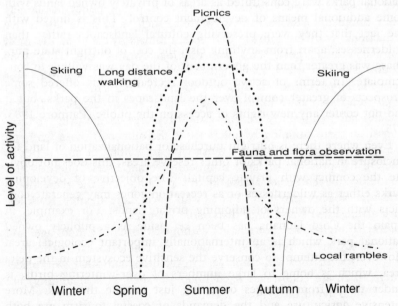

Figure 11.4   Space–time clustering of rural recreational activities

Table 11.1   Types of recreational carrying capacities in rural areas

Type	Characteristics
Ecological carrying capacity	Beyond this, recreational use affects the ability of a site to restore itself by natural means, with or without the assistance of human management
Social carrying capacity	Beyond this, the quality of the recreational experience declines for the participant because of the presence of other users in the same space

Source: after Pigram (1983)

Whether activities do impinge upon each other depends on whether they, individually or collectively, exceed the recreational carrying capacity of an area. The concept is subdivided by Pigram (1983) into two components, as shown in table 11.1.

This raises important management issues of how to regulate access to rural recreation sites. There is, first, the absence of market mechanisms, for there are usually no entrance fees to rural recreational spaces. Direct state intervention is also limited, as rationing access to rural recreational zones has usually been seen as too sensitive an issue for policy formulation. Instead, public policy has largely been confined to less sensitive controls, such as creating alternative attractions to divert tourists and recreationists away from the most popular beauty spots. This was the logic behind the UK's 1968 Countryside Act which facilitated the establishment of country parks near the larger cities; the aim was to create intervening recreational opportunities so as to influence the flows of rural recreation. If such policies fail significantly to relieve the pressures on the prime recreation sites, then rationing by tolerance is the outcome; those who will use the site at prime times are those who are willing or able better to tolerate the presence of large numbers of other users. There is also implicitly uneven social access in this resolution of the recreational carrying capacity problem. Those who have more flexible work/leisure arrangements and high disposable incomes – such as some professionals, high-salary households without children of school age, and the wealthy active retired – are those most able to avoid the peak usage times. In contrast, employees in factories and other workplaces where there are traditional fixed holidays (such as coal mining) are least able to avoid these peak times.

Another issue in the use of the countryside is second homes. Cus-

tomer loyalty is often a feature of rural recreation and tourism, and in
its most extreme form this is manifested as second-home ownership.
Second-home ownership is widespread in Europe, although it varies
considerably between different countries: rates of second-home ownership are 16 per cent in France, 22 per cent in Sweden but only 2
per cent in the UK (Shucksmith 1983). The differences can be
explained in terms of the economics of the housing market, cultural
evaluations of town and country, and the intergenerational links
between urban and rural families. For example, late and rapid urbanization in Greece and Portugal means that there are large numbers
of first- or second-generation city residents. They often inherit or
own old family houses in the countryside which provide them with
second homes.

The use made of second homes is also highly variable. They can,
in effect, be dual first homes, with the family dividing its time
equally between this and the town residence. This is very much the
pattern found around London, New York and other large cities,
where a rural home is used at the weekend as a complement to a city
apartment. Alternatively, the second home may be located in a more
distant region; Parisian families own second homes in the South of
France and German families own second homes in Austria. In these
cases visits may be made less frequently, and may involve seasonal
long stays. Both of these forms of second-home ownership have
implications for local communities (table 11.2). They have similar
impacts on local school rolls (and hence school viability) and housing
markets. However, weekend homes are likely to bring greater economic benefits to the community, offer more custom to local services
and usually lead to greater involvement in community life. Where
second homes form a large proportion of the local housing stock this
can seriously undermine the viability of rural communities, as, for
example, sometimes happens in the English Lake District. Similarly,
Vincent (1987, 117) notes in the Val de Aosta (northern Italy) that
the sale of farmhouses as second homes can mean that 'A culture

Table 11.2 Contrasting effects of second homes

	Weekend homes	Second homes
Economic	Greater	Lesser
Housing market	Equal	Equal
Local schools	Equal	Equal
Local services	Greater	Lesser
Cultural	Greater	Lesser

once meaningful to locals becomes a hollow theatre for tourists'. They can therefore become an object of political conflict and, where this is combined with cultural and linguistic issues, to violent campaigns as in North Wales.

Finally, there are the often neglected issues of rural residents' leisure and recreation. Other than for access to open countryside, there is a hierarchy of recreational facilities which leaves rural residents at a disadvantage. While villages may possess a football pitch and, sometimes, even a swimming pool or a squash court, they will not have cinemas, major spectator arenas or leisure centres. Access to these will depend on mobility and distance, and on the social filter of accessibility. Therefore, in terms of access to facilities, rural leisure deprivation is the mirror image of urban leisure deprivation. The actual extent of rural leisure deprivation is highly variable. This is well documented in the case of the UK: Ventris (1979) has found considerable differences between villages according to their size; Hill (1982) found different patterns between newcomers and locals; and Glyptis (1989) found differences according to location, gender, class, age and mobility. In general, there is little difference between rural and urban populations in terms of their interests, but there are considerable variations in terms of the choice and quality of facilities available.

Farm Tourism and Rural Household Economies

Rural tourism enterprises probably do not differ significantly from tourism enterprises in general (see chapters 5 and 6). The one exception is farm tourism, where the tourist activity is closely intertwined with farming activities, and often with the viability of the household economy. The farm tourism market is already substantial, but it is also subject to strong growth. On the demand side, this is fuelled by the growth in the short-break holiday market, by the demand for more activity-based holidays, and by the growth in the numbers of more critical consumers reacting against mass tourism (see chapter 12). On the supply side, the global crisis of agricultural overproduction is contributing to a drive to farm diversification in both Europe and North America, with tourism being one of the more significant options available to farmers.

There are two main forms of farm tourism – non-accommodation and accommodation-related activities – and some farms participate in both. Non-accommodation activities include farm trails, farm museums, hunting and fishing, horse riding and catering (especially 'farm teas' in the UK). These are based on commercializing existing resources, whether natural, social or simply the 'green' and wholesome image of farm life. Accommodation activities are the second form of farm tourism. This may involve letting serviced rooms in the farmhouse, or self-catering arrangements, whether camping or farm cottages. These two forms tend to involve different social relationships between hosts and guests.

Within Europe, Austria has one of the more highly developed farm tourism sectors. For example, Pevetz (1991) considers that 30 000 farms let approximately 250 000 beds in 150 000 guest rooms in Austria. In the UK it is estimated that almost 20 per cent of farms in 1990 were involved with farm tourism; 9.5 per cent with accommodation, 5.5 per cent with leisure activities, and 4.8 per cent with horse-related activities. Similarly, farm tourism is a vital element in the household economies of several regions in Canada, where there are an estimated 1000 rural hosts, 70 per cent of whom are farmers. In the USA farm tourism is less numerically important and takes two main forms; dude ranches in the west and vacation farms, such as those found in New England (Vogeler 1977). The dude ranch is usually purely concerned with tourism, but the vacation farm has similarities with European farm tourism.

While there is no doubting the empirical evidence for the importance of farm tourism, it has proved to be difficult to conceptualize this in theoretical terms. Friedmann (1980) has suggested a possible theoretical framework for examining the family farm. She emphasizes that there is a balance between the internal and external relationships of households, between the division of labour within the farm and its involvement in larger divisions of labour beyond the farm. Several different strategies for generating additional income are available to the family farm which is seeking to survive in the face of capitalist relationships. Some family members may work off the farm, some may emigrate or the farm economy may be diversified, perhaps into tourism. Each of these involves a different balance between external and internal relationships and has associated divisions of labour.

Friedmann's approach has been criticized. According to the theory, diversification of the farm into tourism as part of a survival strategy is likely to be more important in smaller or part-time farms where there is presumably a greater need for alternative non-agricultural earnings. Yet, farm tourism seems more commonplace on larger rather than on smaller farms in most countries. In addition, Goodman and Redclift (1985) argue that family farms are not an ideal type. Instead, there are many types of family farms and the balance of internal–external relationships changes during the course of the family life-cycle. This is because the amount of time not devoted to looking after dependents, and tourism resources (the number of spare rooms for letting), vary according to the number of children or elderly relatives in the household. Another qualification is the motivation for diversifying into farm tourism; if it is to generate investment for the agricultural sector rather than household survival, then farm tourism is not necessarily more common on smaller farms. Despite these reservations, Friedmann's work does highlight the role of tourism as one element in the balance between external and internal relationships on the farm.

Farm tourism makes demands for additional labour on the farm. While this can be hired labour it is much more likely to be undertaken by family members, usually the women in the household. As Bouquet (1987, 93) writes '. . . in family-based tourist projects, economic relations double with those of kinship'. This will generate new gender divisions of labour and may also affect the distribution of power within the family. There is no inevitable outcome to the new gender division of labour; it is contingent upon the nature of the farm economy, the local economy and culture. It also depends on the role of women within the household prior to the introduction of farm tourism. Gasson (1980), for instance, considers that there are three ideal role types for farm women: as home-centred farm housewives; as working farm wives assisting their husbands within a clear division of labour; or as women farmers on their own account or jointly. The introduction of farm tourism will have very different impacts on the gender division of labour in each of these ideal types.

The diversity of experiences of farm tourism is considerable, but one constant is that women usually carry the burden of tourism-related work on working farms. In Austria, for example, Dernoi (1991) reports that women have a double and often a triple role in the division of labour: 81 per cent of wives involved with farm tourism also have to help with the field work, and almost all do most of the household chores. Similarly in Devon, Bouquet (1982) found that technological changes in milking methods had made it possible for women to redistribute their labour from agricultural activities to farm tourism. Many of the services provided for the tourists – such as cooking or making beds – are similar to those provided for the family. Thus Bouquet (1987, 98) writes that '. . . the women concerned seem to have professionalized, or commoditised, a portion of their domestic labour, at the same time as defining a new field of domestic competence for themselves'. While farm tourism usually involves an increase in the burden of work falling upon the farm wife, it may also increase their power within the family. Bouquet, for example, found that wives could use catering for tourists as a lever to obtain improvements to the family home.

The work implications of farm tourism also touch upon the seasonal rhythm of agricultural work. Farm tourism is usually a summer activity and it may therefore clash with the need for agricultural activities at particular times, such as harvest. This does not follow automatically, and Neate (1987), for example, observed that on the Isles of Scilly farm and tourism work dovetail together rather than being in competition. From November to March flowers are harvested, from April to May is the season of early potatoes, and from June to October is the peak time for tourism. Whatever the precise divisions of work, it seems likely that these are due for further reorganization as the crisis of agricultural overproduction in the developed countries leads to increases in the volume and diversity of farm tourism.

PART V

Future Trends

TWELVE

The Future of Tourism

The Tourism and Leisure System: Manipulations and Reactions

Throughout much of this book we have endeavoured to focus on what Britton (1991, 452) has termed the 'wider structures' of tourism. This has been attempted in two main ways: first, by considering tourism as a system of production and consumption, within a wider leisure context; and secondly, through the recognition that such services '. . . cannot be separated off from the social relations within which they are embedded' (Urry 1990, 23). Such an approach has a number of consequences, including the prospect of developing a more critical perspective on the geography of tourism. This may, eventually, contribute to relocating the geography of tourism within the mainstreams of economic, social, political and cultural geography, thereby rescuing it from the methodological and theoretical isolationism of recent decades.

Underpinning much of this new approach is the premise that within capitalist economies social and production relations are carried over into leisure activities. According to Rojek (1985), there are four major characteristics of such leisure structures; privatization, individuation, commercialization and pacification. We have already commented on these elsewhere (see, for example, chapters 1, 3 and 4), but it is useful at this point to highlight two of these characteristics. The first is the trend for society to identify the individual as distinct from the group; especially, as was shown in chapter 3, the linkage between lifestyles and identity. This is an influential force in much of Western society and an important key to understanding possible future trends in tourism. The second main characteristic, previously identified in chapter 4, relates to the processes of commodification or, as Featherstone (1990) prefers, the culture of consumption, which is strongly related to many tourism and leisure activities. As we have seen, many – if not most – tourism and leisure pursuits have clearly been transformed into 'experiences' that can be marketed, sold and bought just as any other commodities.

Britton has developed these ideas to suggest the formation of a more informed geography of tourism, and has also raised the issue of the 'commodification of place'. This, he argues, works through a process by which 'the tourist production system incorporated them [places] into its products' (Britton 1991, 464). Places and sites can be incorporated into the tourism system in two ways. One is through the tourism industry attempting to give more powerful meanings to their products, by associating them with particular places. We saw in chapter 8, for example, how many regions in England (figure 8.2) were being marketed from the perspective of associations with either particular television programmes, historical events or novels. This in itself, however, is not that new, since in the early twentieth century places such as Cornwall were being marketed by the Great Western Railway in terms of images of the Mediterranean (Shaw and Williams 1991a). The second process of incorporation was also mentioned in chapter 8, and concerns the case in which particular attractions are associated with or assimilated into a tourism product; as in the way that some new shopping centres have taken on leisure and tourism roles. In both cases, the commodification of place occurs through the basic economic mechanisms of advertising, packaging and target marketing. But the essence is the conversion of experiences or images into exchange relationships. The precise form of these depends on the structure of production, including the labour process (chapter 7) and the organization of capital (chapter 9).

The recognition of these mechanisms takes us on to another stage in which particular spatial processes and forms can be identified. As Britton (1991) shows, these can relate to a number of issues, including territorial competition and geographically uneven accumulation. The former is demonstrated by the increasing competition between cities for certain types of visitors (see chapter 10), a process which Harvey (1985) has discussed in terms of the competition for positions as major centres of consumption. Increasingly, such a spatial division of consumption is being driven by the attempts to sell urban areas as major tourist attractions and conference locations. Zukin (1990) sees some of these developments in terms of an investment in cultural capital, which is strongly related to tourist expenditure. Such tourism and cultural capital manifests itself in terms of the construction of four recognizable forms (Britton 1991). First, we can identify the increasing importance of international capital markets within tourism and leisure as investment money is attracted away from industrial property to tourism developments, which offer shorter realization periods. Second, such investment money and the processes of place commodification have produced specific forms of built environments. These range from cultural and convention centres through to theme parks, hotel complexes and new shopping centres. The processes of investment also spill over into major acts of refurbishment, as seen, for example, in the case of Baltimore (see chapter 10). Third, these built forms (either newly developed or refurbished) attract various spectacles such as major sporting contests, which are designed to encourage greater levels of consumption. Fourth, and strongly related to the processes of urban renewal using cultural and tourism capital, are festival markets. These are 'an amalgam of symbolic capital and spectacle combined with a celebration of impulsive shopping' (Britton 1991, 472). Of course, these four forms are all closely related and together create large consumption spaces in or around major urban areas.

In this sense the tourism and leisure system, as described by Rojek (1985), Zukin (1990), Urry (1990) and Britton (1991), plays a pivotal role in understanding the spatial and built form of much of our contemporary landscape. In addition, the tourism system also strongly underpins much of the behaviour of consumers. The processes involved in much of tourism marketing have increasingly attempted to persuade consumers that they are purchasing not only a release from the constraints of their working lives, but also some form of 'lifestyle signifier'. At one level the tourism system is therefore strongly manipulative of consumption levels and behaviour patterns. In its extreme form it leads, as we saw in chapter 9, to mass tourism. However, tourism and consumption levels are not purely the outcome of manipulation by the image-makers. The system is also capable of being restructured by changes in consumer demand and, more importantly, consumer ideas about the ethics of consumption. Such reactions are best seen by taking one significant example, the growth of so-called 'green' or sustainable tourism. This forms the focus of the remainder of this chapter, and serves to illustrate a different area of tourism development.

Critical Consumers and the Growth of Green Tourism

Increasingly, commentators on tourism have noted changing societal notions towards these activities, especially concerning the rise of green tourism. The promotion of environmental issues in tourism appears to have been inspired by the 'green movement' itself, rather than by any original political initiatives, with Krippendorf's (1986) so-called 'critical consumer tourists' leading the demand for environmentally sound holidays. He writes of the need for 'a soft and humane tourism' for which 'the common goal must be to develop and promote new forms of tourism, which will bring the greatest possible benefit to all the participants – travellers, the host population and the tourist business, without causing intolerable ecological and social damage' (Krippendorf 1987, 106). This process represents one of the major forms of change in societal attitudes towards tourism and leisure, although its roots are set within a wider framework of ecological values associated with the green consumer. Gordon (1991) argues that many of these consumers are part of the so-called 'inner-directed' lifestyle group, as discussed in chapter 3. For them, leisure pursuits are strongly motivated by: creativity, health, new experiences, human relations and personal growth. As a consequence, environmental issues become an area of considerable importance and Gordon (1991, 10) believes '. . . it is their growth . . . which has helped to ensure that business and politicians treat the environment as a matter of genuine concern'. Elkington and Hailes (1992), who co-authored *The Green Consumer Guide*, have attempted to spread the notion of green holidays both to consumers and the industry by identifying a simple typology of sustainable tourism. Consumers are asked to consider 'what sort of holidaymaker are you?' (Elkington and Hailes 1992, 22–30) and are given guidelines on how to participate in 'green holidays'.

These changes in holiday tastes and demand, by at least one important set of tourists, do appear to be causing parts of the tourism industry to reassess its image, leading some tour and travel companies to offer 'ecological holidays'. 'Natural Habitat', a US-based operator, and 'Nature Track', who specialize in holidays for observing wildlife on high-quality natural history adventures, are typical of these newer style approaches. Without entering into the debate as to the real value of such tours in environmental terms, these examples do point to the consumer-led form of this type of tourism which has, in some cases, caused a dramatic shift in the relationship between tourism and the environment. Some, such as Urry (1990), argue that this shift is related to postmodernism and the reaction to mass tourism as a form of mass consumption, with the service class (certainly those in the 'inner-directed' lifestyle group) being very much in the vanguard of such movements. Whatever the case, it is certainly more than a passing trend or phase. It may well be, as we argued in the early part of this chapter, that place commodification and mass consumption have produced important structures within society, but we should also recognize that there is a consumer-based counter to these trends. This may only give rise to 'mini mass market segments' (Lickorish 1990), while many tourists will only pay lip-service to 'green holidays', as equally will sections of the tourism system; but this may not ultimately detract from the importance of green tourism.

We should also recognize that political pressure, applied through public policy at all levels of government, is becoming an additional spur to the search for green tourism. At the present time, policy statements and concerns, even within the same country or region, are not consistent – neither are they very often clearly directed. Within the UK, for example, interest in such issues has developed along a number of different lines. One of the more traditional routes has been focused on developing new strategies towards rural tourism (see chapter 11), with the English Tourist Board (1988) and the Countryside Commission (1991) both producing reports which stress that tourism in the countryside should support the objectives of conservation. A more radical departure was the establishment in 1990 of a government task force, charged with finding solutions to tourism's impact on the environment. The terms of reference of the task force were twofold: first, to examine the size and nature of environmental problems caused by large numbers of visitors at particular sites; and second, to draw up guidelines on how tourism activities can be harmonized with the need to conserve and preserve the environment (English Tourist Board 1991, 4–5). The whole project was centred around a series of case studies ranging across historic towns, heritage sites, seaside resorts and rural environments. Moreover, the real significance of the report lies in the fact that it has brought tourism–environment relations onto a national political agenda.

A similar, although more wide-ranging debate, has also been taking place at a European level, based around the European Commission's Charter for Cultural Tourism. This again puts great emphasis on developing a responsible tourism policy, which has implications for both the development of cultural tourism as well as planning to relieve the environmental pressures caused by mass tourism (ECTARC 1989). The basis of the Charter is to move away from the short-term gains of tourism, as presently constructed, towards 'the realisation of longer-term economic, cultural and physical environmental benefits, avoiding the danger of exploitation ultimately damaging the environment' (ECTARC 1989, 92). Such goals tend to cut across most of the established relationships between tourism and the environment, giving a further boost to the ideas of green tourism.

Given these political pressures, together with the growth of demands from green-orientated consumers, it seems likely that future patterns of tourism consumption will be strongly polarized. On the one hand, there will be a strong and still viable market for mass tourism, both from existing participants in this form of leisure and, more importantly, from newer consumers. These will come from those countries (some in the developed world) where, at present, holiday-taking is only weakly established. For many of these people, package holidays will provide the easiest access to international travel. By contrast, there is likely to be a continued growth of these more critical consumers whose leisure interests fall within the realms of green tourism.

Both are likely to produce very different tourism geographies in the sense that new spatial forms may emerge, and there is certainly likely to be much stronger public policy control over tourism developments. Much of this is likely to take the form of constraining policies limiting the consumption spaces for mass tourism. In terms of urban–rural conflict, and access to the countryside, some commentators (Gordon 1991, 12) have suggested that it is possible to imagine the development of a three-tier structure of countryside access. First would be the creation of an intensive-use area, containing theme parks, museums and holiday complexes to satisfy the needs of large volumes of people. The second tier would involve a managed lower-intensity area of forests and woodlands for walking, cycling and riding; activities that could fit in with more sensitive landscapes. Finally, the third tier would be more remote areas catering for limited numbers of visitors who would have minimal impact on the environment.

At present such ideas are couched in terms of management plans around particular urban areas but, of course, these could be expanded to the national scale. What does seem certain is that in terms of production within most developed countries, we are less likely in the future to witness the growth of new centres for mass tourism. This market will be increasingly catered for by the restructuring of existing consumption spaces. The major trend in terms of consumption is likely to be the growth in numbers wishing and able to participate in leisure and tourism activities. The World Tourism Organization (1991, 16) predicts that there will be '. . . an increase in the conversion rate of desire to actuality', based on both the proportions of holiday-taking and of multiple holidays. However, access is likely to reflect the inequalities inherent in society; as such, there will be a strong social filter on the use of the countryside, and the persistence of a disadvantaged underclass. If the predictions of long-term employment decline or of structural unemployment are confirmed, then an issue for society is not only the provision of tourism, but also the distribution of social access to this.

Finally, whatever the balance between mass and critical tourism and leisure, the precise form that this takes will be shaped by production-side changes. Most forms of tourism and leisure provision are becoming locked into larger circuits of capital, and labour markets which overlap with other sectors. Societal and economic development will condition, as well as be conditioned by, tourism and leisure developments.

Bibliography

Airey, D. (1983) 'European government approaches to tourism', *Tourism Management*, vol. 4, pp. 234–44.

Alchain, A. A. (1950) 'Uncertainty, evolution and economic theory', *Journal of Political Economy*, vol. 58, pp. 211–21.

Allen, J. (1988) 'Fragmented forms, disorganized labour?', in J. Allen and D. Massey (eds), *The Economy in Question*, London: Sage.

Alvarez, J. R. D. (1988) *Geografia del Turismo*, Madrid: Editorial Sintesis.

American Express (1989) 'Unique four nation travel study reveals travellers' types', News Release, London, 25 September.

Amin, A. (1983) 'The state and uneven development in advanced capitalism', in A. Gillespie (ed.), *Technological Change and Regional Development*, London Papers in Regional Science, 12, London: Pion.

Anderson, G. and Higgs, D. (1976) *A Future to Inherit: the Portuguese Communities of Canada*, Toronto: McClelland and Stewart.

Andrews, F. M. and Withey, S. B. (1976) *Social Indicators of Well-being*, New York: Plenum Press.

Ascher, F. (1985) *Tourism Transnational Corporations and Cultural Identities*, Paris: Unesco.

Ashworth, G. J. (1989) 'Urban tourism: an imbalance in attention', in C. P. Cooper (ed.), *Progress in Tourism, Recreation and Hospitality Management*, London: Belhaven Press.

Ashworth, G. J. and de Haan, T. Z. (1986) *Uses and Users of the Tourist–Historic City: an Evolutionary Model in Norwich*, Field Studies Series 10, Groningen: GIRUG.

Ashworth, G. J. and Tunbridge, J. E. (1990) *The Tourist–Historic City*, London: Belhaven Press.

Atkinson, J. (1984) *Flexibility, Uncertainty and Manpower Management*, Institute of Manpower Studies, Report 89, Falmer: University of Sussex.

Aubrey, P., Herbert D., Carr, P. G., Chambers, D. A., Clark, S. C. and Cook, F. G. (1986) *Work and Leisure in the 1980s: the Significance of Changing Patterns*, London: Sports Council and Economic and Science Research Council.

Bacvarov, M. and Kazacka, D. (1989) 'Free and recreational time in Bulgaria – geographical aspects', in F. Zimmermann (ed.), *Proceedings of the Aus-*

trian Meeting of the IGU Commission of Geography of Tourism and Leisure, Klagenfurt: Institut für Geographie.

Bagguley, P. (1987) *Flexibility, Restructuring and Gender, Employment in Britain's Hotels*, Lancaster Regionalism Group, Working Paper No. 24, University of Lancaster, Lancaster.

Bagguley, P. (1990) 'Gender and labour flexibility in hotel and catering', *Services Industries Journal*, vol. 10, pp. 105–18.

Banks, R. (1985) *New Jobs from Pleasure–a Strategy for Creating New Jobs in the Tourist Industry*, London: HMSO.

Barbaza, Y. (1970) 'Trois types d'intervention du tourisme dans l'organisation de l'espace littoral', *Annales de Géographie*, vol. 434, pp. 446–69.

Baretje, R. (1982) 'Tourism's external account and the balance of payments'. *Annals of Tourism Research*, vol. 9, pp. 57–67.

Barker, M. L. (1982) 'Traditional landscape and mass tourism in the Alps', *Geographical Review*, vol. 72, pp. 395–415.

Baron, R. R. (1975) *Seasonality in Tourism*, London: Economist Intelligence Unit.

Bath City Council (1987) *Economics of Tourism in Bath*, London: Coopers & Lybrand.

Beechey, V. (1987) *Unequal Work*, London: Verso.

Belisle, J. F. (1983) 'Tourism and food production in the Caribbean, *Annals of Tourism Research*, vol. 10, pp. 497–513.

Bell, D. (1974) *The Coming of Post-industrial Society*, London: Heinemann.

Benington, J. and White, J. (1988) 'Leisure services at a crossroads', in J. Benington and J. White, *The Future of Leisure Services*, London: Longman.

Bernardi, R. (1987) 'The emerging trends in hotel design', in A. Sessa (ed.), *Megatrends in International Tourism*, Rome: Editrice Agnesotti.

Bishop, J. and Hoggett, P. (1989) 'Leisure and the informal economy', in C. Rojek (ed.), *Leisure for Leisure: Critical Essays*, London: Macmillan.

Blank, U. and Petkovich, M. D. (1979) 'The metropolitan area tourist: a comprehensive analysis', *A Decade of Achievement, Proceedings of Travel and Tourist Research Association*, pp. 227–36.

Blank, U. and Petkovich, M. D. (1987) 'Research on urban tourism destinations'. In J. R. Brent Ritchie and C. R. Goeldner (eds), *Travel, Tourism and Hospitality Research: a Handbook for Managers and Researchers*, New York: John Wiley, pp. 165–77.

Blasing, A. L. (1982) 'Prostitution tourism from Japan and other Asian countries', Paper presented to Asian Consultation of Trafficking in Women, Manila.

Böhning, W. R. (1972) *The Migration of Workers in the United Kingdom and the European Community*, Oxford: Oxford University Press.

Bond, M. E. and Ladman, J. R. (1982) 'A strategy for developing tourism', *Research in Tourism*, vol. 2, no. 2, pp. 45–61.

Bonnain-Moerdyk, R. (1975) L'espace gastronomique, *L'Espace Géographique*, vol. 4, pp. 113–22.

Boorstin, O. J. (1964) *The Image: a Guide to Pseudo-events in America*, New York: Harper and Row.
Bouquet, M. (1982) 'Production and reproduction of family farms in Southwest England', *Sociologia Ruralis*, vol. 22, pp. 227–44.
Bouquet, M. (1987) 'Bed, breakfast and an evening meal: commensality in the nineteenth and twentieth century farm household in Hartland', in M. Bouquet and M. Winter (eds), *Who From Their Labours Rest? Conflict and Practice in Rural Tourism*, Aldershot: Avebury Press.
Bourdieu, P. (1984) *Distinction*, London: Routledge.
Bramham, P. and Henry, I. (1985) 'Political ideology and leisure policy in the United Kingdom', *Leisure Studies*, vol. 14, pp. 1–19.
Bramham, P., Henry, I., Mommaas, H. and van der Poel, H. (eds) (1989) *Leisure and Urban Processes: Critical Studies of Leisure Policy in West European Cities*, London: Routledge.
British Tourist Authority (1988) *Digest of Tourist Statistics No. 12*, London: BTA.
Britton, S. (1980) 'A conceptual model of tourism in a peripheral economy' in D. G. Pearce (ed.) *Tourism in the South Pacific: the Contribution of Research to Development and Planning*, Christchurch: University of Canterbury.
Britton, S. G. (1981) 'Tourism, dependency and development: a mode of analysis', Occasional Paper No. 23, Development Studies, Canberra: Australian National University.
Britton, S. (1991) 'Tourism, capital, and place: towards a critical geography', *Environment and Planning D: Society and Space*, vol. 9, pp. 451–78.
Brown, B. (1987) 'Recent tourism research in S.E. Dorset', in G. Shaw and A. M. Williams (eds), *Tourism and Development: Overviews and Case Studies of the U.K. and the S.W. Region*, Working Paper No. 4, Department of Geography, University of Exeter.
Brown, H. (1974) 'The impact of the tourist industries on the agricultural sectors, in the competition for resources and the market for food provided by Jamaica', *Proceedings of the 9th West Indies Agricultural Economics Conference*, University of West Indies.
Bryden, J. (1973) *Tourism and Development: a Case Study of the Commonwealth Caribbean*, Cambridge: Cambridge University Press.
Bryden, J. M. (1974) 'The impact of the tourist industries on the agricultural sectors; the competition for resources and food demand aspects', *Proceedings of the 9th West Indies Agricultural Economics Conference*, University of West Indies.
Buchholtz, C. W. (1983) *Rocky Mountain National Park: a History*, Boulder, Colorado: Associated University Press.
Buckley, P. J. and Witt, S. F. (1985) 'Tourism in difficult areas: case studies of Bradford, Bristol, Glasgow and Hamm', *Tourism Management*, vol. 6, pp. 205–13.
Bull, A. (1990) 'Australian tourism: effects of foreign investment', *Tourism Management*, vol. 11, pp. 325–31.

Burkart, A. J. and Medlik, S. (1981) *Tourism: Past, Present and Future*, London: Heinemann.

Burnet, L. and Valeix, M. A. (1967): 'Equipement hotelier et tourisme', in *Atlas de Paris et de la Région Parisienne*. Paris: Berger-Levrault.

Burtenshaw, D., Bateman, M. and Ashworth, G. J. (1991) *The European City: a Western Perspective*, London: David Fulton.

Butler, R. W. (1980) 'The concept of a tourist area cycle of evolution: implications for management of resources', *Canadian Geographer*, vol. 14, pp. 5–12.

Butler, R. W. (1985) 'Evolution of tourism in the Scottish Highlands', *Annals of Tourism Research*, vol. 12, pp. 371–91.

Butler, R. W. (1991) 'West Edmonton Mall as a tourist attraction', *Canadian Geographer*, vol. 35, pp. 287–95.

Castles, S., Booth, H. and Wallace, T. (1984) *Here for Good: Western Europe's New Ethnic Minorities*, London: Pluto Press.

Cater, E. A. (1987) 'Tourism in the least developed countries', *Annals of Tourism Research*, vol. 14, pp. 202–26.

Cavaco, C. (1980) *Turismo e Demografia no Algarve*, Lisbon: Editorial Progresso Social e Democracia.

Cazes, G. (1972) 'Le role du tourisme dans la croissance économique: reflexions partir de trois examplaires Antillais', *The Tourist Review*, vol. 27, pp. 43–7.

Chadefaud, M. (1981) *Lourdes: un Pélerinage, une Ville*, Aix-en-Provence: Edisud.

Chadwick, R. A. (1987) 'Concepts, definitions and measures used in travel and tourism research', in J. R. Brent Ritchie and C. R. Goeldner (eds), *Travel, Tourism and Hospitality Research: a Handbook for Managers and Researchers*, New York: John Wiley.

Champion, A. G. and Townsend, A. R. (1990) *Contemporary Britain: a Geographical Perspective*, London: Edward Arnold.

Cheek, N. H., Field, D. R. and Burdge, R. J. (1976) *Leisure and Recreation Places*, Ann Arbor: Science Publishers.

Chesney-Lind, M. and Lind, I. Y. (1985) 'Visitors as victims: crimes against tourists in Hawaii, *Annals of Tourism Research*, vol. 13, pp. 167–91.

Clark, R. and Stankey, G. (1979) *The Recreation Opportunity Spectrum: a Framework for Planning, Management and Research*, Seattle: US Department of Agriculture Forest Service, General Technical Report, PNW-98.

Clawson, M. and Knetsch, J. L. (1966) *Economics of Outdoor Recreation*, Baltimore: Johns Hopkins Press.

Clevedon, R. (1979) *The Economic and Social Impact of International Tourism on Developing Countries*, E.I.U. Special Report 60, London: Economist Intelligence Unit.

Clout, H., Blacksell, M., King, R. and Pinder, D. (1989) *Western Europe: Geographical Perspectives*, London: Longman, 2nd edn.

Coates, B. E., Johnston, R. J. and Knox, P. L. (1977) *Geography and Inequality*, Oxford: Oxford University Press.

Cockerell, N. (1988) 'Skiing in Europe – potential and problems', *Travel and Tourism Analyst*, pp. 68–81. London: Economist Intelligence Unit.

Cohen, E. (1972) 'Toward a sociology of international tourism, *Social Research*, vol. 39, pp. 164–82.

Cohen, E. (1979a) 'A phenomenology of tourist experiences, *Sociology*, vol. 13, pp. 179–202.

Cohen, E. (1979b) 'Rethinking the sociology of tourism', *Annals of Tourism Research*, vol. 6, pp. 18–35.

Cohen, E. (1988a) 'Traditions in the qualitative sociology of tourism', *Annals of Tourism Research*, special issue, vol. 15, pp. 29–46.

Cohen, E. (1988b) 'Tourism and AIDS in Thailand, *Annals of Tourism Research*, vol. 15, pp. 467–86.

Cohen, E. (1988c) 'Authenticity and commoditization in tourism', *Annals of Tourism Research*, vol. 15, pp. 371–87.

Cohen, R. B. (1981) 'The new international division of labor, multinational corporations and the urban hierarchy', in M. Dear and A. Scott (eds), *Urbanization and Urban Planning in Capitalist Society*, London: Methuen.

Collinge, M. (1989) *Tourism: a Catalyst for Urban Regeneration*, London: English Tourist Board.

Collins, L. R. (1978) 'Review of hosts and guests an anthropology of tourism', *Annals of Tourism Research*, vol. 5, pp. 278–80.

Collins, M. F. (1982) *Leisure Research, Current Findings and the Future Challenge*, London: Sports Council, Social Science Research Council and Leisure Studies Association.

Colton, C. W. (1987) 'Leisure, recreation, tourism: a symbolic interactionism view', *Annals of Tourism Research*, vol. 14, pp. 345–60.

Commission of the European Communities (1987) *Europeans and their Holidays*, vii/165/87-EN, Brussels.

Confederation of British Industry (1985) *The Paying Guest*, London: CBI.

Cooke, P. (1983) *Theories of Planning and Spatial Development*, London: Hutchinson.

Cooper, C. P. (1981) 'Spatial and temporal patterns of tourist behaviour', *Regional Studies*, vol. 15, pp. 359–71.

Cooper, C. P. (1990) 'The life cycle concept and tourism', Conference Paper presented at 'Tourism Research Into the 1990s', University of Durham, 1990.

Cooper, C. P. and Jackson, S. (1985) 'Changing patterns of Manx tourism', *Geography*, vol. 70, pp. 74–6.

Cordell, H., McLellan, R. and Legg, M. (1980) 'Managing private rural land as a visual resource', in D. Hawkins, E. Shafer and J. Rovelsted (eds), *Tourism Planning and Development Issues: International Symposium on Tourism and the Next Decade*, Washington, DC: George Washington University.

Cornet, J. (1975) 'African art and authenticity', *African Art*, vol. 9, pp. 52–5.

Cosgrove, I. and Jackson, R. (1972) *The Geography of Recreation and Leisure*, London: Hutchinson.

Countryside Commission (1991) *Visitors to the Countryside*, Manchester: Countryside Commission.

Cowan, G. (1977) 'Cultural impact of tourism with particular reference to the Cook Islands, in B. R. Finney and K. A. Watson (eds), *A New Kind of Sugar*, Santa Cruz: Center for South Pacific Studies, University of Santa Cruz, pp. 79–85.

Craig, W. (1972) 'Recreational activity patterns in a small negro urban community: the role of the cultural base', *Economic Geography*, vol. 48, pp. 107–115.

Crandall, J. (1987) 'The social impact of tourism on developing regions and its measurement', in J. R. B. Ritchie and C. R. Goeldner (eds), *Travel, Tourism and Hospitality Research: a Handbook for Managers and Researchers*, New York: John Wiley.

Crompton, J. L. (1979) 'Motivation for pleasure vacation', *Annals of Tourism Research*, vol. 6, pp. 408–24.

Damette, F. (1980) 'The regional framework of monopoly exploitation: new problems and trends', in J. Carney, R. Hudson and J. R. Lewis (eds), *Regions in Crisis*, London: Croom Helm.

Dann, G. (1977) 'Anomie, ego-enhancement and tourism', *Annals of Tourism Research*, vol. 4, pp. 184–94.

de Grazia, S. (1984) *Of Time Work and Leisure*, New York: Anchor Books.

de Kadt, E. (ed.) (1979) *Tourism: Passport to Development*, Oxford: Oxford University Press.

de Kadt, E. (1990) *Making the Alternative Sustainable: Lessons from Development for Tourism*, Brighton: University of Sussex, Institute of Development Studies, Discussion Paper 272.

Debbage, K. G. (1990) 'Oligopoly and the resort cycle in the Bahamas', *Annals of Tourism Research*, vol. 17, pp. 513–27.

Deitch, L. I. (1977) 'The impact of tourism upon the arts and crafts of the Indians of the Southwestern United States' in V. L. Smith (ed.), *Hosts and Guests: an Anthropology of Tourism*, Philadelphia: University of Pennsylvania Press.

Dernoi, L. A. (1991) 'Canadian country vacations: the farm and rural tourism in Canada', *Tourism Recreation Research*, vol. 16, pp. 15–20.

Dex, S. (1985) *The Sexual Division of Labour*, Brighton: Wheatsheaf.

Dicken, P. (1986) *Global Shift: Industrial Change in a Turbulent World*, London: Harper and Row.

Dietvorst, A. (1989) 'Unemployment and leisure: a case-study of Nijmegen', in P. Braham, I. Henry, H. Mommaas and H. van der Poel (eds), *Leisure and Urban Processes: Critical Studies of Leisure Policy in West European Cities*, London: Routledge.

Dimaggio, P. and Useem, M. (1978) 'Social class and arts consumption', *Theory and Society*, vol. 5, pp. 141–61.

Doeringer, P. B. and Piore, M. J. (1971) *Internal Labour Markets and Manpower Analysis*, Lexington: Lexington Books.

Doxey, G. V. (1976) 'When enough's enough: the natives are restless in Old Niagara', *Heritage Canada*, vol. 2, pp. 26–7.

Drexl, C. and Agel, P. (1987) 'Tour operators in West Germany', *Travel and Tourism Analyst*, London: Economist Intelligence Unit.

Dunning, J. H. and McQueen, M. (1982) 'The eclectic theory of the multinational enterprise and the international hotel industry', in A. M. Rugman (ed.), *New Theories of the Multinational Enterprise*, London: Croom Helm.

Earl, P. (1986) *Lifestyle Economics: Consumer Behaviour in a Turbulent World*, London: Wheatsheaf.

Eco, U. (1986) *Travels in Hyper-Reality*, London: Picador.

Economist Intelligence Unit (1988) *International Tourism Report: Spain and Balearic Islands*, London: Economist Intelligence Unit.

ECTARC (1989) *Contribution to the Drafting of a Charter for Cultural Tourism (Tourism and the Environment)*, Llangollen: ECTARC.

Edwards, P. K. (1981) 'Race, residence and leisure style: some policy implications', *Leisure Sciences*, vol. 4, pp. 95–112.

Elkington, J. and Hailes, J. (1992) *Holidays That Don't Cost the Earth*, London: Victor Gollancz.

English Tourist Board (1981) *Tourism and the Inner City*, London: ETB.

English Tourist Board (1984) *Chester Tourism Study*, London: ETB.

English Tourist Board (1988) *Visitors in the Countryside*, London: ETB.

English Tourist Board (1989) *The Inner City Challenge: Tourism Development in Inner City Regeneration*, London: ETB.

English Tourist Board (1990) *British Holiday Intentions*, London: ETB.

English Tourist Board (1991a) *The Future for England's Smaller Seaside Resorts*, London: ETB.

English Tourist Board (1991b) *Tourism and the Environment: Maintaining the Balance*, London: ETB.

Evans, N. J. (1989) *Investigating farm-based accommodation in England and Wales – theoretical framework*, Coventry: University of Coventry, Department of Geography Working Paper 2.

Eversley, D. (1977) 'The ganglion of tourism: an unresolvable problem for London?' *London Journal*, vol. 3, pp. 186–211.

Exhibition Industries Federation (1990) *The UK Exhibition Industry: the Facts*, London: Polytechnic of North London.

Fainstein, S. S. (1983) *Restructuring the City: the Political Economy of Urban Redevelopment*, London: Longman.

Falk, N. (1987) 'Baltimore and Lowell: two American approaches', *Built Environment*, vol. 12, pp. 145–52.

Featherstone, M. (1987) 'Leisure, symbolic power and the life course', in J. Horne, D. Jary and A. Tomlinson (eds), *Sport, Leisure and Social Relations*, London: Routledge and Kegan Paul.

Featherstone, M. (1990) 'Perspectives on consumer culture', *Sociology*, vol. 24, pp. 5–22.

Fedler, A. J. (1987) 'Are leisure, recreation, and tourism interrelated?', *Annals of Tourism Research*, vol. 14, pp. 311–3.

Feldman, J. (1989) 'The growth of international travel service companies', *Travel and Tourism Analyst*, London: Economist Intelligence Unit.

Fenelon, R. (1990) 'The European and international hotel industry', in M. Quest (ed.), *Howarth Book of Tourism*, London: Macmillan.

Ferrario, F. F. (1988) 'Emerging leisure market among the South African Black population', *Tourism Management*, vol. 9, no. 1, pp. 23–38.

Fish, M. (1984) 'On controlling sex sales to tourists: commentary on Graburn and Cohen', *Annals of Tourism Research*, vol. 11, pp. 615–17.

Fitch, A. (1987) 'Tour operators in the UK', *Travel and Tourism Analyst*, London: Economist Intelligence Unit.

Franklin, S. H. (1971) *Rural Societies*, London: Macmillan.

Friedmann, H. (1980) 'Household production and the national economy: concepts for the analysis of agrarian formations', *Journal of Peasant Studies*, vol. 7, pp. 158–84.

Gabriel, Y. (1988) *Working Lives in Catering*, London: Routledge.

Gasson, R. (1980) 'Roles of farm women in England', *Sociologia Ruralis*, vol. 20, pp. 165–80.

Gershuny, J. I. and Jones, S. (1987) 'The changing work/leisure balance in Britain, 1961-1984', in J. Horne, D. Jary and A. Tomlinson (eds), *Sport, Leisure and Social Relations*, London: Routledge and Kegan Paul.

Gershuny, J. I. and Miles, I. (1983) *The New Service Economy*, London: Frances Pinter.

Gershuny, J. I. and Thomas, G. S. (1982) 'Changing leisure patterns in the UK, 1961-1974/5', in M. F. Collins (ed.), *Leisure Research*, London: The Sports Council, The Social Science Research Council, and The Leisure Studies Association.

Gill, S. and Law, D. (1988) *The Global Political Economy: Perspectives, Problems and Policies*, London: Harvester-Wheatsheaf.

Gitelson, R. J. and Crompton, J. L. (1983) 'The planning horizons and sources of information used by pleasure vacationers', *Journal of Travel Research*, vol. 23, pp. 2–7.

Glyptis, S. (1989) 'Recreation in rural areas: a case study in Ryedale and Swaledale', *Leisure Studies*, vol. 1, pp. 49–64.

Glyptis, S. A. and Riddington, A. C. (1983) *Sport for the Unemployed: a Review of Local Authority Projects*, London: Sports Council.

Go, F. (1989) 'International hotel industry – capitalizing on change', *Tourism Management*, vol. 10, pp. 195–99.

Go, F., Pye, S. S., Uysal, M. and Mihalik, B. J. (1990) 'Decision criteria for transnational hotel expansion', *Tourism Management*, vol. 11, pp. 297–304.

Golbey, G. (1985) *Leisure in Your Life: an Exploration*, New York: CBS College Publishing.

Goddard, J. B. (1973) *Office linkages and location*, Oxford: Pergamon Press.

Goeldner, C. R., Buchman, T. A., DiPersio, C. E. and Hayden, G. S. (1991) *Economic Analysis of North American Ski Areas 1989-1990*, Boulder, Colorado: Business Research Division, University of Colorado at Boulder.

Goffee, R. and Scase, R. (1983) 'Class entrepreneurship and the service sector: towards a conceptual clarification', *Service Industries Journal*, vol. 3, pp. 146–60.

Goodall, B. (1988) 'How tourists choose their holidays: an analytical framework' in B. Goodall and G. Ashworth (eds), *Marketing in the Tourism Industry*, London: Croom Helm.

Gooding, E. G. B. (1971) 'Food production in Barbados with particular reference to tourism', in G. V. Doxey (ed.) *The Tourist Industry in Barbados*, Kitchener: DUSCO Graphics.

Goodman, D. and Redclift, M. (1985) 'Capitalism, petty commodity production and the farm enterprise', *Sociologia Ruralis*, vol. 15, pp. 231–47.

Gordon, C. (1991) 'Sustainable leisure', *Ecos*, vol. 12(1), pp. 7–13.

Gormsen, E. (1981) 'The spatio-temporal development of international tourism: attempt at a centre–periphery model', *La Consommation d'Espace par le Tourisme et sa Preservation*, Aix-en-Provence: CHET.

Gottlieb, A. (1982) 'Americans' vacations', *Annals of Tourism Research*, vol. 9, pp. 165–87.

Graburn, N. H. H. (1967) 'The Eskimos and airport art', *Trans-Action*, vol. 4, pp. 28–33.

Graburn, N. H. H. (1983) 'Tourism and prostitution', *Annals of Tourism Research*, vol. 10, pp. 437–43.

Gratton, C. (1990) 'Consumer behaviour in tourism: a psycho-economic approach', Conference paper presented at 'Tourism Research Into the 1990s', University of Durham, 1990.

Gratton, C. and Taylor, P. (1987) *Leisure in Britain*, Letchworth: Leisure Publications.

Gratton, C. and Taylor, P. (1988) *Economics of Leisure Services Management*, London: Longman.

Gray, H. P. (1970) *International Travel: International Trade*, Lexington: Heath Lexington Books.

Greenwood, D. J. (1976) 'Tourism as an agent of change', *Annals of Tourism Research*, vol. 3, pp. 128–42.

Greenwood, D. J. (1977) 'Culture by the pound: an anthropological perspective on tourism as cultural commiditization' in V. L. Smith (ed.), *Hosts and Guests*, Philadelphia: University of Pennsylvania Press.

Greenwood, J., Williams, A. M. and Shaw, G. (1989) *1988 Cornwall Visitor Survey*, Exeter: University of Exeter, Department of Geography, Tourism Research Group.

Griffin, S., Hobson, D., MacIntosh, S. and McCabe, T. (1982) 'Women and leisure', in J. Hargreaves (ed.), *Sport, Culture and Ideology*, London: Routledge and Kegan Paul.

Guitart, C. (1982) 'UK charter flight package holidays to the Mediterranean, 1970–78', *Tourism Management*, vol. 3, pp. 16–39.

Gunn, C. (1980) 'Amendment to Leiper, The framework of tourism', *Annals of Tourism Research*, vol. 7, pp. 253–55.

Gunn, C. A. (1988) *Tourism Planning*, New York: Taylor and Francis, 2nd edn.

Gutiérrez, R. S. (1977) 'Localización actual de la hosteleria madriléna', *Boletin de la Real Sociedad Geografica*, vol. 2, pp. 347–57.

Hall, D. R. (ed.) (1991a) *Tourism and Economic Development in Eastern Europe and the Soviet Union*, London: Belhaven Press.

Hall, D. R. (1991b) 'Evolutionary pattern of tourism development in Eastern Europe and the Soviet Union', in D.R. Hall (ed.), *Tourism and Economic Development in Eastern Europe and the Soviet Union*, London: Belhaven Press.

Hall, J. A. and Braithwaite, R. (1990) 'Caribbean cruise tourism: a business of transnational partnerships', *Tourism Management*, vol. 11, pp. 341–7.

Hall, T. D. (1986) 'Incorporation in the world system: towards a critique', *American Sociological Review*, vol. 51, pp. 390–402.

Hantrais, L. (1989) 'Central government policy in France under the socialist administration 1981–86', in Bramham, I. Henry, H. Mommaas and H. van der Poel (eds), *Leisure and Urban Processes: Critical Studies of Leisure Policy in West European Cities*, London: Routledge.

Harper, M. (1984) *Small Businesses in the Third World: Guidelines for Practical Assistance*, Chichester: John Wiley.

Harrison, C. (1991) *Countryside Recreation in a Changing Society*, London: TMS Partnership.

Hartmann, R. (1986) 'Tourism, seasonality and social change', *Leisure Studies*, vol. 5, pp. 25–33.

Hartmann, R. and Hennig, L. (1989) 'Wilderness recreation, experimental consumerism and the American West – origins, trends and environmental implications', in F. Zimmermann (ed.), *Proceedings of the Austrian Meeting of the IGU Commission of Geography of Tourism and Leisure*, Klagenfurt.

Harvey, D. (1985) *The Urbanisation of Capital: Studies in the History and Theory of Capitalist Urbanisation*, Oxford: Blackwell.

Harvey, D. (1987) 'Flexible accumulation through urbanisation', *Antipode*, vol. 19, pp. 260–86.

Harvey, D. (1989) 'From managerialism to entrepreneurialism: the transformation in urban governance in late capitalism', *Geografiska Annaler B*, vol. 71(1), pp. 3–17.

Haylock, R. (1988) 'Developments in worldwide timeshare', *Travel and Tourism Analysis*, pp. 53–67, London: Economist Intelligence Unit.

Haywood, K. M. (1986) 'Can the tourist area life cycle be made operational?', *Tourism Management*, vol. 7, pp. 154–67.

Henderson, D. M. (1975) *The Economic Impact of Tourism in Edinburgh and the Lothian Region*, Edinburgh: University of Edinburgh, Tourism and Recreation Research Unit.

Henderson, K. A. (1990) 'The meaning of leisure for women: an integrative review of the research', *Journal of Leisure Research*, vol. 22, pp. 228–43.

Hewison, R. (1987) *The Heritage Industry: Britain in a Climate of Decline*, London: Methuen.

Heyzer, N. (1986) *Working Women in South East Asia*, London: Open University Press.

Hill, C. M. (1982) 'Newcomers and leisure in Norfolk villages', in M. J. Moseley (ed.), *Social Issues in Rural Norfolk*, Norwich: Centre for East Anglian Studies.

Hills, T. L. and Lundgren, J. (1977) 'The impact of tourism in the Caribbean: a methodological study', *Annals of Tourism Research*, vol. 4, pp. 248–67.

Hodgson, A. (ed.) (1987) *The Travel and Tourism Industry: Strategy for the Future*, Oxford: Pergamon Press.

Holden, R. (1989) 'British garden festivals: the first eight years', *Landscape and Urban Planning*, vol. 18, pp. 17–35.

Holder, J. (1988) 'Pattern and impact of tourism on the environment of the Caribbean', *Tourism Management*, vol. 9, pp. 119–27.

Holman, R. (1984) 'A values and life styles perspective on human behaviour', in R. E. Pitts and A. G. Woodside (eds), *Personal Values and Consumer Psychology*, Lexington: Lexington Books.

Hopkins, J. (1990) 'West Edmonton Mall: landscape of myths and elsewhereness', *Canadian Geographer*, vol. 34, pp. 2–17.

Horwath and Horwath Ltd (1986) *London's Tourist Accommodation in the 1990s*, London: Horwath and Horwath Ltd.

Hotels (1991) 'Hotels 300 overview', July 1991, pp. 40–50.

Hudson, R. and Williams, A. M. (1989) *Divided Britain*, London: Belhaven Press.

Hughes, H. L. (1987) 'Culture as a tourist resource – a theoretical consideration', *Tourism Management*, vol. 8, pp. 205–16.

Hymer, S. H. (1975) 'The multinational corporation and the law of uneven development', in H. Radice (ed.), *International Forms and Modern Imperialism*, London: Penguin.

Iso-Ahola, S. E. (1980) *The Social Psychology of Leisure and Recreation*, Dubuque: W. C. Brown.

Iso-Ahola, S. E. (1984) 'Social psychological foundations of leisure and resultant implications for leisure counselling', in E. T. Dowd (ed.), *Leisure Counselling: Concepts and Applications*, Illinois: C. C. Thomas.

Jackson, E. L. (1988) 'Leisure constraints: a survey of past research', *Leisure Sciences*, vol. 10, pp. 203–15.

Jackson, E. L. (1991) 'Leisure constraints/constrained leisure: special issue introduction', *Journal of Leisure Research*, vol. 23, pp. 279–85.

Jafari, J. (1973) 'Role of Tourism in the Socio-economic Transformation of Developing Countries', Ithaca, New York: Cornell University Press.

Jafari, J. (1987) 'Tourism models: the sociocultural aspects, *Tourism Management*, vol. 8(2), pp. 151–59.

Jafari, J. (1989) 'Sociocultural dimensions of tourism: an English language literature review', in J. Bustrzanowski (ed.), *Tourism as a Factor of Change: a Sociocultural Study*, Vienna: Economic Coordination Centre for Research and Documentation in Social Sciences, pp. 17–60.

Jakle, J. A. (1985) *The tourist: travel in twentieth-century N. America*, Lincoln: University of Nebraska Press.

Jansen-Verbeke, M. (1986) 'Inner-city tourism: resources, tourists and promoters', *Annals of Tourism Research*, vol. 13, pp. 79–100.

Jansen-Verbeke, M. and Dietvorst, A. (1987) 'Leisure, recreation, tourism: a geographic view on integration', *Annals of Tourism Research*, vol. 14, pp. 361–75.

Jansen-Verbeke, M. (1990) 'Fun shopping: a challenge to planning', in G. J. Ashworth and B. Goodall (eds), *Marketing Tourism Places*, London: Routledge.

Johnson, P. and Thomas, B. (1990) 'Employment in tourism: a review', *Industrial Relations Journal*, vol. 21, pp. 36–48.

Jud, G. D. (1975) 'Tourism and crime in Mexico', *Social Science Quarterly*, vol. 56, pp. 324–30.

Judd, D. R. and Collins, M. (1979) 'The case of tourism: political coalitions and redevelopment in central cities', in G. A. Tobin (ed.), *The Changing Structure of the City: What Happened to the Urban Crises?*, Urban Affairs Annual Reviews, p. 16.

Kando, T. M. (1975) *Leisure and Popular Culture in Transition*, St. Louis: C. V. Mosby.

Karn, V. A. (1977) *Retiring to the Seaside*, London: Routledge and Kegan Paul.

Kassé, M. (1973) 'La théorie du developpement de l'industrie touristique dans les pay sous-dévoloppés, *Annales Africaines* (1971–73), pp. 53–72.

Katz, C. and Kirby, A. (1991) 'In the nature of things: the environment and everday life', *Transactions, Institute of British Geographers*, new series, vol. 16, pp. 259–71.

Kay, T. and Jackson, G. (1991) 'Leisure despite constraint: the impact of leisure constraints on leisure participation', *Journal of Leisure Research*, vol. 23, pp. 301–13.

Kelly, J. (1978) 'Family leisure in three communities', *Journal of Leisure Research*, vol. 10, pp. 38–47.

Kelly, J. R. (1980) 'Outdoor recreation participation: a comparative analysis', *Leisure Sciences*, vol. 3, pp. 129–54.

Kelly, J. R. (1982) *Leisure*, Englewood Cliffs, New Jersey: Prentice-Hall.

Kelly, J. R. (1985) *Recreation Business*, New York: John Wiley.

Keohane, R. O. and Nye, J. S. (1977) *Power and Interdependence*, Boston: Brown.

Key Note (1986) *Tourism in the UK, Key Note Report*, An Industry Sector Overview, London: Key Note Publications.

Key Note (1988) *Fast Food Outlets*, Key Note Report, An Industry Sector Overview, London: Key Note Publications.

King, R. (1986) 'Return migration and regional economic development: an overview', in R. King (ed.), *Return Migration and Regional Economic Problems*, London: Croom Helm.

King, R., Mortimer, J., Strachan, A. and Trono, A. (1985) 'Return migration and rural economic change: a south Italian case study', in R. Hudson and J. R. Lewis (eds), *Uneven Development in Southern Europe*, London: Methuen.

Knoll, G. M. (1988) *Grosstadttourismus der Innenstadt von Köln im 19. und 20. Jahrhundert*. Köln: Hundt Druck.

Knox, P. L. (1974) 'Spatial variations in the level of living in England and Wales', *Transactions, Institute of British Geographers*, vol. 62, pp. 1–24.

Knox, P. and Agnew, J. (1989) *The Geography of the World Economy*, London: Edward Arnold.

Krippendorf, J. (1986) 'The new tourist turning point for travel and leisure', *Tourism Management*, vol. 7, pp. 131–35.

Krippendorf, J. (1987) *The Holiday Makers*, London: Heinemann.

Kuhn, W. (1979) 'Geschaftsstrassen als Freizeitsraum', *Münchner Geographie*, vol. 42.

Landgren, J. O. J. (1974) 'On access to recreational lands in dynamic metropolitan hinterlands', *Tourist Review*, vol. 29, pp. 124–31.

Lanfant, M.-F. (1980) 'Introduction: tourism in the process of internationalisation', *International Social Science Journal*, vol. 23, pp. 14–43.

Lanfant, M.-L. (1989) 'International tourism resists the crisis', in A. Olszewska and K. Roberts (eds), *Leisure and Life-Style: a Comparative Analysis of Free Time*, London: Sage Publications.

Latimer, H. (1985) 'Developing-island economies – tourism v agriculture', *Tourism Management*, vol. 6, pp. 32–42.

Lavery, P. and van Doren, C. (1990) *Travel and Tourism: a North American–European Perspective*, Huntingdon: Elm Publications.

Law, C. M. (1985a) The British Conference and Exhibition Business, Urban Tourism Project, Department of Geography, University of Salford.

Law, C. M. (1985b) *Urban Tourism: Selected American Case Studies*, Urban Tourism Project, Department of Geography, University of Salford.

Law, C. M. (1985c) *Urban Tourism: Selected British Case Studies*, Urban Tourism Project, Department of Geography, University of Salford.

Law, C. M. (1987) 'Conference and exhibition tourism', *Built Environment*, vol. 13, pp. 85–95.

Law, C. M. (1988) 'Public, private partnerships in urban revitalisation in Britain', *Regional Studies*, vol. 22, pp. 446–51.

Law, C. M. (1991a) 'Tourism and urban revitalization', *East Midland Geographer*, vol. 14, pp. 49–60.

Law, C. M. (1991) *Tourism as a Focus for Urban Regeneration: the Role of Tourism in the Urban and Regional Economy*, London: Regional Studies Association.

Law, C. M. (1992) 'Urban tourism and its contribution to economic regeneration', *Urban Studies*, vol. 29, pp. 597–616.

Laws, E. (1991) *Tourism Marketing: Service and Quality Management Perspectives*, Cheltenham: Stanley Thornes.

Lawson, F. R. (1982) 'Trends in business tourism management', *Tourism Management*, vol. 3, pp. 298–302.

Lea, J. (1988) *Tourism and Development in the Third World*, London: Routledge.

Leontidou, L. (1991) 'Greece: prospects and contradictions of tourism in the

1980s', in A. M. Williams and G. Shaw (eds), *Tourism and Economic Development: Western European Experiences*, London: Belhaven Press, 2nd edn.

Lew, A. A. (1987) 'A framework of tourist attraction research', *Annals of Tourism Research*, vol. 14, pp. 553–75.

Lewis, J. R. and Williams, A. M. (1986) 'The economic impact of return migration in Central Portugal', in R. King (ed.), *Return Migration and Regional Economic Problems*, London: Croom Helm.

Lewis, J. R. and Williams, A. M. (1988) 'No longer Europe's best-kept secret: the Algarve's tourist boom', *Geography*, vol. 74, pp. 170–2.

Lewis, J. R. and Williams, A. M. (1991) 'Portugal: market segmentation and regional specialisation', in A. M. Williams and G. Shaw (eds), *Tourism and Economic Development: Western European Experiences*, London: Belhaven Press, 2nd edn.

Ley, D. and Olds, K. (1988) 'Landsape as spectacle: world's fairs and the culture of heroic consumption', *Environment and Planning D: Society and Space*, vol. 6, pp. 191–212.

Lickorish, L. L. (1990) 'Tourism facing change', in M. Quest (ed.), *Howarth Book of Tourism*, London: Macmillan.

Llinas, M. S. (1991) 'Nature et tourism – l'équilibre indispensable pour l'avenir de l'îsle de Majorque', *Méditeranée*, pp. 15–20.

Lloyd, P. E. and Mason, C. M. (1984) 'Spatial variations in new firm formation in the U.K.: comparative evidence from Merseyside, Greater Manchester and South Hampshire', *Regional Studies*, vol. 18, pp. 207–20.

Lowyck, E., Van Langenhove, L. and Bollaert, L. (1990) 'Typologies of tourist roles', Conference paper presented at 'Tourism Research into the 1990s', University of Durham, 1990.

Lumley, R. (1988) *The Museum Time-machine: Putting Cultures on Display*, London: Routledge.

Lundberg, D. E. (1972) *The Tourist Business*, Boston: Cahners.

Lundberg, D. E. (1974) 'Caribbean tourism: social and racial tensions', *Cornell Hotel and Restaurant Administration Quarterly*, vol. 15, pp. 82–7.

Lundgren, J. O. J. (1972) 'The development of tourist travel systems – a metropolitan economic hegemony par excellence', *Jahrbuch für Fremdenverkehr*, vol. 20, pp. 86–120.

Lundgren, J. O. J. (1973) 'Tourist impact/island entrepreneurship in the Caribbean', Conference paper quoted in Mathieson and Wall (1982).

MacCannell, D. (1973) 'Staged authenticity: arrangements of social space in tourist settings', *American Sociological Review*, vol. 79, pp. 589–603.

MacCannell, D. (1976) *The Tourist: a New Theory of the Leisure Class*, New York: Sulouker Books; see also revised edition, 1989.

MacCannell, D. (1984) 'Reconstructed ethnicity: tourism and cultural identity in Third World Communities', *Annals of Tourism Research*, vol. 11, pp. 375–91.

MacNulty, W. K. (1985) 'U.K. social change through a wide-angle lens', *Futures*, August, pp. 18–25.

McConnell, J. E. (1986) 'Geography of international trade', *Progress in Human Geography*, vol. 10, pp. 471–83.

McGuire, C. (1984) 'A factor analytical study of leisure constraints in advanced adulthood', *Leisure Sciences*, vol. 6, pp. 313–26.

McPheters, L. R. and Stronge, W. B. (1974) 'Crime as an environmental externality of tourism: Florida', *Land Economics*, vol. 50, pp. 288–92.

Mandel, E. (1975) *Late Capitalism*, London: New Left Books.

Mannell, R. C. and Iso-Ahola, S. E. (1987) 'Psychological nature of leisure and tourism experience', *Annals of Tourism Research*, vol. 14, pp. 314–31.

Mansfield, Y. (1990) 'Spatial patterns of international tourist flows: towards a theoretical framework', *Progress in Human Geography*, vol. 4, pp. 372–90.

Markusen, A. R. (1985) *Profit Cycles, Oligopoly and Regional Development*, Cambridge, Massachusetts: MIT Press.

Mars, G. and Nicod, M. (1984) *The World of Waiters*, London: Allen & Unwin.

Marshall, G. (1986) 'The workplace culture of a licensed restaurant', *Theory, Culture and Society*, vol. 3, pp. 33–48.

Marshall, J. N. (1989) *Uneven Development in the Service Economy: Understanding the Location and Role of Product Service*, Oxford: Oxford University Press.

Maslow, A. H. (1954) *Motivation and Personality*, New York: Harper and Row.

Massey, D. (1983) 'Industrial restructuring as class restructuring: production decentralization and local uniqueness', *Regional Studies*, vol. 17, pp. 73–90.

Massey, D. (1984) *Spatial Divisions of Labour: Social Structures and the Geography of Production*, London: Macmillan.

Mathieson, A. and Wall, G. (1982) *Tourism: economic, physical and social impacts*, London: Longman.

Mayo, E. J. (1974) 'A model of motel-choice', *Cornell Hotel and Restaurant Administration Quarterly*, vol. 15(3), pp. 55–64.

Meeker, J. W., Woods, W. K. and Lucas, W. (1973) 'Red, white and black in the national parks', *North American Review*, Fall, pp. 3–7.

Mendonsa, E. L. (1983) 'Tourism and income strategies in Nazare, Portugal', *Annals of Tourism Research*, vol. 10, pp. 213–38.

Meyer-Arendt, K. J. (1987) Resort evolution along the Gulf of Mexico littoral: historical, morphological and environmental aspects, unpublished PhD thesis, Louisiana State University.

Middleton, V. T. C. (1982) 'Tourism in rural areas', *Tourism Management*, vol. 5, pp. 52–8.

Middleton, V. T. C. (1989) 'Marketing implications for attractions', *Tourism Management*, vol. 10, pp. 229–34.

Mihovilovic, M.A. (1980) 'Leisure and tourism in Europe', *International Social Science Journal*, vol. 32, pp. 99–113.

Mill, R. C. and Morrison, A. M. (1985) *The Tourism System*, Englewood Cliffs, New Jersey: Prentice Hall.

Miossec, J. M. (1976) 'Eléments pour une théorie de l'espace touristique', *Les Cahiers du Tourisme*, vol. C-36, Aix-en-Provence.

Mitchell, A. (1983) *The Nine American Life Styles*, New York: Warner.

Mommaas, H. and van der Poel, H. (1989) 'Changes in economy, politics and lifestyles: an essay on the restructuring of urban leisure', in P. Bramham, I. Henry, H. Mommaas and H. van der Poel (eds), *Leisure and Urban Processes: Critical Studies of Leisure Policy in West European Cities*. London: Routledge.

Momsen, J. M. (1986) 'Linkages between tourism and agriculture: problems for the smaller Caribbean economies', Seminar Paper No. 45, Department of Geography, University of Newcastle-Upon-Tyne.

Monopolies and Mergers Commission (1989) *Thomson Travel Group and Horizon Travel Ltd.*, London: HMSO.

Moore, K. (1976) 'Modernization in a Canary Island village', in J. B. Aceves and W. A. Douglass (eds), *The Changing Faces of Rural Spain*, New York: Schenkman.

Morrell, J. (1985) *Employment in Tourism*, London: British Tourist Authority.

Morton, A. (1988) 'Tomorrow's yesterdays: science museums and the future', in R. Lumley (ed.), *The Museum Time-machine: Putting Cultures on Display*, London: Routledge.

Mullins, P. (1991) 'Tourism urbanization', *International Journal of Urban and Regional Research*, vol. 15, pp. 326–42.

Murakami, K. and Go, F. (1990) 'Transnational corporations capture Japanese market', *Tourism Management*, vol. 11, pp. 348–53.

Murphy, P. E. (1980) 'Tourism management using land use planning and landscape design: the Victoria experience', *Canadian Geographer*, vol. 24(1), pp. 60–71.

Murphy, P. E. (1985) *Tourism: a Community Approach*, London: Routledge.

Murphy, P. E. (1988) 'Community driven tourism planning', *Tourism Management*, vol. 9, pp. 96–104.

Nash, D. (1977) 'Tourism as a form of imperialism', in V. L. Smith (ed.), *Hosts and Guests: the Anthropology of Tourism*, Philadelphia: University of Pennsylvania Press.

Neate, S. (1987) 'The role of tourism in sustaining farm structures and communities on the Isles of Scilly', in M. Bouquet and M. Winter (eds), *Who From Their Labours Rest? Conflict and Practice in Rural Tourism*, Aldershot: Avebury Press.

Newman, O. (1983) 'The coming of a leisure society?' *Leisure Studies*, vol. 2, pp. 97–109.

Nicholls, L. L. (1976) 'Tourism and crime: a conference', *Annals of Tourism Research*, vol. 3, pp. 176–82.

Nolan, S. D. (1976) 'Tourists' use and evaluation of travel information sources: summary and conclusions', *Journal of Travel Research*, vol. 14, pp. 6–8.

Nunez, T. A. (1977) 'Touristic studies in anthropological perspectives', in V.

L. Smith (ed.), *Hosts and Guests: an Anthropology of Tourism*, Philadelphia: University of Pennsylvania Press.

OECD (1974) *Government Policy in the Development of Tourism*, Paris: OECD.

OECD (1990) *Tourism Policy and International Tourism*, Paris: OECD.

Ogilvie, F. W. (1933) *The Tourist Movement*, London: P. S. King.

Palloix, C. (1975) *L'Économie Mondiale Capitaliste et Les Firmes Multinationals*, Paris: Maspero.

Parker, S. (1983) *Leisure and Work*, London: Allen & Unwin.

Patmore, J. A. (1983) *Recreation and Resources: Leisure Patterns and Leisure Places*, Oxford: Blackwell.

Pearce, D. G. (1978) 'Tourist development: two processes', *Journal of Travel Research*, vol. 16, pp. 43–51.

Pearce, D. G. (1987a) 'Mediterranean charters – a comparative geographic perspective', *Tourism Management*, vol. 8, pp. 291–305.

Pearce, D. G. (1987b) 'Spatial patterns of package tourism in Europe', *Annals of Tourism Research*, vol. 14, pp. 183–201.

Pearce, D. G. (1987c) *Tourism Today: a Geographical Analysis*, London: Longman.

Pearce, D. (1988a) 'Tourism and regional development in the European Community', *Tourism Management*, vol. 9, pp. 13–22.

Pearce, D. G. (1988b) 'Tourist time budgets', *Annuals of Tourism Research*, vol. 15, pp. 106–21.

Pearce, D. (1989) *Tourist Development*, London: Longman, 2nd edn.

Pearce, P. L. (1982) *The Social Psychology of Tourist Behaviour*, Oxford: Pergamon Press.

Peck, J. G. and Lepie, A. S. (1977) 'Tourism and development in three North Carolina coastal towns', in V. L. Smith (ed.), *Hosts and Guests: an Anthropology of Tourism*, Philadelphia: University of Pennsylvania Press.

Peneff, J. (1981) *Industriels Algériens*, Paris: Editions du CNRS.

Perez, M. (1987) 'New trends in international tourism viewed in the light of a quantitative interpretation', in A. Sessa (ed.), *Megatrends in International Tourism*, Rome: Editrice Agnesotti.

Perry, M. (1975) 'Planning and evaluating advertising campaigns related to tourist destinations', in S. P. Ladany (ed.), *Management Science Applications to Leisure Time Operations*, New York: American Elsevier.

Petersen, J. and Belchambers, K. (1990) 'Business travel – a boom market', in M. Quest (ed.), *Howarth Book of Tourism*, London: Macmillan.

Pevetz, W. (1991) 'Agriculture and tourism in Austria', *Tourism Recreation Research*, vol. 16, pp. 57–60.

Phelps, A. (1988) 'Seasonality in tourism and recreation: the study of visitor patterns. A comment on Hartman', *Leisure Studies*, vol. 7, pp. 33–9.

Phongpaichit, P. (1980) 'Rural women of Thailand', *ISIS International Bulletin* No. 13, Geneva: International Labour Office.

Pigram, J. (1983) *Outdoor Recreation and Resource Management*, London: Croom Helm.

Pimlott, J. (1976) *The Englishman's Holiday: a Social History*, Sussex: Harvester.

Pine, R. (1987) *Management of Technological Change in the Catering Industry*, Aldershot: Avebury Press.

Pizam, A. (1982) 'Tourism manpower: the state of the art', *Journal of Travel Research*, vol. 21, pp. 5–9.

Pizam, A. and Pokela, J. (1988) 'The perceived impacts of casino gambling on a community', *Annals of Tourism Research*, vol. 12, pp. 147–65.

Pizam, A., Reichel, A. and Shieh, C. F. (1982) 'Tourism and crime: is there a relationship?', *Journal of Travel Research*, vol. 20, pp. 7–11.

Plog, S. C. (1972) 'Why destination areas rise and fall in popularity', Paper presented at Southern California Chapter of the Travel Research Association.

Plog, S. C. (1987) 'Understanding psychographics in tourism research', in J. R. Brent Ritchie and C. R. Goeldner (eds), *Travel, Tourism and Hospitality Research: a Handbook for Managers and Researchers*, New York: John Wiley.

Pocock, D. (1992) 'Catherine Cookson country: tourist expectation and experience', *Geography*, vol. 77, pp. 236–44.

Préau, P. (1968) 'Essai d'une typologie de stations de sporte d'hiver dans les Alpes du Nord', *Revus de Géographie Alpine*, vol. 58, no. 1, pp. 127–40.

Préau, P. (1970) 'Principe d'analyse des sites en montagne', *Urbanisme*, vol. 116, pp. 21–5.

Pyo, S., Cook, R. and Howell, R. L. (1988) 'Summer Olympic tours and market-learning from the past', *Tourism Management*, vol. 9, pp. 137–44.

Rapoport, R. and Rapoport, R. N. (1975) *Leisure and the Family Lifecycle*, London: Routledge and Kegan Paul.

Relph, E. (1976) *Place and Placelessness*, London: Pion.

Richter, L. K. (1983) 'Tourism politics and political science: a case of not so benign neglect', *Annals of Tourism Research*, vol. 10, pp. 313–35.

Richter, L. K. (1985) 'Fragmented politics of US tourism', *Tourism Management*, vol. 6, pp. 162–73.

Ritchie, J. R. and Zins, M. (1978) 'Culture as a determinant of the attractiveness of a tourist region', *Annals of Tourism Research*, vol. 5, pp. 252–67.

Rivers, P. (1973) 'Tourist troubles', *New Society*, vol. 23, pp. 250.

Roberts, K. (1981) *Leisure*, London: Longman, 2nd edn.

Roberts, K. (1989) 'Great Britain: socioeconomic polarisation and the implications for leisure', in Olszewska, A. and Roberts, K. (eds), *Leisure and Life-Style: a Comparative Analysis of Free Time*, London: Sage Publications.

Rojek, C. (1985) *Capitalism and Leisure Theory*, Andover: Tavistock.

Romeril, M. (1989) 'Tourism and the environment – accord or discord?' *Tourism Management*, vol. 10, pp. 204–8.

Rosemary, J. (1987) *Indigenous Enterprises in Kenya's Tourism Industry*, Geneva: Unesco.

Rothman, R. A. (1978) 'Residents and transients: community reaction to seasonal visitors', *Journal of Travel Research*, vol. 16, pp. 8–13.

Sawicki, D. S. (1989) 'The festival marketplace as public policy', *Journal of the American Planning Association*, vol. 55, pp. 347–61.

Schmidhauser, H. (1989) 'Tourist needs and motivations', in S. F. Witt and L. Moutinho (eds), *Tourism Marketing and Management*, Hemel Hempstead: Prentice-Hall.

Seager, J. and Olsen, A. (1986) *Women in the World: an International Atlas*, London: Pan.

Seaton, A. V. (1992) 'Social stratification in tourism choice and experience since the war: part 1', *Tourism Management*, vol. 13, pp. 106–11.

Sessa, A. (1983) *Elements of Tourism Economics*, Rome: Catal.

Shaw, G. (1992) 'Culture and tourism: the economics of nostalgia', *World Futures*, vol. 33, pp. 199–212.

Shaw, G. and Williams, A. M. (1987) 'Firm formation and operating characteristics in the Cornish tourism industry', *Tourism Management*, vol. 8, pp. 344–48.

Shaw, G. and Williams, A. (1990) 'Tourism, economic development and the role of entrepreneurial activity', *Progress in Tourism, Recreation and Hospitality Management*, vol. 2, pp. 67–81.

Shaw, G. and Williams, A. M. (1991a) 'From bathing hut to theme park: tourism development in South West England', *Journal of Regional and Local Studies*, vol. 11, pp. 16–32.

Shaw, G. and Williams, A. M. (1991b) 'Tourism and Development', in D. Pinder (ed.), *Western Europe: Challenge and Change*, London: Belhaven Press.

Shaw, G., Williams, A. M. and Greenwood, J. (1987) *Tourism and the Economy of Cornwall*, University of Exeter: Tourism Research Group.

Shaw, G., Williams, A., Botterill, D. and Greenwood, J. (1990) *Visitor Patterns and Visitor Behaviour in Plymouth*, Exeter: Tourism Research Group, University of Exeter.

Sheldon, P. J. (1983) 'The impact of technology on the hotel industry', *Tourism Management*, vol. 4, pp. 269–78.

Sheldon, P. J. (1988) 'The US tour operator industry', *Travel and Tourism Analyst*, pp. 25–48. London: Economist Intelligence Unit.

Shivers, J. S. (1981) *Leisure and Recreation Concepts: a Critical Analysis*, Boston: Allyn and Bacon.

Shiviji, J. G. (1973) *Tourism and Socialist Development*, Dar-es-Salaam: Tanzania Publishing House.

Shucksmith, D.M. (1983) 'Second homes, a framework for policy', *Town Planning Review*, vol. 54, pp. 174–93.

Sidaway, R. and Duffield, B. S. (1984) 'A new look at countryside recreation in the urban fringe', *Leisure Studies*, vol. 3, pp. 249–71.

Sillitoe, K. (1969) *Planning for Leisure*, London: HMSO.

Simms, J., Hales, C. and Riley, M. (1988) 'Examination of the concept of internal labour markets in UK hotels', *Tourism Management*, vol. 9, pp. 3–12.

Slattery, P. and Roper, A. (1988) *UK Hotels Group Directory 1988*, London: Cassell.

Smith, D. M. (1977a) *Human Geography: a Welfare Approach*, London: Edward Arnold.

Smith, D. (1980) *New to Britain: a Study of Some New Developments in Tourist Attractions*, London: English Tourist Board.

Smith, G. V. (1989) 'The European conference market, *Travel and Tourism Analyst*, no. 4, pp. 60–76. London: Economist Intelligence Unit.

Smith G. V. (1990) 'The growth of conferences and incentives', in M. Quest (ed.), *Howarth Book of Tourism*, London: Macmillan.

Smith, J. (1987) 'Men and women at play: gender, lifecycle and leisure'. In J. Homes, D. Jary and A. Tomlinson (eds), *Sport, Leisure and Social Relations*, London: Routledge and Kegan Paul.

Smith, S. L. J. (1983) 'Restaurants and dining out: geography of a tourism business', *Annals of Tourism Research*, vol. 10, pp. 515–49.

Smith, V. L. (ed.) (1977b) *Hosts and Guests: an Anthropology of Tourism*, Philadelphia: University of Pennsylvania Press.

Spink, J. (1989) 'Urban development, leisure facilities and the inner city: A case study of inner Leeds and Bradford'. In P. Bramham, I. Henry, H. Mommaas and H. van der Poel (eds), *Leisure and Urban Processes: Critical Studies of Leisure Policy in West European Cities*, London: Routledge.

Spreitzer, E. and Snyder, E. E. (1987) 'Educational–occupational fit and leisure orientation as related to life satisfaction', *Journal of Leisure Research*, vol. 19, pp. 149–58.

Stallinbrass, C. (1980) 'Seaside resorts and the hotel accommodation industry', *Progress in Planning*, vol. 13, pp. 103–74.

Stamps, S. M. and Stamps, M. B. (1985) 'Race, class and leisure activities of urban residents', *Journal of Leisure Research*, 17, pp. 40–56.

Standing Bear, L. (1989) *Your House is Mine*, New York: Storefront for Art and Architecture.

Stansfield, C. A. and Rickert, J. E. (1970) 'The recreational business district'. *Journal of Leisure Research*, vol. 2(4), pp. 213–25.

Stockdale, J. (1985) *What Is Leisure?*, London: Sports Council and Economic and Social Research Council.

Sundelin, A. (1983) 'Tourism trends in Scandinavia', *Tourism Management*, vol. 4, pp. 262–68.

Talbot, M. (1979) *Women and Leisure: a Review for the Joint Panel on Recreation and Leisure Research*, London: The Sports Council and Social Science Research Council.

Tarrant, C. (1989) 'UK hotel industry – market restructuring and the need to respond to customer demands', *Tourism Management*, vol. 10, pp. 187–91.

Taylor, M. and Thrift, N. (1986) 'Introduction: new theories of multinational corporations', in M. Taylor and N. Thrift (eds), *Multinationals and the Restructuring of the World Economy*, London: Croom Helm.

Teuscher, M. (1983) 'Social tourism for all: the Swiss Travel Savings Fund', *Tourism Management*, vol. 4, pp. 216–19.

Theodorson, G. A. and Theodorson, A. C. (1969) *Modern Dictionary of Sociology*, New York: Thomas Crowell.

Thomas, J. (1964) 'What makes people travel?', *Asia Travel News* (August), pp. 64–5.

Thrift, N. (1989) 'Images of social change', in C. Hamnett, L. McDowell and P. Sarre (eds), *The Changing Social Structure*, London: Sage Publications.

Thurot, J. and Thurot, G. (1983) 'The ideology of class and tourism', *Annals of Tourism Research*, vol. 10, pp. 173–89.

Todaro, M. (1977) *Economic Development in the Third World*, London: Longman.

Townsend, A. R. (1992) 'New directions in the growth of tourism employment?: Propositions of the 1980s', *Environment and Planning A*, vol. 24, pp. 821–32.

Travis, A. S. (1982) 'Leisure, recreation and tourism in W. Europe', *Tourism Management*, vol. 3, pp. 3–15.

Truett, D. B. and Truett, L. J. (1987) 'The response of tourism to international economic conditions: Greece, Mexico and Spain', *Journal of Developing Areas*, vol. 21, pp. 177–90.

Turner, L. and Ash, J. (1975) *The Golden Hordes: International Tourism and the Pleasure Periphery*, London: Constable.

Tuynte, J. C. M. and Dietvorst, A. G. J. (1988) 'Musea anders bekeken: vier Nijmegse musea bezien naar vitstralingseffecten en complexvorning', quoted in Ashworth and Tunbridge (1990).

Tyrell, B. (1982) 'Work, leisure and social change', in M. F. Collins (ed.), *Leisure Research*, London: The Sports Council, The Social Science Research Council and The Leisure Studies Association.

Unesco (1976) 'The effects of tourism on sociocultural values', *Annals of Tourism Research*, vol. 4, pp. 74–105.

Unger, K. (1986) 'Return migration and regional characteristics: the case of Greece', in R. L. King (ed.), *Return Migration and Regional Economic Problems*, London: Croom Helm.

United Nations (1982) *Transnational Corporations in International Tourism*, New York: UN.

Urry, J. (1987) 'Some social and spatial aspects of services', *Environment and Planning D: Society and Space*, vol. 5, pp. 5–26.

Urry, J. (1988) 'Cultural change and contemporary holiday-making', *Theory, Culture and Society*, vol. 5, pp. 35–55.

Urry, J. (1990) *The Tourist Gaze: Leisure and Travel in Contemporary Societies*, London: Sage Publications.

Valenzuela, M. (1991) 'Spain: the phenomenon of mass tourism', in A. M. Williams and G. Shaw (eds), *Tourism and Economic Development: Western European Experience*, London: Belhaven Press, 2nd edn.

van Doorn, J. W. M. (1979) 'The developing countries: are they really affected by tourism? Some critical notes on socio-cultural impact studies', Paper presented at Leisure Studies and Tourism Seminar, Warsaw, December.

van Duijn, J. J. (1983) *The Long Wave in Economic Life*, London: Allen & Unwin.

Vandermey, A. (1984) 'Assessing the importance of urban tourism', *Tourism Management*, vol. 5, pp. 123–35.

Vaughan, R. (1990) *Assessing the Economic Impact of Tourism: the Role of Tourism in the Urban and Regional Economy*, London: Regional Studies Association.

Veal, A. J. (1987a) *Leisure and the Future*, London: Allen & Unwin.

Veal, A. J. (1987b) *Using Sports Centres*, London: Sports Council.

Veblen, T. (1925) *The Theory of the Leisure Class*, London: Allen & Unwin.

Ventris, N. (1979) 'Recreational and cultural provision in rural areas', in J. M. Shaw (ed.), *Rural Deprivation and Planning*, Norwich: Geo Books.

Vetter, F. (ed.) (1985) *Big City Tourism*, Berlin: Reimer Verlag.

Vickerman, R. W. (1980) 'The new leisure society – an economic analysis', *Futures*, vol. 10, pp. 191–200.

Vincent, J. (1987) 'Work and play in an Alpine community', in M. Bouquet and M. Winter (eds), *Who From Their Labours Rest? Conflict and Practice in Rural Tourism*, Aldershot: Avebury Press.

Vogeler, J. (1977) 'Farm and ranch vacationing', *Journal of Leisure Research*, vol. 9, pp. 291–300.

Walvin, J. (1978) *Leisure and Society, 1830–1950*, London: Longman.

Washburne, R. F. (1978) 'Black under-participation in wildland recreation: Alternative explanations', *Leisure Sciences*, vol. 1, pp. 175–89.

Weber, M. (1968) *Economy and Society*, New York: Bedminster Press.

Whatmore, S., Munton, R., Little, J. and Marsden, T. (1987) 'Towards a typology of farm businesses in contemporary British agriculture', *Sociologia Ruralis*, vol. 27, pp. 21–37.

Wheatcroft, S. (1982) 'The changing economies of international air transport', *Tourism Management*, vol. 3, pp. 71–82.

Wheatcroft, S. (1990) 'Towards transnational airlines', *Tourism Management*, vol. 11, pp. 353–8.

White, P. E. (1974) The social impact of tourism on host communities: a study of language change in Switzerland, Research paper No. 9, School of Geography, University of Oxford.

White, P., Wall, G. and Priddle, G. (1978) 'Anti-social behaviour in Ontario provincial parks', *Recreational Research Review*, vol. 2, pp. 13–25.

Wilensky, C. H. (1960) 'Work, careers and social integration', *International Social Science Journal*, no. 4, pp. 543–60.

Williams, A. M. and Shaw, G. (1988) 'Tourism: candy floss industry or job generator?', *Town Planning Review*, vol. 59, pp. 81–104.

Williams, A. M. and Shaw, G. (1990) 'Tourism in urban and regional development Western European experiences', in S. Hardy, T. Hart and T. Shaw (eds), *The Role of Tourism in the Urban and Regional Economy*, London: Regional Studies.

Williams, A. M. and Shaw, G. (1991) *Tourism and Economic Development: Western European Experiences*, London: Belhaven Press, 2nd edn.

Williams, A. M., Greenwood, J. and Shaw, G. (1989a) *Tourism in the Isles of Scilly: a Study of Small Firms on Small Islands*, University of Exeter: Tourism Research Group.

Williams, A. M., Shaw, G. and Greenwood, J. (1989b) 'From tourist to tourism entrepreneur, from consumption to production: evidence from Cornwall, England', *Environment and Planning A*, vol. 21, pp. 1639–53.

Williams, A. V. and Zelinsky, W. (1970) 'On some patterns in international tourist flows', *Economic Geography*, vol. 46, pp. 549–67.

Willits, W. L. and Willits, F. K. (1986) 'Adolescent participation in leisure activities: 'the less, the more or the more, the more'', *Leisure Sciences*, vol. 8, pp. 189–206.

Winpenny, J. T. (1982) 'Some issues in the identification and appraisal of tourism projects in developing countries', *Tourism Management*, vol. 3, pp. 218–21.

Wolfe, R. I. (1983) 'Recreational travel, the new migration revisited', *Ontario Geography*, vol. 19, pp. 103–24.

Wood, S. (1981) A Tale of Two Markets: contrasting approaches to developments in Covent Garden and Les Halles, Paper given at PTRC summer meeting.

World Tourism Organization (1981) *Estudio Piloto Sobre las Consecuencias Sociales y Culturales de los Movimentos Turistocos*, Madrid: WTO.

World Tourism Organization (1983) *Development of Leisure Time and the Right to Holidays*, Madrid: WTO.

World Tourism Organization (1984) *Economic Review of World Tourism*, Madrid: WTO.

World Tourism Organization (1985) *The Role of Transnational Tourism Enterprises in the Development of Tourism*, Madrid: WTO.

World Tourism Organization (1989a) *Yearbook of Tourism Statistics, Volume 1*, Madrid: WTO.

World Tourism Organization (1989b) *Yearbook of Tourism Statistics, Volume 2*, Madrid: WTO.

World Tourism Organization (1990) *Current Travel and Tourism Indicators, January 1990*, Madrid: WTO.

World Tourism Organization (1991) *Tourism to the Year 2000: Qualitative Aspects Affecting Global Growth, A Discussion Paper (Executive Summary)*, Madrid: WTO.

Wynne, D. (1990) 'Leisure lifestyle and the construction of social space' *Leisure Studies*, vol. 9, pp. 21–34.

Yokeno, N. (1968) 'La localisation de l'industrie touristique: application de l'analyse de Thunen–Weber', *Les Cahiers du Tourisme*, vol. C-9, Aix-en-Provence.

Young, G. (1973) *Tourism: Blessing or Blight?* London: Penguin.

Young, Lord (1985) *Pleasure, Leisure and Jobs – the Business of Tourism*, London: HMSO.

Young, M. and Willmott, P. (1973) *The Symmetrical Family*, London: Routledge and Kegan Paul.

Zimmermann, F. (1991) 'Austria: contrasting tourist seasons and contrasting regions', in A. M. Williams and G. Shaw (eds), *Tourism and Economic Development: Western European Experiences*, London: Belhaven Press, 2nd edn.

Zukin, S. (1990) 'Socio-spatial prototypes of a new organisation of consumption: the role of real cultural capital', *Sociology*, vol. 24, pp. 37–56.

Recommended Reading

ONE Introduction

Jansen-Verbeke, M. and Dietvorst, A. (1987) 'Leisure, recreation, tourism: a geographic view on integration', *Annals of Tourism Research*, vol. 14, pp. 361–75.

Kelly, J. R. (1982) *Leisure*, Englewood Cliffs, New Jersey: Prentice-Hall.

Pearce, D. (1989) *Tourist Development*, London: Longman/New York: John Wiley, 2nd edn.

Rojek, C. (1985) *Capitalism and Leisure Theory*, Andover: Tavistock.

Smith, D. M. (1977) *Human Geography: a Welfare Approach*, London: Edward Arnold.

Urry, J. (1990) *The Tourist Gaze: Leisure and Travel in Contemporary Societies*, London and Newbury Park, California: Sage Publications.

TWO The International Dimension

Lea, J. (1988) *Tourism and Development in the Third World*, London and New York: Routledge.

Smith G. V. (1990) 'The growth of conference and incentives', in M. Quest (ed.), *Howarth Book of Tourism*, London: Macmillan.

Williams, A. M. and Shaw, G. (eds), (1991) *Tourism and Economic Development: Western European Experience*, London: Belhaven Press, 2nd edn.

World Tourism Organization (1991) *Tourism to the Year 2000: Qualitative Aspects Affecting Global Growth, A Discussion Paper (Executive Summary)*, Madrid: World Tourism Organization.

THREE Social Access to Tourism and Leisure

Bramham, P., Henry, I., Mommaas, H. and van der Poel, H. (eds) (1989) *Leisure and Urban Processes: Critical Studies of Leisure Policy in West European Cities*, London and New York: Routledge.

Jackson, E. L. (1988) 'Leisure constraints: a survey of past research', *Leisure Sciences*, vol. 10, pp. 203–15.

Newman, O. (1983) 'The coming of a leisure society?' *Leisure Studies*, vol. 2, pp. 97–109.

Seaton, A. V. (1992) 'Social stratification in tourism choice and experience since the war: part', *Tourism Management*, vol. 13, pp. 106–11.

FOUR   Individual Consumption of Tourism

Cohen, E. (1979) 'A phenomenology of tourist experience, *Sociology*, vol. 13, pp. 179–202.

Jafari, J. (1987) 'Tourism models: the sociocultural aspects, *Tourism Management*, vol. 8(2), pp. 151–9.

Jafari, J. (1989) 'Sociocultural dimensions of tourism. An English language literature review', in J. Bustrzanowski (ed.), *Tourism as a Factor of Change: a Sociocultural Study*, Vienna: Economic Coordination Centre for Research and Documentation in Social Sciences, pp. 17–60.

Krippendorf, J. (1987) *The Holiday Makers*, London: Heinemann.

MacCannell, D. (1976) *The Tourist: a New Theory of the Leisure Class*, New York: Sulouker Books. See also revised edition, 1989.

Mathieson, A. and Wall, G. (1982) *Tourism Economic, Physical and Social Impacts*, London: Longman.

Murphy, P. E. (1985) *Tourism: a Community Approach*, London and New York: Routledge.

FIVE   The Tourism Industry

Ascher, F. (1985) *Tourism Transnational Corporation and Cultural Identities*, Paris: Unesco.

Burkart, A. J. and Medlik, S. (1981) *Tourism Past, Present and Future*, London: Heinemann.

Dunning, J. H. and McQueen, M. (1982) 'The eclectic theory of the multinational enterprise and the international hotel industry', in A. M. Rugman (ed.), *New Theories of the Multinational Enterprise*, London and New York: Routledge.

Laws, E. (1991) *Tourism Marketing: Service and Quality Management Perspectives*, Cheltenham: Stanley Thornes.

Pearce, D. (1989) *Tourist Development*, London: Longman/New York: John Wiley, 2nd edn.

Urry, J. (1987) 'Some social and spatial aspects of services', *Environment and Planning D: Society and Space*, vol. 5, pp. 5–26.

Williams, A. M. and Shaw, G. (eds) (1991) *Tourism and Economic Development: Western European Experience*, London: Belhaven Press, 2nd edn.

SIX   Tourism and Entrepreneurship

Britton, S. (1991) 'Tourism, capital, and place: towards a critical geography', *Environment and Planning D: Society and Space*, vol. 9, pp. 451–78.
Mathieson, A. and Wall, G. (1982) *Tourism: Economic, Physical and Social Impacts*, London: Longman/New York: John Wiley.
Shaw, G. and Williams, A. M. (1987) 'Firm formation and operating characteristics in the Cornish tourism industry', *Tourism Management*, vol. 8, pp. 244–8.

SEVEN   Tourism Employment and Labour Markets

Bagguley, P. (1990) 'Gender and labour flexibility in hotel and catering', *Service Industries Journal*, vol. 10, pp. 105–18.
Bishop, J. and Hoggett, P. (1989) 'Leisure and the informal economy', in C. Rojek (ed.), *Leisure for Leisure: Essays*, London: Macmillan.
Simms, J., Hales, C. and Riley, M. (1988) 'Examination of the concept of internal labour markets in UK hotels', *Tourism Management*, vol. 9, pp. 3–12.
Urry, J. (1990) *The Tourist Gaze: Leisure and Travel in Contemporary Societies*, London and Newbury Park, California: Sage Publications.
Williams, A. M. and Shaw, G. (1988) 'Tourism: candy floss industry or job generator?', *Town Planning Review*, vol. 59, pp. 81–104.

EIGHT   Tourism and Leisure Environments

Butler, R. W. (1980) 'The concept of a tourist area cycle of evolution: implications for management of resources', *Canadian Geographer*, vol. 14, pp. 5–12.
Haywood, K. M. (1986) 'Can the tourist area life cycle be made operational?', *Tourism Management*, vol. 7, pp. 154–67.
Law, C. M. (1987) 'Conference and exhibition tourism', *Built Environment*, vol. 13, pp. 85–95.
Pearce, D. G. (1987) *Tourism Today: a Geographical Analysis*, London: Longman/New York: John Wiley.

NINE   Mass Tourism

Krippendorf, J. (1987) *The Holiday Makers*, London: Heinemann.
Pearce, D. G. (1987) 'Spatial patterns of package tourism in Europe', *Annals of Tourism Research*, vol. 14, pp. 183–201.
Sessa, A. (1983) *Elements of Tourism Economics*, Rome: Catal.
Williams, A. M. and Shaw, G. (1991) 'Western European tourism in per-

spective', in A. Williams and G. Shaw (eds), *Tourism and Economic Development: Western European Experiences*, London: Belhaven Press, 2nd edn.

Urry, J. (1990) *The Tourist Gaze: Leisure and Travel in Contemporary Societies*, London and Newbury Park, California: Sage Publications.

TEN   Urban Tourism

Ashworth, G. J. (1989) 'Urban tourism: an imbalance in attention', in C. P. Cooper (ed.), *Progress in Tourism, Recreation and Hospitality Management*, London: Belhaven Press.

Ashworth, G. J. and Tunbridge, J. E. (1990) *The Tourist–Historic City*, London: Belhaven Press.

Law, C. M. (1992) 'Urban tourism and its contribution to economic regeneration', *Urban Studies*, vol. 29, pp. 597–616.

Law, C. (1993) *Urban Tourism*, London: Mansell.

ELEVEN   Rural Tourism

Bouquet, M. and Winter, M. (eds), (1987) *Who from Their Labours Rest? Conflict and Practice in Rural Tourism*, Aldershot: Avebury Press.

Kelly, J. R. (1980) 'Outdoor recreation participation: a comparative analysis', *Leisure Science*, vol. 3, pp. 129–54.

Middleton, V. T. C. (1982) 'Tourism in rural areas', *Tourism Management*, vol. 5, pp. 52–8.

TWELVE   The Future of Tourism

Britton, S. (1991) 'Tourism, capital, and place: towards a critical geography', *Environment and Planning D: Society and Space*, vol. 9, pp. 451–78.

Krippendorf, J. (1987) *The Holiday Makers*, London: Heinemann.

Index